Framing Piracy

Framing Piracy

Globalization and Film Distribution in Greater China

Shujen Wang

ROWMAN & LITTLEFIELD PUBLISHERS, INC.
Lanham • Boulder • New York • Toronto • Oxford

ROWMAN & LITTLEFIELD PUBLISHERS, INC.

Published in the United States of America
by Rowman & Littlefield Publishers, Inc.
A Member of the Rowman & Littlefield Publishing Group
4501 Forbes Boulevard, Suite 200, Lanham, Maryland 20706
www.rowmanlittlefield.com

P.O. Box 317, Oxford OX2 9RU, United Kingdom

Chapter 2 is based on "Re-Contextualizing Copyright: Piracy, Hollywood, the State, and
Globalization," by Shujen Wang, from *Cinema Journal* 43:1. Copyright © 2003 by the
University of Texas Press. All rights reserved.

Chapter 6 is based on an original paper that was first published in *Theory, Culture and
Society* 20(4) in August 2003. Reprinted by permission of Sage Publications Ltd. from
Shujen Wang, "Mapping Film Piracy in China." Copyright © 2003 *Theory, Culture and
Society* Ltd.

British Library Cataloguing in Publication Information Available

Library of Congress Cataloging-in-Publication Data

Wang, Shujen, 1963–
  Framing Piracy : globalization and film distribution in greater China / Shujen Wang.
    p. cm.
Includes bibliographical references and index.
ISBN 0-7425-1979-1 (alk. paper)—ISBN 0-7425-1980-5 (pbk. : alk. paper)
  1. Motion pictures—China. 2. Motion pictures, American—China. 3. Copyright—
Motion pictures—China—History—20th century. 4. Piracy (Copyright)—China—
History—20th century. I. Title.

PN1993.5.C4W268 2003
384'.8'0951–dc21

                                                              2003046652

Printed in the United States of America

⊖™ The paper used in this publication meets the minimum requirements of American
National Standard for Information Sciences—Permanence of Paper for Printed Library
Materials, ANSI/NISO Z39.48-1992.

To the Loving Memory of My Parents

Wang Chieh (1926–1997)
Kuo Chung-Hsiou (1935–1995)

Contents

Part II: Case Studies

Figures

Photographs

Tables

Acknowledgments

I am most indebted to Henry Geddes. From the inception to the completion of this book, Henry's help was invaluable. He read the manuscript in its various stages numerous times and made insightful suggestions and comments. Without his continuous support, encouragement, and friendship this book would not have been possible.

Two other individuals to whom I am deeply indebted are independent film distributor Wolf Chen in Taiwan and Professor Jonathan Jian-Hua Zhu in Hong Kong. Wolf opened the door for me to a fascinating world of film distribution. Jonathan generously helped me secure a crucial City University of Hong Kong research grant that funded my research fieldwork in China for two years.

I would like to acknowledge the institutional support I received from Emerson College in the form of multiple course reductions and research grants. I would like to thank Dorothy Aram, David Bogen, Grafton Nunes, Rob Sabal, and Stuart Sigman for their ongoing support. Librarians Sarah Graham, Beth Joress, and Tabitha Lee also deserve special thanks for their expertise and patience in locating valuable materials for my research.

Several colleagues read my manuscript and provided helpful comments: Yuan-Horng Chu, Chris Fujiwara, Junhao Hong, Katrien Jacobs, Anandam Kavoori, Ed Mckluskie, and Ned Rossiter.

The following individuals are my support network, whose friendship and support in one form or another kept me sane in the process: Dianne Brooks, Briankle Chang, Christina Fong, Timur Friedman, Chris Fujiwara, Katrien Jacobs, Lori Landay, Maria Koundoura, Matthew Leeds, Gini Ma, Jeff Perk, Jackie Romeo, Helen Wang, and Xueping Zhong.

I would like to thank all those who accepted my interview requests. Their interviews are the highlights of this book. In particular I would like to thank Michael Werner of Fortissimo and Twentieth Century Fox, Sam Ho of MPA, Zhang Lihui and John Alonte of Warner Bros, Simon Huang of UIP, Tim Meade and Chow Li of Columbia, Rudy Tseng of Buena Vista International, Huang Xiaoxin of the PRC Press and Publication Administration, and Duncan E. E. Chang of Linfair Engineering and Trading.

Jack Chang, Lin Wenchi, Lu Fei-I, and Yang Tsu-Chuen helped me locate some of the most useful information in Taiwan.

My editor Brenda Hadenfeldt has been most wonderful and patient. Her sense of humor has made the process much more enjoyable than I could have hoped. Special thanks are due to Kirstyn Leuner and Kärstin Painter for their help in editorial production. My graduate assistants Shun Liang and Jen Mitchell helped with the preparation of the manuscript. Steve Scipione gave me valuable advice.

I would like to thank Professor Ray Hiebert, the late Professor Ouyang Shun, and Mrs. Ouyang Shia Ho, my mentors, for believing in me. They are the most important influence in my academic and scholarly life.

My deepest gratitude goes to my parents, whose love, encouragement, guidance, and many sacrifices made it possible for me to pursue scholarship. It is to the loving memory of my parents that I dedicate this book. My sister Wang Shiao-Shiou, her husband Shao Shien-Tai, and their three beautiful sons have been a wonderful presence in my life.

Finally, I would like to thank Qin Feng for putting things in perspective and for giving me that most needed final push to finish this book. His passion for art, and life as art, has been most inspiring and contagious.

Introduction

> The two extremes, local and global, are much less interesting than the interme-
> diary arrangements that we are calling networks.
> —Bruno Latour (1993:122)

This is a book about film distribution, both legal and illegal, within the context of a changing digital media environment that calls for a reassessment of key dimensions: networks, space, globalization, technology, and the state. More specifically, it focuses on film piracy and Hollywood's global film distribution networks in Greater China (including the Mainland, Hong Kong, and Taiwan), and it examines the functional and regulatory roles of the state in an age of transnational trade and intellectual property regimes. Such examination is especially significant given that both Mainland China and Taiwan gained their respective accession into the World Trade Organization (WTO) in 2001 and 2002, with great implications for media and intellectual property rights policies in both territories.

So, why distribution? Why Hollywood? Why Greater China? In the discussion of global cultural production, or "the becoming cultural of the economic, and the becoming economic of the cultural," to quote Jameson (1998:60), Hollywood occupies a unique and highly contested space. Viewed in the classical (macro) framework of political economy, Hollywood is the ultimate symbol of American cultural and economic hegemony. Capitalism and commodity form reign supreme in all aspects of life. The economic, formal, and political triumph of Hollywood is perceived to be one of the major forces that have shattered national cinemas, while potentially affecting national and local cultures as a whole.

In a world that increasingly functions as a net or a web (see, for example, Haraway, 1997; Jameson, 1998; Irvine 1998; and Robert Reich via Castells, 1997), distribution is precisely those lines that give objects their mobility and enable the flow among different nodes and hubs. The success of a global strategy hinges therefore upon a stable distribution system. Hollywood's early emphasis on distribution and exhibition strategy, for example, has contributed greatly to its dominance of the worldwide film industry. While distribution has been widely recognized as one of the key factors for Hollywood's global success

1

as well as survival (e.g., Hoskins, McFadyen, and Finn, 1997; Askoy and Robins, 1992), it has not been adequately examined or theorized.

The centrality of the role of a distributor lies in the fact that it is the distributor who controls the flow of information to both the consumers (through marketing, promotion, branding, and positioning) and the sources of finance (see Hoskins et al., 1997). This role is especially significant in a global economy as it links the global and the local, and is indeed the part where boundaries are redefined and where translation, transformation, deformation, leakage, and overlapping take place (see discussion of the Actor Network Theory in chapter 1). In other words, it is where different networks intersect and interact with significant cultural, economic, and political implications and consequences.

Distribution is especially crucial in the transnationalization of Hollywood in a global information economy. After the Justice Department's Paramount Decree of 1948, the major Hollywood studios ("the majors") had essentially become distributors and financiers (e.g., Wyatt, 1998; Donahue 1987). It is important to note that distribution and financing are closely related. With the common practice of pre-selling, the securing of financing is often contingent upon a distribution deal. It becomes clear that the control over distribution is a key to control over finance (Christopherson and Storper, 1986). Increasingly bankers have come to depend on the large distributors to control *all* processes of film practice: script selection, development, production, and finally distribution. The increasing proliferation and importance of ancillary windows and foreign markets further accentuate the critical role distribution plays. The new global conglomerate and convergent entertainment marketplace is a centrally controlled network in which distribution has tremendous influence over the complex movement and ultimate reception of a product. Monopolistic distribution schemes are in place to ensure Hollywood's dominance of the world market, while a handful of the major distributors still control the industry.

Digital technology has disrupted this balance of power in the film industry. If power in this mode of late capitalist expansion lies in one's capacity to overcome constraints of both time and space (see, for example, Graham and Marvin, 1996), then digital technologies present a major challenge to existing forms of power and control due to their capacity to erase space and reward speed. While technological innovation is instrumental in furthering capitalist market expansion, when used by pirates it also seriously undermines and challenges the copyright industries' critical need to command space and control time. Piracy has interrupted the spatial securities of (legitimate) distribution. If digital technology rewards speed and partnership, the worldwide entertainment piracy networks are often far better connected and more flexible than their legitimate counterparts. The windowing strategies of sequencing sales to different territories at different times (Hoskins et al., 1997) long practiced by Hollywood are rendered ineffective with the formidable rate and velocity of optical disc and online piracy. Jack Valenti, president of the Motion Picture Association of America (MPAA), has indeed named piracy one of the "emerging global issues" in the new "digital millennium" (2000:85).

The key, however, is not simply revenue losses for legitimate entertainment and software industries. The crucial issue remains the fact that in the information economy, intellectual property becomes the real property (e.g., Hoskins et al., 1997). What are traded in many cases are precisely intellectual property *rights*. What ensures the proper functioning of the global information economy then is copyright protection, which often takes the form of transnational as well as national copyright legislature, agreements, and enforcement. Herein lies the essential role the state plays in global copyright regulation and management, as piracy not only challenges conventional centers of power (e.g., "legitimate" transnational media rights holders, international intellectual property rights regimes), it also tests a state's internal regulatory and enforcement capacity as well as external negotiation and trade leverage.

Given China's geopolitical influence, its formidable market size (for both legitimate and illegitimate products), its long coast lines and shared borders (i.e., multiple entry, egress, and connecting points for smugglers), and its uniquely hybrid and ambivalent politico-economic-cultural system, distribution and piracy in China make for a particularly important case study. It highlights some of the most interesting and intricate insights into issues of power, control, technology, network, speed, global-regional-national dynamics, subjectivities, reflexivity, and theory.

It is important to note that the remarkable economic growth witnessed in China in the past two decades has had much to do with the collaboration among the triangular economies of Taiwan, Hong Kong, and the Mainland, which is integral to the global trend of regionalism. The study of the three culturally similar, yet politically and economically different territories offers an important site in which the roles of the state and its sovereignty are tested and most pronounced.

Given the complexity of the issues, existing theoretical frameworks (e.g., political economy, some of the recent writings on globalization) are largely inadequate when it comes to a comprehensive assessment of global film distribution and piracy. Focusing on piracy and distribution is an effort to move beyond a tendency in existing literature to treat aspects of global production and local distribution as isolated phenomena. To focus on distribution is to stress the specific links, relations, and connections that transport and translate images, products, ideas, and meanings among various nodes and hubs on the global web (e.g., Hollywood as central distribution networks and its overseas operations, transnational IP and trade regimes and local enforcement, the state in transition). It is to examine the directions, movements, and velocity of the lines that connect the nodes and points (e.g., where are piracy networks located and how do they operate in relation to their legitimate counterparts), as well as the ever-shifting alignment and configuration of the circulating networks (e.g., what are the complex and dynamic relations among the state, transnational corporations and trade regimes, pirates, optical-disc production line makers and distributors, and consumers).

This book has two parts. Part one (chapters 1 through 4) provides historical, theoretical, and politico-economic-technological contexts, while part two (chapters 5 through 11) offers case studies of film piracy and distribution in Greater China. Chapter 1 provides a historical overview of Hollywood's global distribution practices, followed by a discussion of viable theoretical and methodological frameworks. An examination of distribution, piracy, and copyright would not be complete without situating these in the larger contexts of power, technology, the state, and the networking logic of globalization.

Chapter 2 surveys the global intellectual property rights issues in the contexts of digital technology, space, and globalization. It also reviews the complexity of copyright issues in light of the dynamics between the state and transnational trade regimes.

Given that both China and Taiwan's respective accessions to the WTO had had great impact on media policies in the two territories, chapter 3 examines the profound implications of the WTO and the state. It is in this chapter that the concept of "Greater China" is problematized, as there are paradoxes and conflicts inherent in such grouping that inevitably seeks to manage differences, enforce similarities, and mark boundaries. It is also in these contexts of regionalism and transnational trade regimes that the changing roles of the state are addressed.

One of the most significant developments in optical disc piracy is that of Video Compact Disc (VCD) technology in Asia. The development of VCD highlights some of the most interesting issues of the reversed flow of technology and the local translation of a global format. Chapter 4 provides a brief examination of the VCD phenomenon and its implications for piracy in Greater China.

Chapters 5 through 10 map, compare, and contrast distribution systems and piracy networks in Mainland China (chapters 5 and 6), Taiwan (chapters 7, 8, and 9) and Hong Kong (chapter 10), and how they shape, and are shaped by, local film industries and local cultural, economic, and political dynamics. Some of the foci include media policies and histories, technological developments, intraregional networks and flows, market dynamics, and WTO accessions. The concluding chapter discusses the theoretical implications.

Appendix A provides a brief note on methodology and a list of interviewees. Appendix B presents optical-disk piracy check sheet and appendix C lists Hollywood major studios' video releases in China.

Part I

Contexts

1

Global Film Distribution Revisited: Network, Technology, and Space

Three Cases

"A Quiet but Bloody Revolution"—Case #1

Described by *Variety* (Dunkley and Harris, 2001:1) as a "quiet but bloody revolution" and the "day-and-date revolt," the recent changes in the ranks of international film distribution executives at major Hollywood studios (the "majors") reflect important shifts in the direction of the film industry. In 2001–2002, the respective international distribution heads at Sony (Columbia TriStar), Universal, Twentieth Century-Fox, and Warner Bros. were replaced by their domestic distribution or marketing counterparts. These new and expanded positions oversee responsibilities that include both domestic and international distribution and marketing. Such a shift not only signals a rapidly shrinking world in which international and domestic distribution are now *perceived* to have more in common than in previous eras, as was pointed out by the report, it also brings out complex issues of technology, the new mega merger environment, and control of space, time, and flow.

The "VCD Menace"—Case #2

Figure 1.1 traces the flow and routes of pirated *Star Wars Episode 1: The Phantom Menace* video compact discs (VCDs) from the U.S. theatrical release to Malaysia and then to other parts of the Asia-Pacific region. It demonstrates the efficiency and extraordinary speed with which piracy networks operate to undermine authorized film distribution networks. Within three days of the U.S. theatrical release (on 19 May 1999), three different versions of pirated VCDs were found in Malaysia. Within a week of U.S. release, pirated VCDs were found in China, the largest market in the world for both legitimate and illegitimate goods.[1]

Figure 1.1. Piracy Map: *Star Wars Episode 1: The Phantom Menace*

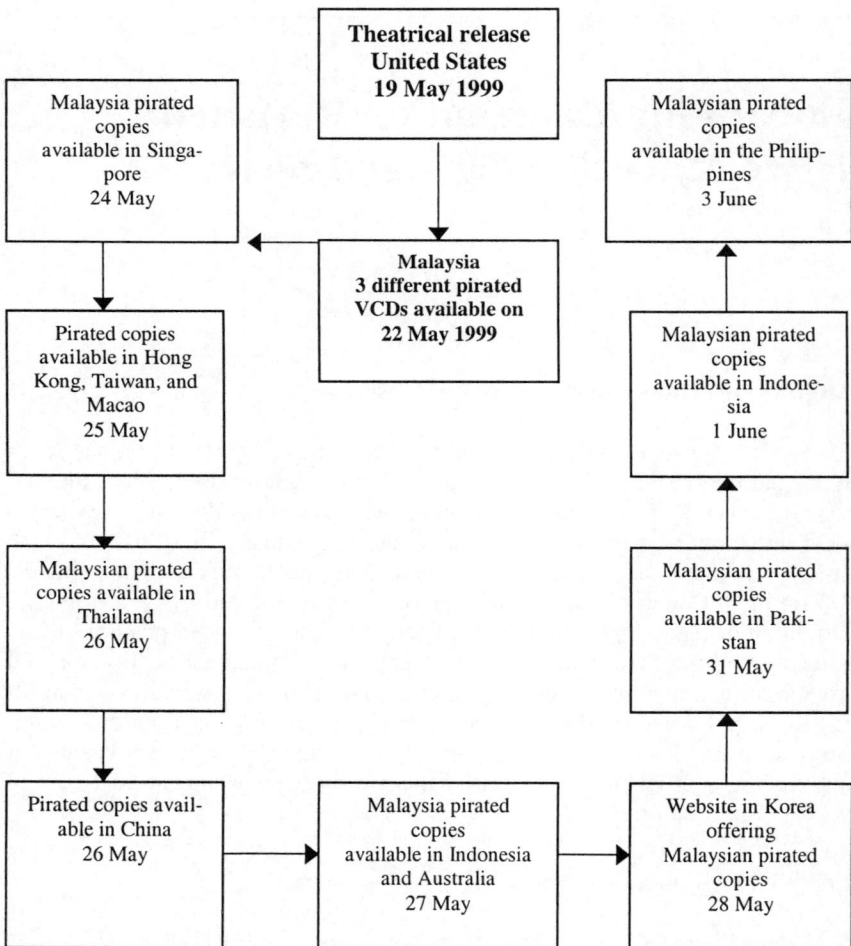

Source: Michael C. Ellis, vice president and director, Asia/Pacific Anti-Piracy Operations, Motion Picture Association. Personal interview, 1 June 2000, Hong Kong.

E-Commerce or Gray Market?—Case #3

According to *Variety* (7–13 February 2000), as much as 30 percent of total DVD sales outside of North America are conducted online via American E-tailers. Such sales not only take profits away from the majors' (overseas) local home entertainment branches, they also have serious implications for the price discrimination strategy "windowing," which the majors have practiced since the 1970s and 1980s when video and cable channels started to proliferate. Windowing is an attractive distribution strategy in that it extends markets by sequencing sales to different territories through time (Hoskins, McFadyen, and Finn, 1997). Thus, by sequencing different exhibition windows according to whichever customer class is willing to pay the next highest price, the windowing strategy as a price discrimination method maximizes the distributor's profits. The sequential order usually begins with theatrical exhibition (domestic and overseas), followed by home video (including DVD), pay-per-view, pay cable, network television, and syndication (see Litman, 1998). In other words, it is how space is maneuvered through time, and vice versa. What this *Variety* report demonstrates is the Internet's ability to erase distance and make windowing obsolete. Digitization destroys distance.

These seemingly unrelated cases are in fact inextricably interconnected. They highlight some of the most pressing issues and challenges the majors face and must manage to remain in control: piracy, global expansion and issues of control (or lack thereof), digital technology, and the subsequent disintermediation possibility, among others. They also demonstrate the significance of distribution in this global information economy, where speed is increasingly one of the most essential elements in a successful global operation, legitimate or otherwise.

To fully understand the centrality of film distribution and how it has come to define Hollywood's global dominance, one has to take into account several crucial contexts in which the film industry has taken shape. The following sections examine distribution in the contexts of policy, technology, space, and control, followed by a further discussion of the above cases and their theoretical implications.

Policy, Industry Structure, and Globalization

How has policy come to shape the market structure? And how have the market structure and other larger economic, political, and cultural contexts, in turn, informed policies and regulations? While policy has changed the structure of Hollywood in general and its spatial organization and strategies in particular, new digital technology and global market environment have also rendered policy and regulation ineffective. And most important, policy provides an avenue through which one can get a glimpse of the configurations of the state in this rapidly

changing global economy informed by technological developments and the resulting transnational expansion, mergers, and trade regime operations.

As mentioned in the introduction, the Paramount Decree of 1948 (*U.S. v.
Paramount*, 334 U.S.131) marked a profound change in the structure of the U.S.
film industry. It was a decision that shifted and altered the power relations
among various components of the industry. It also signaled the new strategies
the studios adopted to remain in control. Prior to the Paramount Decree, Hollywood majors were vertically integrated and firmly in control of production, distribution, and exhibition. They had, since the 1910s, expanded cooperatively to
control the film industry and create an oligopoly (Thompson and Bordwell,
1994). In 1938 the Justice Department initiated the Paramount case and accused
the Big Five (Paramount, Warner Bros., MGM, Twentieth Century-Fox, and
RKO) and the Little Three (Universal, Columbia, and United Artists) of collud-
ing to monopolize the film business and hence were in violation of the antitrust
laws (see Thompson and Bordwell, 1994). The Big Five owned theater chains,
block-booked films, and engaged in other unfair practices. The Little Three were
also accused of unfair practice and of cooperating to exclude other firms from
entering the market, even though they did not own theaters. To prevent these
monopolistic practices of the majors from further development, the Paramount
Decree prohibited the Big Five from owning theater chains. Such policy change
had profound impact on the market structure and proved to be detrimental to the
Big Five, as for them exhibition had contributed more to profits than either production or distribution (Hillier, 1993).

Consequently, with the emergence of television and the new postwar demo-
graphic changes (i.e., baby boom and suburbanization), the Paramount divorce-
ments set off the decline of the studio era (e.g., Gomery, 1998; Thompson and
Bordwell, 1994) and broke down the vertical integration of the majors. Without
secured outlets for their products, the major studios began to reduce and disintegrate production. Major functions hence moved to the market (see Christopherson, 1996) in an effort to expand and deepen control over worldwide distribution. What became clear about the profound influence of the Paramount Decree
was the strategic position distribution occupied: control over distribution was
indeed a key to control over finance (Aksoy and Robins, 1992; see also Guback,
1969, and Thompson and Bordwell, 1994), and thus the industry.

Foreign markets also took on even greater importance after the decline of
the studios in the post-Paramount Decree era. While the transnationalization of
Hollywood has been intensified in recent decades, it is certainly not something
new. As early as 1914, the United States supplied half of the motion picture production in the world; and by 1917 the United States supplied almost all of it. By
1925 and 1926 Hollywood had become a large-scale operation generating $1.25
billion from the global mass market (see Donahue, 1987). As early as 1928, foreign revenue already represented 25 to 40 percent of the total earnings of a film.
After the Paramount Decree, the majors started to lower production outputs to
reduce overhead while trying to differentiate film projects to maximize audience
consumption. Amidst the majors' efforts to diversify and disintegrate in terms of

production and contents (i.e., involvements and developments in television production), they remained centralized in their distribution operations. To recoup losses incurred in domestic markets in the 1960s, they emphasized international distribution even more (see, for example, Christopherson and Storper, 1986). In the 1950s, foreign rentals generated 40 percent of revenue. By the early 1960s, approximately 53 percent of all theatrical revenue came for foreign markets (Donahue, 1987). Foreign markets now provide 65 percent of box office grosses (see Dunkley and Harris, 2001), they are no longer just one of the ancillary markets, but rather an indispensable revenue source essential for the survival of the major studios. As table 1.1 and table 1.2 show, both in terms of global admissions and box office grosses, overseas markets outweigh domestic ones.[2] An international distribution strategy holds the key to the financial well-being of the majors.

Hollywood's dominance of overseas distribution and markets is not a coincidence. It is largely due to the policy and regulation that permitted the "collusion" among firms in foreign markets (see Christopherson, 1996), while domestically such collusions were prohibited. Under the provisions of the Webb-Pomerene Export Trade Act of 1918, the Motion Picture Export Association of America (MPEAA, formerly the Foreign Department of Motion Picture Association of America) was organized in 1946[3] as a legal cartel (see Donahue

Table 1.1. Split of Admissions by Continent (Percentage)

	1995	2001	2010 (forecast)
Asia Pacific	71	66	65
Europe	9	11	11
Latin America	2	3	4
Middle East/Africa	3	3	4
North America	15	17	16

Source: Informa Media Group (2001).

Table 1.2. Split of Gross Box Office by Continent (Percentage)

	1995	2001	2010 (forecast)
Asia Pacific	23	18	18
Europe	25	28	29
Latin America	4	6	7
Middle East/Africa	1	1	1
North America	46	47	44

Source: Informa Media Group (2001).

1987 and Guback, 1969). This act was set up so that competitors were allowed to cooperate in foreign trade by building associations that would otherwise be considered illegal under the two earlier antitrust acts of 1890 (the Sherman Antitrust Act) and 1914 (the Clayton Antitrust Act).[4] The MPEAA was then able to act as the sole export sales agent for the majors and to effectively regulate and fix prices, allocate customers in foreign markets, control the flow of products, set the terms of trade for the films, and arrange the distribution abroad (see Donahue, 1987; Guback, 1969; and Christopherson, 1996).

Finally, the 1970s witnessed major restructuring in Hollywood in which ownership patterns were altered. Even though the film industry was in financial troubles in the 1960s, the major studios still represented a good investment opportunity with such assets as prime real estate, film libraries, and well-established distribution networks (Hillier, 1993). Changes in ownership and structure ensued when conglomerates started to take over studios. Examples include Gulf and Western's takeover of Paramount in 1966, Transamerica's purchase of United Artists in 1967, Kinney National Services' takeover of Warner Bros. in 1969 (and the studio's amalgamation into Warner Communications Inc. in 1971), and Kirk Kerkorian's control of MGM in 1969 (see Hillier, 1993).

By the 1980s, the film industry had become profitable again. It also became apparent that the way to remain cost effective on a meaningful level in the film industry was to be a major, since only the majors are able to gain worldwide dominance through economies of scale and through their strategies of consolidating overseas distribution with other majors. This realization prompted another wave of mergers. With the reversal of the Paramount Decree in 1985, furthermore, the majors started to buy into theater chains and started a "re-assertion of vertical integration" (Hillier, 1993:23). In fact, this trend of vertical reintegration has extended to global markets. Many of the major international exhibitors are linked to major Hollywood studios. For example, Warner Bros. International Theaters has a global deal with Village Roadshow of Australia; Sony and Universal have part ownership of Loews Cineplex Entertainment while Universal also co-owns United Cinemas International; Paramount is linked to National Amusements through Viacom; and Fox owns a 16 percent share in the Hong Kong-based Golden Harvest (see Thomas and O'Brien, 2001).

With policy and foreign distribution systems in place, the majors survived the Paramount Decree setbacks, while reintegrating themselves both horizontally and vertically into the new global economy. These structural and policy changes reflect the working of global market forces and developments. One can see how the state actively functions in the new global economy to ensure the working of an expansionist and capitalist global spatial strategy. To operate on a global scale, national as well as transnational regulations are essential. With the collusion between MPEAA and the government, Hollywood was able to expand its global operations.

The new challenges resulting from digital technology, however, prove to be formidable, as they render regulations futile and inadequate. New technology has had a great impact on distribution and poses serious implications for both theory and practice.

Technology, Windowing, and Piracy

Power in this mode of late capitalist expansion lies in one's capacity to overcome constraints of both time and space (see, for example, Graham and Marvin, 1996; Harvey, 1990). Digital technology has disrupted the balance of power and forms of control in the film industry by erasing space and rewarding speed (see also introduction, pp. 2–3). Consequently, while new production technologies have certainly altered the process of film production, it has been the new technologies of distribution and delivery that have had the most far-reaching and profound impact on the industry structure. This is so partly because new technologies bring about the proliferation of ancillary markets. The ancillary markets (or the end markets/new exhibition windows) include all means of exploiting a motion picture other than that of theatrical exhibition (Donahue, 1987), such as video (including DVD and VCD), cable television, pay per view, broadcast television, and the Internet. To extend markets and to maximize consumption and revenues, the majors use strategies to segment audiences, to differentiate among different outlets of distribution and their times of release, and to use price discrimination strategies, charging audience different prices to see the same film via different outlets depending on where and when the film is seen (See Aksoy and Robins, 1992; Christopherson, 1996). The ability to control a range of new delivery and distribution outlets and to maximize exhibition possibilities is of great importance for the majors, allowing them to spread risks among the increasingly segmented audiences and to retain their dominance.

In addition, the significance of a proper working windowing strategy is closely related to one of the unique characteristics of film: it is a joint consumption good (see Hoskins, Finn, and McFayden, 2000:127).[5] Joint consumption has to do with cultural goods' property as a "public good," by which the viewing by one person of a film does not use up the product or detract from the experience by others. In other words, an additional viewer for a specific product has no effect on cost, while the replication of such a product is very low compared to the original costs. Films thus become an infinitely exportable commodity; since a print shipped abroad would not deprive the domestic market of anything (see Guback, 1969). Table 1.3, for example, shows release windows in Hong Kong, Taiwan, and Japan. One can see that the less secure (in terms of copyright protection) and less profitable means of distribution normally appear at the end of the release sequence (e.g., broadcast free TV, see also Bettig, 1997). Hence, the windowing strategies are only possible with proper copyright protection since market extension relies fully on the transfer and ownership of exclusive rights to reproduction, distribution, performance, and display.

Table 1.3. Release Windows (Months after Theatrical Release)

	Video Rental	Video Sale	PPV	Pay TV	Free-to-Air
Hong Kong	3–6	N/a	10	12	24–30
Japan	6	12	12	15–18	30–36
Taiwan	6	12	N/a	13–14	N/a

Source: Informa Media Group (2001).
Note: Data on China and the United States are not available.

For the consumers, the new delivery technologies have inevitably changed the way they use the media. The development of the VCR, for example, afforded the consumers with means for time-shift recording and content sharing. The Internet further provides users with even greater capability to copy and share audio and video files free of charge. Ultimately it is an issue of control, of when and where the films are watched, by whom, and through what channels. Technologies give consumers such control.

These developments also have implications for piracy. Named as one of the "Emerging Global Issues 2000" (*The Business of Film*, 2000), piracy has proved to be able to move products around the globe in a much faster and more efficient fashion than its legitimate counterparts. The annual losses due to piracy are estimated at $9 billion in 1999, $8.1 billion in 2000, $8.4 billion in 2001, and $9.21 billion in 2002 (see USTR 2001 and 2002 "Special 301" Decisions, and IIPA Press Release, 2003). While revenue losses for legitimate entertainment and software industries are an immediate concern, the fact that intellectual property becomes the real property in the information economy has more far-reaching implications (e.g., Hoskins et al., 1997).

If mobility equals profitability and if speed in this digital world translates into profit, then the ultraflexible local, regional, and global piracy networks prove to be among the greatest challenges the film industry has ever had to face. Thus, speed becomes a major goal of, and challenge to, participants in this global informational structure and capitalist expansion. It is certainly one of the determining factors of the success and prevalence of the piracy networks. Viewed in this context, the windowing strategies practiced by Hollywood illustrate the major studios' endeavor to manage time and control speed through space in order to minimize the threat posed by new technologies and to reestablish control. Technologically savvy pirates and their ever more efficient and flexible networks have, nevertheless, seriously undermined the majors' control and endeavors.

Facing these challenges brought about by the new technology, namely, pirates' increasing command of speed and the global audience's demand for faster and more affordable products and releases, the majors are put in a position to speed up and expand their global distribution networks. The shrinking of windows and the shortening of the release intervals has been one strategy employed by the majors to combat piracy and meet the global audience demand for speedy delivery.[6]

Viewed in this context, the aforementioned "quiet but bloody revolution" in some of the majors' decisions to subsume international distribution operations under their domestic counterparts (see case 1) is but a logical step toward the speeding up and the stretching out of the global distribution network.[7] The tendency toward international day and date release (i.e., simultaneous domestic and overseas releasing), a strategy most of these newly appointed distribution and marketing heads endorse, is an effort on the part of the majors to maintain control and to curb piracy and parallel import.

Toward a Network-Oriented Theoretical and Methodological Framework

> For the sociologist then the question of method boils down to knowing where to place oneself. Like Hobbes himself, he or she sits just at the point where the contract is made, just where forces are translated, and the difference between the technical and the social is fought out, just where the irreversible becomes reversible and where the chreods reverse their slopes. *There, only a tiny amount of energy is necessary to drag a maximum of information about its growth from the newborn monster.*
> —Michel Callon and Bruno Latour (1981:301, emphasis added)

As structure necessarily affects the trajectory through which one moves, a theoretical framework determines the direction which research might take and the outcomes that it would produce. As the above quote indicates, the space and time from which a researcher speaks, as well as the research tool he or she chooses to use, inevitably shape the results of the research. Too often, unfortunately, they are limited because of a pre-determined framework for the study based a priori on a subject's size. Callon and Latour (1981) have pointed out that few, if any, sociologists examine macro-actors and micro-actors with the same tools or arguments. Such a tendency, while logical, can create detrimental effects as theorists anticipate the actors' strengths and sizes and, with their analysis, would help these actors to grow even stronger and more vigorous. Or they would deny their existence altogether.[8] Such a problem would be especially significant in times of flux. A fixed research tool and framework can be seriously limiting. Conversely, a flexible research framework and method allows much crucial space for changes and variations to take place. Such a framework is especially essential when dynamics are in formation and when multiple lines, both theoretical and practical, blur and interact.

As mentioned, because of new globalization and information technological developments, film piracy and distribution underline interesting and intricate insights into issues of power, control, network, speed, and global-regional-

16 Chapter 1

national dynamics. A major area of international trade and legal disputes and negotiations, piracy in particular accentuates some of the most complex, paradoxical, and contradictory developments of globalization. On the one hand, the deterritorialized flow of capital and intellectual property products (e.g., filmic imageries) thrive in a deregulated and code-free environment. On the other hand, however, transnational copyright industries require strong government protection in maintaining market order and monopolies. Piracy occurs at the point where deterritorialized forces of capitalism intersect with the reterritorized forces of the nation (see Deleuze and Guattari, 1987), where the cross-bordered flows of informational and copyright goods require national law and enforcement to contain, if not eliminate, piracy. Without strong national legal regimes, the global information economy as we know it would cease to exist. Is the nation-state necessarily in decline?

Indeed, with digital technology, the "tyranny of real time" has overcome the "tyranny of distances" (Virilio, 1993:10). That there are no fixed trajectories in what Castells (1996) calls the space of flows has every indication for the rethinking of power and control. Given the complexity of the issues and the yet to be fully co-opted "power of flows" (as opposed to the "flows of power," see Castells, 1996:469) that digital technology can still offer, existing theoretical frameworks (e.g., political economy, some of the recent writings on globalization) where the focus tends to be on the dichotomy between the center and the peripheral, the local and the global are inadequate. Consider instead a spatial-, network-, and process-oriented *relational* theoretical framework. The intersecting and circulating networks of distribution and piracy call for such an integrated theoretical approach that addresses process and relations rather than totality, spatiotemporal specificities as opposed to historical or epochal inevitability, and the overlapping, intersecting, and interfacing places, spaces, and border zones in contrast to fixed and demarcated territories.

By relational I refer to Massey's (1994) "thinking in terms of relations."[9] In her work on space, place, and gender, Massey argues for a (feminist) relational view on space and place. By focusing on the relational rather than the absolute, on the relative rather than the fixed, on the dynamic simultaneity rather than the bounded/demarcated, we would be able to see "a simultaneous multiplicity of spaces: cross-cutting, intersecting, aligning with one another, or existing in relations of paradox or antagonism" (p. 2). In the case of distribution and piracy, multiple networks such as the state, transnational corporations, criminal organizations, trade associations, hardware and software manufacturers and distributors, transnational trade regimes, and consumers are all inextricably linked and interconnected.

To focus more specifically on film distribution and piracy is an effort to dissect and understand the complex processes and the multiple linkages of the deterritorializing flows of global filmic products and images, as well as the processes by which they are reterritorialized in various regional, national, and local loci through distribution and consumption, both legitimate and illegitimate. Film distribution and piracy are what constitute the links and relations of these networks of circulating images, products, and capital. They are also the connecting lines that bridge the gaps among these otherwise separate entities. To focus on piracy and distribution, then, is to add the middle part to what traditional analyses have misleadingly dichotomized into the macro/global/production and the micro/local/reception aspects.

Focusing on "peripheral vision," Sinclair, Jacka, and Cunningham (1996) also argue for a middle-range analytical approach that shifts the emphasis from both the macro-analysis of political economy and the micro-emphasis of reception and textual studies to a middle-range geolinguistic regional approach. Now that the global economy is increasingly marked by simultaneous concentration and regionalization (Stallings, 1993, cited in Castells, 1996), a mid-range theory complements existing frameworks in studying these dynamic *processes* of movements at different levels. It is important to note that this is not to minimize the importance of macro or micro approaches of studies, nor to make light of the serious effects of Hollywood dominance in the world. Quite the contrary. It is simply to fill the gaps in existing frameworks and to also study the flows and "the economies of space, of *how* objects and subjects are amazingly mobile and that these mobilities are themselves structured and structuring" (Lash and Urry, 1994:3, emphasis mine). It is the study of flows and the various "-scapes" that Appadurai (1990) theorizes. It is the "mediating factors" that Sinclair et al. are emphasizing: for example, who are the gatekeepers to the global cultural industries? Who acquire global cultural products and how are they acquired? Once acquired, through what channels and in what forms are they relayed to consumers? How have digital technologies changed the balance of the existing power structure and what are the real, perceived, and potential impacts digital technologies have on distribution? What are the relations between authorized distributors and illegitimate pirates? What is the significance of parallel or gray markets in this global market? What are their implications for the transnational corporations' (TNCs) control over space? If digital technologies have made space irrelevant, what constitutes boundaries? Are there necessarily fewer boundaries in this global information economy? What are the roles of the state? Is state sovereignty necessarily declining? Finally, what constitutes legality in intellectual property right? What are these rights and whose rights are we talking about anyway?

Given the complex and fast-changing nature of distribution and, especially, piracy networks, then, a relational *methodological* approach such as the Actor Network Theory (ANT) might be able to address some of these complex issues and relations that other approaches have failed to. One of the most important, liberating and, indeed, counterintuitive characteristics of ANT is the fact that, despite its name, the Actor Network Theory is *not* a theory (see Callon, 1999; Latour, 1999). Rather, it is a methodology, one that enables the social scientists to access sites and to travel from one field site to the next. The potentialities of the ANT lie thus in the fact that they "would not claim to explain the actors' behaviour and reasons, but only to find the procedures which render actors able to negotiate their ways through one another's world-building activity" (Latour,

1999:21). Furthermore, because ANT is not a theory, it indeed involves a "background/foreground reversal" (Latour, 1996:370). In other words, instead of attempting to be a universalistic grand theory that "fills in" the whole surface at the cost of explaining away local contingencies, ANT begins with the disorderly and the seemingly unconnected and incommensurable localities and contingencies. It does not attempt to explain the surface, nor does it intend to "fill in what is *in between* local pockets of orders or *in between* the filaments relating these contingencies" (Latour, 1996:370, original emphasis). Therefore, as a change of topology and metaphors to describe essences, ANT focuses on filaments, and on nodes that have "*as many dimensions* as they have connections" instead of surfaces (two dimensions) or spheres (three dimensions) (Latour 1996:370, original emphasis). In so doing, ANT does not assume the totalizing explanatory power of a theoretical paradigm, grand or otherwise, and thus provides much room for concept and theory development. After all, the act of theorizing should be a happening and process that is never concluded (see Wang, 2001).

By reassessing piracy and distribution in Greater China in the context of a highly dynamic and paradoxical process of globalization, one can utilize ANT's strengths in allowing flexibility for actors and networks to change. Because globalization processes have to do with substantial cross-border dispersals and the subsequent need for centralization of ownership and control (see Sassen, 2002), it is important to study simultaneously associations *and* dissociations as well as the ensuing multiplying and changing configurations of networks and actors. In so doing one hopes to avoid confining these complex and intersecting networks and actors to a predetermined notion of power relations.

Thus, for the case studies of piracy networks in Greater China, it is to study, for example, Sony and Philips' dumping of the VCD technology in China, and how this "plane of pure action"[10] subsequently, and *unexpectedly*, connected and interacted with various local, regional, and global players, thereby *creating* multiple circulating networks with forces that were unforeseen by any of the parties involved, including transnational electronics corporations, consumers, hardware manufacturers, transnational copyright industries, and the state (see chapter 4). It is also to study how respective copyright governance regimes in Taiwan, Hong Kong, and the Mainland, while *all* compliant with TRIPS requirements, are each drastically different in characteristics and enforcement actions. Through active and intersecting local interpretations, national maneuverings, regional interactions, and global forces, international treaties and agreements go through complex processes of translation and transformation, thereby producing vastly different results (chapters 6, 9, and 10). Finally, it is to study how three territories with fundamental differences in size, system, and power, by strategically connecting with, and working through, multiple moving networks, can exert similar threats to transnational copyright industries (chapters 6, 9, and 10).

Notes

1. Another more recent example is *Mission Impossible 2*, which was released in the United States on 25 May 2000. Pirated copies were found in Hong Kong on 28 May 2000 (shot in theater and with local subtitles). Personal interview with Mike Ellis, director, MPA Asia-Pacific Anti-Piracy Operations, 1 June 2000, Hong Kong.

2. Note the discrepancy between the above *Variety* estimate of 65 percent foreign box office grosses and the one presented here in table 1.2 of roughly 55 percent.

3. The timing is crucial. Because many foreign markets were closed during World War II, quite a number of unplayed films were stocked up to be released overseas (Donahue, 1987).

4. Even though the majors often collude and collaborate in overseas operations, the fact that overseas distribution has become increasingly competitive has caused the majors to become competitive overseas to maximize profits (Hillier, 1993).

5. Two other characteristics of film are that it suffers a cultural discount when traded across international boundaries, and it may result in external benefits (see Hoskins, Finn, and McFayden, 2000:127). Cultural discount happens when viewers of one territory or culture find it difficult to understand or identify with the content, themes, or values of the imported cultural goods due to different culture, language, or other such elements. And external benefits in economics indicate the benefits the product might bring to people other than the producer or the viewer.

6. Note, however, the implications for exhibitors. Theatrical exhibits greatly affect the performance of ancillary markets as the theatrical exposure and marketing would enhance subsequent performances of ancillary markets. Furthermore, because downstream purchase prices of movies by pay and free TV are mostly determined by a formula in which the film's box office gross is a crucial factor, the majors continue their emphasis on wide release. Additionally the increasingly hefty theatrical marketing and advertising would not be considered wasteful it they could benefit downstream end market prospects for a theatrical film (see Thomas and O'Brien, 2001).

7. It is also a side product of the recent wave of mega merger developments (e.g., Vivendi-Universal, AOL-Time Warner). As the *Variety* report points out, because film studios are now only a small part of these mega conglomerates, joining domestic and international distribution and marketing efforts appears to be a more efficient way of global operations.

8. While there are clear consequences of power difference, power is relational and fluid. Taiwan, for example, is an island with questionable political status with little power. Its piracy networks, on the other hand, have proven to be too much of a threat to the global copyright industries. In this case what is to be made of the question of size and power of a small island nation?

9. See also Foucault's (1978) writing on power as relational.

10. See Brown and Capdevila, 1999:35.

2

Recontextualizing Copyright: Technology, Transnational Trade Regimes, and the State

The rapidly changing environment of copyright regulations highlights the increasing importance, centrality, and complexity of issues surrounding intellectual property (IP) *and* piracy for economies worldwide. It is also an indication of how transnational corporations and industrial states strive to maintain control over property and markets in the face of technological challenges and changes. Suffice it to use two recent examples, one national (United States) and one international, to briefly illustrate such significant development in IP right regulation. In the United States, Congress in 1998 enacted the Digital Millennium Copyright Act (DMCA) to implement a World Intellectual Property Organization (WIPO) treaty.[1] One of the first and most important DMCA legal proceedings is the DeCSS[2] case in which the Motion Picture Association of America (MPAA) accused Eric Corley (a.k.a. Emmanuel Goldstein), editor of *2600: The Hacker Quarterly*, of helping to pirate MPAA member studio films by posting the DVD decryption code DeCSS on the Internet (*The Economist*, 2000:29). The U.S. District Court ruled in favor of MPAA on 17 August 2000, declaring that the defendants' posting of DeCSS on the Internet was a violation of the Digital Millennium Copyright Act, 17 U.S.C.§§1201 *et seq.* (MPAA website), a ruling with grave implications for questions of access, free speech and ownership in the "digital millennium."

On the global level, there is the World Trade Organization's (WTO) Agreement on Trade-Related Aspects of Intellectual Property Rights (TRIPS), which includes basic trade and international IP principles, protection, enforcement, dispute settlement, and transition arrangements (see WTO website). It also dictates that all state laws of its member countries (including developed countries, developing countries, and transition economies, as well as "least developed" countries) must conform to the TRIPS agreement by 2006.[3] There was also the signing, on 1 January 1996, of an agreement between WIPO and the WTO, providing cooperation concerning the implementation of the TRIPS agreement. In July 1998 WIPO and WTO further launched a joint initiative to help developing countries meet their TRIPS obligations in 2000 and beyond (see WIPO website). The Uruguay Round of the GATT negotiations that created WTO and TRIPS (under the auspices of WTO) therefore became a historically significant event as it marked a new era in transnational regime in general and IP regulation in particular. Not only did the Uruguay Round build IP protection into the fabric of GATT itself, TRIPS also established the highest level of IP protection in any international agreement.[4]

These transnational as well as national legal developments are inextricably linked. They epitomize not only the centrality of knowledge and IP in global trade as mentioned above but also other complex issues that require critical examination and contextualization: questions of control, power, and access in a digital age; the intricate relations among technology, content, and distribution; optical disc and online piracy and its implications for Hollywood's global operations; the significant role MPAA plays in American as well as global trade policy making; the dynamic relations between the state and transnational regimes; the North-South divide; and the changing role of the state in a global environment, among others. Copyright and piracy therefore provide a critical site where multiple issues play out and where such matters can be examined. As Boyle (1996) argues, the "sanctity of intellectual property" has replaced earlier issues of international importance to serve in an iconic role in the making of the developed world's foreign policies (p. 3), while "piracy of intellectual property" will replace nationalization as the main fear of the developed countries for the next fifty years (p. 4).

Furthermore, the increasing dominance of copyright industries in global trade is also symptomatic of a "new kind of structure" (Lash and Urry, 1994:112), one that extends on analysis of social structure with a focus on information structure, and of an "economy of signs and space" or a "de-centered set of economies of signs in space" (p. 4), in which the traded and circulated objects are increasingly signs and are thus postmodern (objects emptied out of meanings), post-industrial (objects emptied out of material content), and spatial (increased velocities of mobility and flows in the information structure). The control of intellectual property rights becomes crucial since what constitutes the global economy of signs is the trading of the rights to those signs. Likewise, in theorizing the rise of the network society in a global web, Castells (1996:91) advocates "informationalism" and an information technology paradigm. He argues that the current global network economy is "informational," rather than simply "information-based," because "the cultural-institutional attributes of the whole social system must be included in the diffusion and implementation of the new technological paradigm," and that the industrial economy is based increasingly on the emergence of an industrial culture, which is characterized by a "new social and technical division of labor," and not simply on the use of new sources of energy for manufacturing. The global informational economy, therefore, is viewed as distinct from the industrial economy but not opposed to its logic. Indeed, he sees the new global informational economy as subsuming the industrial economy and as, therefore, both capitalist (in terms of production) and informational (as a mode of development, see Bromley, 1999).

Power in this context is viewed as existing in the space of flows. While this line of theorization is not without its totalizing and technology-deterministic bias, it sheds light on some of the most important characteristics of the global informational structure. If indeed the new global economy is informational, post-industrial, and postmodern (as the cultural logic of late capitalism) as Castells and Lash and Urry have argued, it is then crucial to examine questions of how markets and property are organized, how information technologies and the ensuing networking logic have impacted the patterns of production, distribution, and exchange, how consumers figure in such structures, how the state is implicated in this process, and how and where power is constituted (see also Bromley's critique of Castells, 1999:14).[5]

This chapter focuses on Hollywood's global film practices as they relate to issues of piracy and copyright. Because of its reliance on the operations of distribution networks and windowing strategies (see chapter 1) for its global dominance, and because of its unique economics and market structure, Hollywood provides an important case study for the examination of issues of copyright, technology, piracy, the state, and globalization. The crucial role MPAA plays in shaping national and international trade policies and anti-piracy efforts further underscores Hollywood's unique involvement in the matter.

An examination of piracy, copyright, and the film industry would not be complete without situating them in the larger context of power, technology, the state, and the networking logic of globalization.[6]

Copyright, Piracy, and the Film Industry

[The] freshly formed Copyright Assembly . . . enlists into its membership the vast array of American enterprises involved in sports . . . music, song-writing, advertising, software, broadcasters . . . cable, movies, publishing, television programs, home video. These are the enterprises which [sic] are *America's most wanted exports*, in addition to being the favorites of the viewing, reading and listening public. . . . The simple fact is this: The protection of copyright and copyrights is not antagonistic to the New Technologies, such as the Internet. Not at all. The Internet is widened and made more fruitful by our high velocity involvement in it. *But if we cannot protect what we invest in, create and own, then we don't own anything.*

—Jack Valenti (15 June 2000, emphasis added)

There are two categories of intellectual property: industrial property, which includes inventions, patents, trademarks, trade secrets and industrial designs, and copyrights (see, for example, Benko, 1987). Copyright covers "original works of authorship fixed in any tangible medium of expression, which includes *inter alia* literary, musical, scientific, dramatic and artistic works and sound recordings" (17 U.S.C.§102, 1994, cited in Jayakar, 1997:531). There are two things worth noting here: One, copyright protects only the *expression* of ideas, not the ideas themselves. Copyright, therefore, favors the publisher and distributor, not necessarily the author. Two, with the development of digital technology, "works of authorship" are no longer fixed in any tangible medium of expression. Content is separated from the medium, hence the implications for piracy, as well as the resultant DMCA as an effort to curb the problems (see later discussion).

According to the 2002 International Intellectual Property Alliance (IIPA)[7] "Copyright Industries in the U.S. Economy" report (Siwek, 2002), copyright industries have continued to be one of the fastest growing segments of the U.S. economy for the eleventh straight year. There are two classifications of the copyright industries: (1) the *core* copyright industries include those that create copyrighted works as their primary product: the motion picture industry, the recording industry, the music publishing industry, the book, journal and newspaper publishing industry, the computer software industry, as well as legitimate theater, advertising, and the radio, television, and cable broadcasting industries; and (2) the *total* copyright industries encompass the core industries plus portions of other industries which either create, distribute, or depend on copyrighted works: for example retail trade (e.g., sales of video, audio, software, and books), the doll and toy industry, and computer manufacturing (see IIPA website).

Based on three economic indicators—value added to gross domestic product (GDP); share of national employment; and revenues generated from foreign sales and exports—the 2002 Siwek/IIPA report details the importance of the copyright industries to the U.S. economy. In 2001, the core copyright industries contributed an estimated $535.1 billion to the U.S. economy, accounting for approximately 5.24 percent of GDP.[8] The total copyright industries, in addition, contributed an estimated $791.2 billion to the U.S. economy, accounting for approximately 7.75 percent of GDP. Viewed in terms of the real annual growth rate, the core copyright industries have grown more than double the growth rate of the economy as a whole, with average annual growth rate between 1977 and 2001 at 7.0 percent while the rest of the U.S. economy grew at 3.0 percent (see table 2.1). Within the film industry, it saw a much greater growth between 1985

Table 2.1. Estimated Average Annual Real Growth Rate 1977–2001

	1977–2001	1987–2001	1991–2001
Core Copyright Industries	7.0	7.0	9.4
Remainder of U.S. Economy	3.0	3.2	3.0

Source: Copyright Industries in the U.S. Economy—the 2002 Report (Siwek, 2002).

and 1990 (from $21.5 billion in 1985 to $40 billion in 1990, close to 100 percent growth in five years). The annual growth rate in the 1990s is comparable to that of the copyright industries' average (between 6 and 7 percent for the period of 1993–1997, see table 2.2).

According to the Siwek/IIPA report, the copyright industries' foreign sales/exports are also larger than almost all other leading industry sectors. For 2001, for instance, the copyright industries' foreign sales exceeded the combined automobile and automobile parts industries, as well as the agricultural sector (tables 2.3 and 2.4). The film industry's foreign sales are roughly 10 percent that of the core copyright industries.

Table 2.2. Annual Receipts of Taxable Firms: 1985–1997 (in billions of dollars)

	1985	1990	1993	1994	1995	1996	1997
Motion Pictures	21.5	40.0	49.8	53.5	57.2	60.3	63.0

Source: U.S. Census Bureau (Statistical Abstract of the United States: 1999).

Table 2.3. Annual Growth Rate of Copyright Industry: Foreign Sales and Exports

1991	1995	1996	1997	1998	1999	2000	2001
6.4%	9.9%	13.3%	11.1%	3.5%	14.7%	7.6%	4.1%

Source: Copyright Industries in the U.S. Economy—the 2002 Report (Siwek, 2002).

Table 2.4. Foreign Sales/Exports for Selected Industries 2000 and 2001 (in billions of dollars)

Industry	Foreign Sales/Exports	
	2000	2001
Core Copyright Industries	85.46	88.97
Chemicals and Allied Products	74.43	74.68
Motor Vehicles, Equipment, and Parts	59.81	56.52
Aircraft and Aircraft Parts	51.52	55.31
Agricultural Sector	50.90	53.00
Electronic Components and Accessories	63.34	48.26
Computer and Peripherals	44.19	36.99

Source: Copyright Industries in the U.S. Economy—the 2002 Report (Siwek, 2002).

According to 1998–2002 IIPA "Special 301" Recommendations (see IIPA reports), conversely, total losses to piracy were estimated at $10.4 billion in 1998, $8.54 billion in 1999, $8.1 billion in 2000, and $8.38 billion in 2001, while total losses in the motion pictures industry were at $1.42 billion in 1998 (close to 14 percent of the total copyright industries' losses), $1.32 billion in 1999 (over 15 percent of the total losses), $1.22 billion in 2000 (15 percent of total losses), and $1.29 billion in 2001 (15.4 percent of total losses).

While the copyright industries have indeed suffered huge profit losses due to piracy, the accuracy and validity of the above estimates, however, are questionable. Because illegal sales and distribution are private acts, the needed data have to be based on extrapolation from very limited information. Furthermore, it is problematic to assume that each illegal copy would displace a sale at standard market prices. Finally, the estimates are based on reduction in "gross revenues" rather than on net loss to the industries (National Research Council, 2000).

Like other copyright industries, film industry is faced with the *appropriability problem*, where the costs of product development are high and where the costs of product imitation may be low (or, the high investment-to-reproduction costs, see Ryan, 1998, and Bettig, 1996). Furthermore, because of the capital intensiveness and the enormously high barriers to entry in the film industry, the seven major studios dominate production and distribution, representing 90 percent of total revenue. [9] To recoup the high costs, the majors have to also rely on the overseas markets. Indeed, Hollywood has been an international industry since the 1920s, counting on international markets for its profit. According to *Variety* (Dunkley and Harris, 2001), today roughly 65 percent of all seven majors' total box office income comes from international box office (see also tables 2.5 and 2.6; note that some of the figures differ from the *Variety* estimate).

Table 2.5. International Box Office as a Percentage of Global Box Office by Distributor, 1993–1997

	1993	1994	1995	1996	1997
Disney	43.2	47.5	48.6	47.6	58.6
Fox	34.0	48.7	49.2	50.8	59.1
MGM/UA	23.4	26.7	30.2	52.8	39.8
Paramount	50.5	43.9	44.5	39.5	27.7
Sony	45.6	50.0	52.8	49.6	45.6
Universal	54.0	55.6	53.8	64.7	59.7
Warner					
Bros.	53.0	49.6	54.0	47.4	51.7
Other	23.7	25.6	47.2	34.6	33.2
Total	45.8	46.1	49.5	48.2	48.5

Source: Cruttenden Roth; Baskerville Communications Corp. From TableBase™, Copyright 2000 Accession# 1683277.

Table 2.6. International Box Office by Distributor 1993–1999 [e] (in $ million)

	1993	1994	1995	1996	1997	1998	1999
Disney	650	963	1,007	1,090	1,253	1,173	1,320
Fox	290	481	426	787	1,000	1,970	1,016
MGM/UA	30	55	150	331	106	n/a	295
Paramount	500	600	445	491	280	491	310
Sony	768	514	805	610	1,070	780	574
Universal	860	850	812	901	910	683	1,258
Warner	1,100	870	1,070	836	725	760	1,070
Other	162	287	675	454	656	963	817
Total	4,360	4,620	5,390	5,500	6,000	6,820	6,660

[e] Estimated
Source: Cruttenden Roth; Baskerville Communications Corp. From TableBase™, Copyright 2000
Accession# 2318882.

The importance of foreign markets has made centralized distribution networks essential to the majors' overseas operations and their ultimate survival.[10] Piracy and copyright infringement can be incapacitating if unchecked or pervasive. Thus, the key to profit making and the solution to the appropriability problem lie in copyright protection when periods of exclusivity and monopoly are established, thereby creating economic incentives for the creators, the rights holders, and the distributors (e.g., Bettig, 1996; Ryan, 1998; Benko, 1987). The windowing strategies (or the sequencing of films through different exhibition outlets and price differentiation approaches) practiced by Hollywood are possible only with proper copyright protection, since market extension relies fully on the transfer and ownership of exclusive rights to reproduction, distribution, performance, and display. The fact that the less efficient means of distribution in terms of copyright exclusion normally appear at the end of the cycle or release sequence (e.g., broadcasting) attests to the importance of copyright exclusion and protection (See Bettig, 1996, and Litman, 1998).

Referring to itself as "a little State Department," the Motion Picture Association (MPA) is MPAA's international arm and was formed in 1945 to "reestablish American films in the world market, and to respond to the rising tide of protectionism resulting in barriers aimed at restricting the importation of American films" (See MPAA website). Its name was changed from the Motion Picture Export Association of America (MPEAA) to the MPA in 1994 to "more accurately reflect the global nature of audiovisual entertainment in today's international marketplace" (MPAA website). It prides itself in having expanded its operations to cover not only film or cultural activities but also those that fall in diplomatic, economic, and political arenas. It has historically worked closely with the U.S. Department of Commerce and other trade and foreign policy offices. Will Hays, for example, argued as early as the 1920s that trade no longer followed the flag, instead "trade followed the film" (cited in Maltby, 1995:69).

Jack Valenti, MPAA and MPA chairman, has been a leading figure in the copy-right industries' anti-piracy efforts. More recently, he worked closely with the USTR during the Uruguay Round of GATT negotiations. With MPA's global anti-piracy operations, Valenti's highest priority now is fighting "earthbound and cyberspace" piracy (cited in Bromley, 2000:40).

Meanwhile, in this new global informational economy of signs, intellectual property has become the real property (e.g., Hoskins, McFadyen, and Finn, 1997) while copyright becomes the "main form of capital" since a major source of copyright industries' profit comes from the copying and selling of copyrights (Lash and Urry, 1994:136). This new postindustrial structure has implications for relations of production and distribution since what is being exploited interna-tionally is no longer exclusively labor but capital in the form of copyright (Lash and Urry, 1994). The discussion above, then, demonstrates the film industry's efforts (and struggles) to organize and control access to this "property" and "capital" as it expands on a global scale to maximize profits. The windowing strategies, the use of encryption codes, the policing of DVD zones (see later discussion), and other such measures are but a few of the strategies Hollywood uses to maintain control, and to ensure control of access and exclusive rights to the value-added postmodern goods. As the following section will show, the emergence of digital technologies has disrupted the traditional balance of power in managing the circulation of informational goods, and thus has great implica-tions for issues of power, space, and control.

Hardware, Software, and the Floating Content: Power and the Digital Challenge

> [B]ut the journey [*trajet*], because it lacks a trajectory, is fundamentally out of control. Thus the *interface* in real time definitely replaces the *interval* that had formerly constructed and organized the history and geography of our societies, leading to an obvious culture of paradox, in which everything *arrives* without there being any need either to *travel* or to *leave* in the slightest physical sense.
> —Paul Virilio (1993:10, original emphasis)

Issues of piracy and copyright protection have always been closely connected to technology. The origin of literary property rights in the sixteenth century, in effect, was tied to the development of the printing press (see Benko, 1987).

For the U.S. film industry, piracy emerged as a problem in the late 1970s when Sony introduced the VCR to the consumer electronics market. Video pi-racy became a serious concern for Hollywood in the early 1980s when it real-ized that wherever there was hardware capacity, there was a market for pirated videos (see Bettig, 1996). In Bettig's 1996 study of copyright and the political economy of IP, he listed some of the contributing factors of video piracy in Asia and the Middle East: lack of IP laws and weak enforcement of existing laws, minimal participation in bilateral and multilateral international IP agreements, a proliferation of recording technologies, underdeveloped local production industries, and public demand for content due to screen quotas, state-controlled broadcasting, or censorship. While most of these factors are still relevant and prevalent today, the development of digital technologies has increased the scale of piracy and intensified the complexity of the issues. In the case of the VCR, the technology affords consumers with means for time-shift recording and content sharing and pirates with the ease to duplicate and distribute on a mass scale. In the case of digital technologies, the potential for piracy has been radically transformed.

When information is stored digitally, content is liberated from the medium and it is the information alone that flows (or floats) to the recipient; the costs of reproduction accordingly decrease and the volume and speed increase, while quality remains unchanged with each generation of duplication. Optical disc and online piracy, for instance, have become major threats to the film, music, and software industries because of the low cost, high speed, extraordinary quality of the copies, and ease of distribution made possible by digital technologies. Further still, with digital production and online delivery and distribution potential, the need for intermediaries (e.g., distributors, publishers, etc.) is decreasing, thereby creating the possibility of "disintermediation" where creators (*and* pirates) and consumers are able to connect more directly. In other words, digital information and technologies as well as computer networking logic are revolutionizing and radically transforming the economics and character of information production, distribution, and reception/consumption (e.g., National Research Council, 2000).

With progressive devaluation of the medium and the hardware, and the increasing costs and overvaluation of the content and software, on the other hand, the content is further decontextualized and becomes indispensable (see Boyle, 1996). Control over access to, and ownership of, the content is ever more crucial.[11] When information is stored digitally, however, access also inevitably means copying. Complete control of copying would therefore mean control of access. Technical protection measures such as cryptography (e.g., encryption) thus become a logical mechanism for the copyright industries to control access to their content. The goal of encryption is to scramble the information so that it is not readable or usable until it is unscrambled or decrypted. Here "access" means whether one can "read" the document, whereas "use" focuses on what one does with it (see National Research Council, 2000:174–175).

It is illuminating then that Congress included in the DMCA two kinds of anti-circumvention regulations: (1) The *access-control provision* that outlaws circumventing technical protection measures used by rights holders to control access. It is therefore illegal to break an encryption such as CSS (Content Scramble System) licensed to DVD hardware manufacturers by DVD Copy Control Association (DVD CCA)(see DVD CCA website). (2) The *anti-device provisions* that outlaw devices that are intended for purposes of circumventing technical protection measures (National Research Council, 2000). In other words, DMCA indirectly encourages entertainment industries to use strong encryption to protect their products while criminalizing efforts to break those codes and the possession of any tools designed for that purpose (see Barlow, 2000). The court decision on the aforementioned MPAA-DeCSS case was based on these provisions. The indication was that, in the digital era, rights holders' control over access far outweighs the importance of free speech.[12]

In addition to technical protection measures, MPAA and DVD CCA (an organization loosely associated with MPAA) also use the classification and policing of DVD zones to prevent foreign DVD markets from stepping out of line, and therefore to ensure the proper functioning of the windowing strategies. DVDs are manufactured with a code that allows the DVD to be played only on DVD players sold in a particular geographic area of the world. Regional DVD coding thus prevents foreign viewers from watching and playing, for example, DVDs sold in other regions (e.g., in the United States via the Internet) before the film is scheduled for theatrical release in the area.[13]

Not only do these cases speak to the industries' need to use technology to control time and command space, they are also about speed: speed by which the computer networks function, speed by which legitimate *as well as* illegitimate distribution networks operate, and speed with which the increasingly technology-savvy global audiences demand their day and date releases of Hollywood products and instant gratification. Electronic networks have made worldwide distribution inexpensive and very fast, both for legitimate content rights holders and for pirates. Global audience demand, which is progressively more informed by instantaneous webcasting and other media reports about new releases in the United States and which appears to be less willing to wait for their respective local theatrical releases (usually several months behind the U.S. releases), has created an instant market for pirated products.[14] The speed of digital networking also has consequences for law enforcement (and thus implications for the state), as global piracy (and other criminal) networks are usually much more efficient and flexible in their operations than their legitimate counterparts.[15]

The Global Context: Transnational Regimes and the State

> By becoming signatories to TRIPS, however, states have for the first time through their membership in the World Trade Organization ceded to a global organization significant elements of their sovereignty over their administrative and judicial structures and procedures—essential features of polity, not policy.
> —Michael Ryan (1998:143)

In the world of legitimate (transnational corporations) and illegitimate (global, regional, local pirates) distribution networks, and of transnational copyright regulations, what becomes of the state? Has the sovereignty of states further eroded with their signing of TRIPS and through their membership of the WTO? Has the state become simply "one node in a wider network of private and public, legal and illegal, powers?" (see Bromley's critique of Castells, 1999:10). An analysis of recent global copyright governance development can help explain the dynamics between the state and transnational regimes and the implications for national cultural/film policies.

With the move toward a global information society, the IP regime has also been increasingly globalized through WIPO, WTO, and TRIPS (see table 2.7). More specifically, the establishment of TRIPS under the auspices of the WTO attests to the further expansion of global copyright issues into the arena of global *trade* (as opposed to treating it only in the area of international legal regime, see May, 1998). It is also important to note the imperative role the U.S. intellectual property industries play in ensuring that the U.S. negotiating team would take up the industries' specific position (given these industries' importance to the U.S. economy) first in the Uruguay Round of GATT negotiations, and later in TRIPS. The interests and requirements of the IP industries, consequently, were fore-grounded in the negotiations. That there are no international laws per se governing global copyright protection, only agreements and treaties, further complicates the situation (see Benko, 1987:5). Regardless of how far-reaching TRIPS or WIPO agreements are, the success of the said international agreements or treaties and the protection of copyrights still lie in the effectiveness of individual national laws and enforcement efforts, hence the crucial role the state plays in transnational copyright governance. Additionally, while such trade fora as the WTO meetings further erode state sovereignty, a developing country is not completely without leverage in how it negotiates its position in global trade and IP issues vis-à-vis the global trade regimes and with the United States. A case in point is China's leverage in its trade and IP negotiations with the United States, as demonstrated in its passage of the Permanent Normal Trade Relation (PNTR) in 1999–2000 and in its accession into the WTO in 2001. China's tough stand in restricting the import of Hollywood films further illustrates some of the possibilities, albeit slim, of maneuvering and resistance by developing nations (see chapter 5).

Frow (2000) defines the postwar period as marked by the struggle for dominance between two opposing models of international information and knowledge governance: *development* versus *trade*, with the former represented

Table 2.7. Transnational IP Governance

The UN System (one nation one vote)
        Paris Convention (1883) + Berne Convention (1886) = United International Bureaux for the Protection of IP (BIRPI, 1893)
        ➔WIPO (1960) ➔ WIPO became a specialized UN agency (1974)

International Trade Regime
        The Uruguay Round of the GATT negotiation (1986–1995) ➔ WTO created and TRIPS took effect (January 1995, Geneva)

---

by the New World Information and Communication Order (NWICO), along with such regimes and organizations as WIPO and UNESCO, and the latter by TRIPS, plus WTO, the International Monetary Fund (IMF), and the World Bank. With NWICO being defeated in 1985 upon the U.S. withdrawal from UNESCO, and with the ratification of TRIPS in 1995, the trade approach has clearly become the dominant model in governing global IP issues.[16]

While his examination is insightful and illuminating, and while it is true that the development and dominance of global *trade* regimes in regulating world-wide IP issues has been most significant, Frow's views are not without questions. First of all, as much as NWICO was a movement espoused by a large bloc of the Third World nations, and as much as WIPO and UNESCO do embody a "development" component in their operations, it would be overly optimistic to believe that they were established in the true sense of a *development orientation*. Alleyne (1995), for example, points out that the United Nations was set up by the wartime Allied nations from the outset to form a specific *international order* as opposed to establishing justice or equality as a development model would suggest. Furthermore, even with the UN's one-nation-one-vote system, a few powerful states still get to dominate the decision-making structures of the international organizations and regimes in two major ways: (1) dominance of technical expertise and the resulting majorities on the technical related committees that inform the operations of the institutions, and (2) the financial support of the international bureaucratic operations (Alleyne, 1995:30–31).

As noted earlier, the Uruguay Round of the GATT negotiations had drastically changed the structure of global copyright governance. Before the Uruguay Round, international IP rights governance was performed by "obscure administrators at the World Intellectual Property Organization (WIPO) and its predecessors," while trade diplomacy was conducted by "high-profile trade and economic ministers at the GATT forum" (Ryan, 1998:12). Since the Uruguay Round, the international IP governance is mainly regulated through the WTO's Agreements on Trade-Related Aspects of Intellectual Property Rights (TRIPS).

Instead of defining the changes of international copyright governance from a UN system to a global trade body solely in terms of competition for dominance between the development and the trade models, it might be more fruitful to also treat such a crucial shift as a move toward the convergence and integration of functionalism and linkage-bargain models that Ryan (1998:18) has summarized. WIPO, being a function-specific UN agency, is the "law creation mill," while WTO, as a linkage-bargain trade regime, "fixes the breakdowns." Further, because the making of international IP laws is viewed as both function-specific and linkage-bargain diplomacy, it would make sense for policymakers to use both the WIPO and WTO fora. The role of the state vis-à-vis the global is far more implicated in such a framework while the tensions—between North and South, the local and the global—are much more pronounced.

In Ryan's (1998) view, the GATT forum was much preferred by the U.S. trade diplomats over the one-nation-one-vote WIPO regime for governing global IP rights precisely because of GATT's linkage bargaining forum and its economic power-based decision-making structure. Theoretically such linkage bargain and deep integration (i.e., "harmonizing the policies and laws of developing countries with those of the global community," Ryan 1998:141) diplomacy could attain unprecedented multilateral IP agreement that WIPO treaties could not. For example, under such linkage bargain agreements the developing countries would provide universal minimum IP protection standards as well as relaxation of foreign direct investment restrictions that industrialized countries normally demand, in exchange for much needed breaks and reductions in tariffs on, say, apparel and agriculture that they usually seek. The United States was therefore instrumental in expanding intellectual property rights into a trade issue. By doing so the United States, as the world's largest market, could effectively exert structural power at a trade forum such as WTO.

To rely exclusively on multilateral agreements for IP protection, however, was still deemed too risky by the copyright industries. Under the leadership of MPAA, in 1984 the U.S. copyright industries created IIPA as a separate strategy to strengthen international copyright right protection.[17] The main IIPA strategy was to support an agenda for the USTR's Section 301 mandate, because the bilateral Section 301 strategy, with sanction possibilities, would increase enforcement levels in developing countries.[18] As Ryan (1998) has clearly pointed out, the formation of IIPA as well as its bilateral (e.g., Special 301) and unilateral (e.g., economic sanctions and other retaliation measures) preferences, as opposed to multilateral through GATT and WIPO, were greatly influenced by Hollywood because of the piracy problems the major studios were facing. Based on the IIPA Special 301 Recommendations and under the 1988 Omnibus Act, USTR would announce which countries are to be identified under Special 301.[19] In addition to countries already subject to 301 discipline or being monitored under Section 306 of the Trade Act,[20] USTR would name TRIPS Copyright Cases,[21] Potential Priority Foreign Countries,[22] Priority Foreign Countries,[23] Priority Watch List, Watch List, and Special Mention according to the severity of their offenses and if the countries do not begin to "solve their copyright protection deficiencies, improve enforcement, and dismantle market access barriers."[24] The unilateral trade retaliations and bilateral Section 301 and Special 301 actions undertaken by the USTR have proved to be a useful tool in securing better copyright protection overseas and removing trade barriers.[25]

The above discussion has, on the one hand, demonstrated the significant and active role the state plays in global trade and copyright issues. Global financial and media markets, therefore, need to be viewed as "social constructs" and "products of regulation" that have been established with "particular speeds, balances of forces, degrees of openness" (Frow, 2000:178).[26] With TRIPS's linkage bargain and deep integration orientation, on the other hand, the state is even further linked to the global. States now need to bargain not just with other states but also with their own domestic groups, making domestic concessions while redefining the importance of various issues to domestic policy makers. Under TRIPS, then, the key to achieving international agreement is to get "the right mix of issues on the table so that previously unrelated issues can be *linked*"

(Ryan, 1998:12, emphasis added). Consequently, the emerging global interdependence under GATT and WTO does appear to have further eroded state sovereignty by demanding wide-ranging trade policy restructuring in exchange for trade benefits and advantages from industrialized countries. As Sassen (1996) has pointed out, by participating in the implementation of globalization the state is being transformed. Many governments are experiencing their roles as going beyond traditional foreign policy to extend to global trade, environment, and economic issues. By adhering to the WTO agenda, governments are also placing the principle of free trade above all other criteria.[27] Thus, what she terms as the "strategic geography" or a "new geography of power" is related to the "unbundling of national territory" (2000:225) due partly to the issues of the spaces of the global economy, the ascendance of legal regimes, and the growing importance of electronic space (1996:5).

The crucial question is, then, does the institutional order of the capitalist economy and the state have to be necessarily treated in constant-sum terms, "assuming that any increase in power in one sphere implies a diminution in the other?" (Bromley, 1999:16). Why couldn't it be treated, as Bromley (1999) has suggested, as both a constant-sum phenomenon in some aspects and a positive-sum one in others since power can be both competitive and collective? States do derive their power from being members of a system of states, while regional and international organizations do not always represent only an erosion of sovereignty as much as a form of multilevel consolidation. In the case of copyright governance and TRIPS, for example, the state power is not only indispensable and instrumental in implementing and enforcing international agreements but also in reflexively negotiating and maneuvering its positions vis-à-vis transnational regimes and regional and domestic influences (both legitimate and illegitimate) while shaping national policies pertaining to the working of information structures. It raises critical questions, for instance, concerning the protection of local film industry vis-à-vis transnational copyrights holders and agreements, which in the age of regional/global trade agreements tend to favor the North or larger industrialized nations.

Overlapping Domains

Even a longer network remains local at all points.

—Bruno Latour (1993:117)

In consequence, analysis of these circumstances cannot be accomplished merely by "modest modification of existing neo-Marxist models of uneven-development and state formation." Today social actors are likely to live, and entities likely to operate, in overlapping domains of the national and the global. The distinct formations produced of these dynamics require empirical specification and theorization on their own terms.

—Saskia Sassen (2000:221)

At first glance, the increasingly trade-oriented global governance of copyright and the further subjugation of the state to global trade regimes seem to point to the inevitable conclusions of the formidable power of transnational capital as represented by copyright industries, the embeddedness of technology and transnational legal and trade regimes in capitalism, and the still firmly entrenched North-South divide. Political economists have pointed to the inherent bias of ownership and control, and the ensuing full inscription of information, technology, and laws into "the political, economic and social relations of capitalism."[28] A deeper look, however, reveals the complexity of the processes involved and the insufficiency of such (politico-economic) frameworks. Because there is a growing intersection between the national and the global, and the yet to be fully co-opted "power of flows"[29] that digital technologies can still offer, there are uncertainties and disorders, and hence opportunities, yet to be accounted for or realized. After all, "globalization" as "a noun of *becoming*" should be treated as such, and as a continual evolvement of "processes" where the planning, intervention, changes, and anomalies are taken into account (Frow, 2000:174, emphasis added). The dynamic and interconnecting relations between the state and the global, consequently, deserve and require serious examination since they set up the "contents" and "conditions" of the global. As Sassen (2000:217) has pointed out, the two key elements in the formulation of the conditions and contents are "the degree of economic globalization's embeddedness in the national and the specificity and social thickness of the global," because the global economy is "something that has to be actively implemented, reproduced, serviced, and financed."

This is not to negate political economy as a worthy area of study or as a useful tool of research. Quite the contrary, political economy has been an especially powerful approach in assessing and critiquing the workings of the enduring architecture of global capitalism. This is instead to point out the insufficiency and blind spots inherent in such a framework (e.g., in dealing with the variable geometry aspect such as the fast changing digital environment and its effects) while looking for complementary approaches and methods of inquiry. In Bettig's study (1996:33) of the political economy of intellectual property, for example, he summarizes three fundamental categories of radical politico-economic communications theory in examining IP issues: (1) the economic structure of communications industries; (2) the effects of the logic of capital on the production, distribution, and consumption of culture and information; and (3) the contradictions and forms of resistance within capitalist communications systems. In other words, in this sort of political economy framework issues of copyright and piracy can only be understood in, and are reduced to, the context of a totalizing capitalistic inscription. While these categories are useful in explaining the underlying structure of global economy, they fail to acknowledge the cultural, national, and regional dynamics that have presented some of the most interesting cases of local differences and specificities in, for instance, how national and regional laws and enforcements vary; how "late industrializers" such as Taiwan, Korea, and China are good learners (Ryan, 1998:149); how governments and consumers collude directly or indirectly with domestic as well as regional and global pirates; or how some of the hardware electronics industries are actively involved in such practices and operations.[30] Further, although resistance within the capitalist system is acknowledged in Bettig's work, it is subsumed in the overall logic of capital and hegemony and hence treated only as an afterthought.

As Latour (1993) argues, while concepts such as *local* and *global* work well for geometry and surfaces, they are ill suited to describe networks or topology. The continuous paths that connect the local and the global, instead, are what enable the network to function. In other words, it is important not to focus exclusively on aspects of global production and local distribution as isolated phenomena. Rather, one should look at the specific links and connections that transport and translate between the local and the global. In studying issues of copyright and piracy, therefore, it is critical to review the nodes and hubs on the web (e.g., Hollywood as central distribution networks and its overseas operations, transnational regimes and local enforcements), the directions, movements, and forces of the lines that connect the nodes and points (e.g., where are piracy networks located and how do they operate in relation to legitimate ones, how are legitimate as well as illegitimate informational goods transported and translated), as well as the ever-changing alignment and configuration of the web itself (e.g., the complex and dynamic relations among the state, transnational corporations, pirate networks, optical-disc production line makers and distributors, and consumers). It would be seriously remiss, in studying issues of copyright and piracy, to insist on a fixed underlying structure of global capitalism while ignoring specific middle and local specificities and anomalies that could affect or condition the movements of the network. It becomes crucial to enlist a network- and process-oriented spatial framework, as discussed in chapter 1, to adequately study the complexity of issues pertaining to media and economic globalization such as copyright and piracy. Castells (1998:366), for example, argues for a "new structure of power" dominated by a "*network geometry*, in which power relationships are always specific to a given configuration of actors and institutions" (emphasis added).

Similarly, Appadurai (2000:5) stresses "relations of disjuncture" in that he understands "the paths or vectors taken by [the various flows] have different speeds, axes, points of origin and termination, and varied relationships to institutional structures in different regions, nations, or societies." He uses as an example of such disjuncture the media flows across national boundaries producing images of luxury or well-being that cannot be satisfied by consumer capabilities or national living standards. Piracy, then, can also be partially understood in such relations of disjuncture. If, for example, the capability to watch a first-run Hollywood film or to buy certain brand names as shown in these images or to use the latest computer software have come to represent a certain desirable status, the counterfeit products would then be a cheap and easy replacement for the real, and a quick solution to the perceived disjuncture or disparity. By consuming these counterfeit products, the consumers are actively reorienting and negotiating their local existence in relation to the global and the regional, as the local is immersed in the global, and vice versa. As long as they are on the network, they can be reflexive learning subjects. Thus, drawing on Lash and Urry (1994:15), I argue that consumers are reflexive "agents of aestheticization," as opposed to passive recipients, in their consumption of pirated goods and, hence, complicity in piracy. Do I then dare to suggest that the consumers' complicity in piracy, especially in the developing countries, is in some cases a form of self-empowerment (see more discussion in chapter 5)?

Notes

1. Unlike prior copyright legislation, DMCA contains no allowance for "fair use" and is therefore slanted heavily in favor of content owners. See Parker, Dana. 2000. Copyrights vs. free speech: DeCSS case may be the first test of the DMCA. *EMedia Professional*, 13(3):18

2. CSS stands for *Content Scrambling System*, it is an encryption used for movie DVDs. DeCSS is the software that breaks the CSS encryption. See DeCSS Central site: http://web.lemuria.org/DeCSS/ (accessed 15 April 2003).

3. See WTO website: www.wto.org/english/thewto_e/whatis_e/agrm6_e.htm. When TRIPS took effect on 1 January 1995, it provided "transition arrangements" of one, five, or eleven years for its member countries to fall into line: developed countries were given one year to make sure that their IP laws conform with the TRIPS agreement; developing countries and transition economies were given five years; while "least developed" countries eleven years.

4. Boyle, 1996. It is also important to note that initially it was at the urging of the United States Trade Representative (USTR) that the GATT membership agreed to include IP protection on the Uruguay Round agenda (see Ryan 1998). And as a result of the Uruguay Round negotiations, WIPO and GATT joined forces and such changes have contributed to the further reconfiguration of the state in this new global trade environment.

5. Current literature on intellectual property rights pertaining to media and economic globalization has been valuable in contributing to our understanding of IP issues. Most of these works, however, are one-dimensional in their approach. They mostly address issues of technology (e.g., National Research Council, 2000), laws (e.g., Benko, 1987; Boyle, 1996), political economy (e.g., Bettig, 1996 and 1997; May, 1998), and international information order (Frow, 2000; Ryan, 1998; Jayakar, 1997). With a few exceptions, most of these works also tend to be descriptive and diagnostic, rather than theoretical and critical. Finally, most of the existing works fail to (1) differentiate among different types of intellectual property rights; and (2) within the domain of copyright, distinguish among different industries. Such clarifications and distinctions are crucial, as each industry and each IP right is unique with vastly different theoretical and practical implications.

6. The state is very much an active participant, rather than a waning influence, in the processes of globalization in general, and in global IP and IT policy making and negotiations in particular.

7. IIPA is a "coalition of associations representing U.S. copyright-based industries in bilateral and multilateral efforts to open up foreign markets closed by piracy and other market access barriers" (www.iipa.com/html/022398_press_release.html). IIPA member

associations include MPAA, American Film Marketing Association (AFMA), the Recording Industry Association of America (RIAA), the Association of American Publishers (AAP), the Business Software Alliance (BSA), the Interactive Digital Software Association (IDSA), and the National Music Publishers' Association (NMPA).

8. Furthermore, 1997 saw the growth rate of value added to GDP by the core copyright industries of 241 percent over a twenty-year period (1977–1997, see the 1999 IIPA report).

9. See Ryan, 1998. Also, in the first issue of the 2001 Weekly *Variety* (1–7 January, pp.1 and 48), Roger Smith analyzes the profit records of the film industry in 2000. In the column he points out the extremely high barriers to entry in the movie business, that it has taken seven years for Spielberg, Katzenberg and Geffen to make *DreamWorks* into the first new major in fifty years (with $2.7 billion of "OPM"—Other People's Money).

10. In the film industry we see the practice of flexible/de-centralized productions (outsourcing productions) working with centralized distribution (i.e., Hollywood Majors' global distribution networks).

11. An example would be how MGM was crippled by the sale of the bulk of its library seventeen years ago. See Smith (2001).

12. In the MPAA-DeCSS case, "free speech" comes in the form of DeCSS dissemination on the Internet. See *Economist*, "Freedom of Speech," 5 August 2000, p. 29 for a discussion of the issue and of the origin of DeCSS. In 1999 a young Norwegian programmer created DeCSS to decrypt CSS. In early 2000, Norwegian police raided the house of the sixteen-year-old Jon Johansen and confiscated his computer equipment. In the belief that information wants to be free and in the tradition of the open-source Internet community, however, DeCSS was still widely distributed. The MPAA DeCSS case would soon change that.

13. There are currently eight DVD zones. Zone 1: Canada, U.S., U.S. Territories; 2: Japan, Europe, South Africa, Middle East (including Egypt); 3: Southeast Asia, East Asia (including Hong Kong); 4: Australia, New Zealand, Pacific Islands, Central America, Mexico, South America, Caribbean; 5: Former Soviet Union, Indian Subcontinent, Africa (also North Korea, Mongolia); 6: China; 7: Reserved and not in use yet; 8: Special international venues (e.g., airplanes, cruise ships, etc.). See DVD CCA and Infrench websites.

14. Ang Lee's *Crouching Tiger Hidden Dragon* (2000) is an interesting case that reverses the usual sequence, direction, and flow of piracy. This Hong Kong—Taiwan — China co-production was released in Asia five months before its U.S. release. Pirated video copies of the film were circulating in the U.S. market long before the film's formal U.S. release in December 2000. Personal interviews.

15. Castells in part three of his three-volume work on the network society, *End of Millennium* (1998), has an extensive discussion on the operations of global criminal networks in the informational structure.

16. Because of TRIPS's trade orientation and pro-North stand, it is viewed as imposing a definition of IP rights directly disadvantageous to developing countries, as they are almost always the net importers of IP rights while the developed world are the net exporters. Such conditions cause more outflow of much needed foreign exchange in the Third World while further increasing their indebtedness. Furthermore, developing countries also view IP protection as having negative effects on technological developments and the acquisitions of know-hows.

17. At the outset the copyright industries did not advocate a multilateral, GATT-based diplomatic effort for fear that the United States might lose its economic sovereignty to a global regime (see both Ryan, 1998 and Alleyne, 1995).

18. Initially, the Trade and Tariff Act of 1974 enabled the United States to take retaliatory action against any country that denied it rights granted by a trade agreement or unfairly restricted U.S. commerce (Jayakar, 1997). The cooperation among the copyright industries and the resulting lobbying leverage IIPA possessed had led to the expansion and the change of language of the 1974 Trade Act: the Trade and Tariffs Act of 1984 extended the definition of unfair trade practices to include intellectual property rights violations. The 1984 Trade Act also empowered the USTR to undertake annual review of problem countries, which could result in a USTR investigation and subsequent trade sanctions (see Jayakar, 1997 and Ryan, 1998). Under the same trade act, the U.S. president would also consider a country's IP protection record when deciding on its eligibility for the Generalized System of Preferences (GSP), and whether a country's actions are "unjustifiable" or "unreasonable" according to Section 301 (Alleyne, 1995:133). Additionally, the Omnibus Trade and Competitiveness Act of 1988 granted more power to the United States to retaliate against foreign trade barriers. It detailed measures through which the USTR could investigate, identify, and retaliate against foreign countries that had failed to provide adequate IP protection to U.S. copyright industries' overseas operations (see Bettig, 1996 and Jayakar, 1997).

19. It is called the special 301 trade policy. See Ryan, 1998:71.

20. For example, China and Paraguay in 1998–1999.

21. For example, Denmark, Greece, and Ireland in 1998–1999.

22. For example, Ukraine—GSP in 1998–1999. Examples taken from the "USTR 2000 'Special 301' Decisions and IIPA 1998–1999 Estimated Trade Losses Due to Copyright Piracy." See IIPA website.

23. That is, those with the "most onerous or egregious" policies that deny U.S. rights holders IP protection or market access. See Jayakar, 1997:534.

24. IIPA (1998), "Copyright Piracy in 55 Countries Causes $10.8 Billion in Trade Losses in 1997." IIPA Press Release, 23 February 1998. See IIPA website: http://www.iipa.com/html/022398_press_release.html

25. Jayakar (1997) lists four factors that have contributed to the foreign countries' compliance with U.S. pressures: receipt of GSP benefits, the importance of the United States as an export market and source of investment, local industrial and technological competence and policies, and domestic political equations.

26. John Frow (2000:176) views the recent development of global IP right regime in the context of a "Gramscian" view of globalization, in which it is not considered a sweeping process, but rather "a series of moves, strategically coordinated and implemented, which are complexly related to the dynamics of capital accumulation and which have uneven effects on different fields." The establishment of TRIPS, Frow suggests, should then be viewed as a result of the careful planning in transnational bureaucracies to create the legal instruments necessary for ensuring the unimpeded flow of goods and capital. It denotes an apparent historical demarcation in the global control of information.

27. Sassen (1996) has pointed out that even here in the United States many people who had supported GATT did not like the idea of the WTO because it would mean binding the nation to an international dispute-resolution tribunal that is not entirely controlled by the United States.

28. See Graham and Marvin (1996:94). In their work they discuss four approaches to the studying of relations between cities and telecommunications. Some of the discussions are applicable to the examination of global copyright issues.

29. As opposed to the "flows of power." See Castells (1996:469), who concludes, "the power of flows takes precedence over the flows of power," to argue that the net-

working logic that has induced "a social determination of a higher level than that of the specific social interests expressed through the networks."

30. Personal in-depth interviews conducted with optical-disc production line distributors, optical-disc production plant owners, and other industry representatives in summer 1999, winter 1999–2000, and summer 2000 in Taiwan, Hong Kong, and China.

3

WTO and the Greater China Economic Circle: Local, Regional, and Global Dynamics

> I believe that as this century unfolds and people look back on this day, they will conclude that in admitting China to the WTO we took a decisive step in shaping a global economic and commercial system.
> —Robert B. Soellick, U.S. Trade Representative
> (*New York Times*, 11 November 2001)

It would be remiss to discuss film distribution and piracy issues in Greater China without examining the impacts that China's and Taiwan's respective accessions to WTO have had on their media policies. It is important to note that while the Hong Kong Special Administrative Region (HKSAR) is not directly linked to the WTO accession, its special position as the connection between the Mainland and Taiwan, and as the gateway between the Mainland and a major part of the world, would be greatly affected by the WTO-induced further trade liberalization both on the Mainland and between the Mainland and Taiwan. Meanwhile, the examination of the WTO accession sheds light on how processes of reterritorialization and translation of the global into the regional, the national, and the local in turn shape the multiple and complex processes of globalization, as the above USTR quote indicates. It also puts the formation of the Greater China economic circle in the context of a new regionalism and associationalism that complements these processes of globalization (see later discussion).

41

The WTO Accession

It is not a coincidence that both the role of distribution in global film and entertainment operations and the unprecedented scale of optical media piracy expanded during the decade of the 1990s. With the collapse of the socialist economies of Eastern Europe in the early 1990s, and the dizzying array of advanced digital technology developments through the 1990s, there was much celebration and talk of a new market-driven global informational economy that rendered boundaries obsolete. It is amidst such changes that the WTO was founded in the mid-1990s, adding to the International Monetary Fund and the World Bank as the "third pillar" and a rule-based global system that serves as a guardian of, and a legal and institutional scaffolding for, the new global economic order (Bello, 2001: xi).

Long before China's and Taiwan's respective WTO accessions on 11 December 2001 and 1 January 2002, their efforts in gaining the accession had already shaped individual film policies in these two territories. Meanwhile, the long-awaited accession to the WTO has meant significant diplomatic achievements to both China and Taiwan. To China, the WTO accession is a crucial step that put China on the global economic map, as it grants China equal status with advanced nations for its fast-growing economy.[1] This achievement complements the first step that put China on the global political map in 1971 when China displaced Taiwan to become a UN Security Council member, which granted China political parity with the United States and the former Soviet Union (see Kahn, 2001). To Taiwan, conversely, WTO membership means the end of political and economic isolation that has long haunted Taiwan since 1971. It also signifies the beginning of an equal trade status that Taiwan would share with its archrival, Mainland China.

Given that the state figures prominently in the much-celebrated Asian capitalism, it is especially important to examine the dynamic, intersecting, and complex relations between the national and the global in these cases. The Asian financial crisis of 1997 and 1998, for instance, exemplifies how the West used IMF policies to dismantle the structures of state-assisted Asian capitalism, instead of promoting expansionary policies to help restore the "Asian miracle" in which strong government involvement had been instrumental (Bello, 2001). Indeed, the United States views these structures as formidable barriers to the entry of American goods and investments to the area. In part global trade regimes were employed to remove these barriers while ensuring "free trade."

In general, the WTO accession agreements dictate tariff concessions and restrictions and nontariff barriers. More specifically, two principles apply to these general provisions. The Most Favored Nation (MFN) treatment requires that whatever benefits a WTO member country grants to any other exporting country it must grant to all. Second, the National treatment calls for a WTO member country to provide equal treatments to domestic and imported products, trade and investments alike (see Tiefer, 2001; Master 2001; and the WTO website). Both principles have significant implications for overall economic developments within Taiwan and the Mainland, for cross-strait relationships between them, and for Hong Kong in its role as the major link between Taiwan and the Mainland.

In addition to agreeing to multilateral accession provisions, a country wishing to gain accession to the WTO would also need to sign bilateral treatments with the United States, Canada, and the European Union detailing particular industries to be affected by the WTO accession. These bilateral agreements offer a glimpse of more specific costs a WTO accession would bring to a member nation. To use the film industry as an example, the bilateral agreement between the PRC and the United States indicates further market access for American audiovisual products, a mandated foreign film import of twenty revenue sharing films (see chapters 5 and 6 for more discussion), a 49 percent joint-venture stake (for foreign investors) in exhibition sector, and the right to form joint ventures for video and sound recordings distribution, among others (see, for example, Potter, 2001; and the WTO website). While these compromises are not as extensive as those that Taiwan made, where all foreign film import restrictions were lifted on 1 January 2002, upon Taiwan's accession to WTO, they no doubt constitute a significant departure from those pre-WTO protectionist PRC film and cultural policies.

Regionalism and the Greater China Economic Circle

The formation of the Greater China Economic Circle has been the focus of much scholarly and policy interest and query (see, for example, Hsing, 1998; Ong and Nonini, 1997; and Cunningham and Sinclair, 2001). The trope of Greater China (*Da Zhonghua*) of an overseas Chinese capitalist zone founded on overseas Chinese capital has been coined by economists to describe the increasing integration of the economies of Taiwan, Hong Kong, and the Mainland produced by globalization (see Ong, 1997). While the concept celebrates transnational hybridity and flexibility, it is deceptively unifying if not oppressive in oversimplifying and assuming a single China-centered identity, ignoring significant historical, political, cultural, and economic differences. Furthermore, the concept itself is not without its overall nationalistic overtones given that many take great pride in the fact that the "Chinese bloc" of the combined foreign currency reserves of the Greater China economies, plus those of the heavily ethnic-Chinese populated and dominated Singapore, would replace Japan as Asia's top economic giant (see Ong, 1997:176).

Thus, with globalization comes the realization that the twenty-first century will be one that is marked by both fierce competition and increasing cooperation. The formation of regional and subregional economic blocs that consist of geographically adjacent territories is precisely a result of such an understanding (Lin and Lin, 2001). It is against this backdrop that we understand the growing importance of regionalism as complementary to the forces and processes of globalization. In addition to promoting global economic cooperation, hence, WTO also supports subregional economic collaborations. As Lin and Lin (2001)

have pointed out, there are at least two reasons why expanding regional cooperation would complement the WTO system of multilateral trading. First, given the
geographic, if not also cultural and economic, proximity the adjacent territories
share and the smaller number of parties involved, regional pacts would provide
deeper liberalization whereby specific economic interests of member countries
can be taken care of. With a multilateral and global organization like the WTO,
conversely, it is the broader range of interests that the organization would have
to cater to. Second, it is more probable that regional pacts would be able to
promulgate new issues before they advance to the multilateral WTO trade
agenda. Many nations therefore opt for forsaking political or economic rivalries
and differences for strategic alliances and cooperative relationships. The close
yet indirect trade relations between archrivals Taiwan and the Mainland in the
last decade and a half serve as a good example of such strategic alliances.

Consequently, it would be instrumental to discuss the formation of Greater
China as integral to the global trend of regionalism (see Lin and Lin, 2001; and
Martin and Dixon, 2001). The remarkable economic growth witnessed in China
in the past two decades has had much to do with the collaboration among the
triangular economies of Taiwan, Hong Kong, and the Mainland. In other words,
it is necessary to examine the Greater China economic circle against the backdrop of a "new regionalism" and "associationalism." These concepts have come
to define the working of advanced capitalism whereby reflexive governance
structures among the state, economic actors, and civil society stakeholders are
considered a preferred mold of operations to that of a national government and
an interventionist economic policy (see Martin and Dixon, 2001:2–3). Such operations no doubt have great implications for the changing roles of the state. In
this context, entrepreneurial networks and the state are not necessarily opposed;
in fact, they can be complementary in that a decentralized state structure can
reinforce networks of entrepreneurs, as Hsing (1998) has suggested, and vice
versa.

It is in this light that we understand "resource complementarity" as the most
important drive behind the Greater China economic circle's cooperation (Lin
and Lin, 2001:698; see also Master, 2001). Each of the three territories offers
unique assets that complement those of the others. China, with its cheap and
abundant labor base, its rich and sizable land, and its billion-plus untapped consumer market, becomes an attractive investment site. Given its free port and
financial center status, as well as its excellent natural port location, Hong Kong,
on the other hand, not only provides management know-how, capital, and financial services, but also serves as a natural link between the Mainland and Taiwan.
Finally, with its high-tech competition edge and its economic achievements,
Taiwan offers capital and expertise in high-tech manufacturing and enterprise
management.

This resource complementarity has translated to a very impressive double-
digit economic growth in China in the 1990s, with the most impressive figures
ranging from 13.6 percent real GDP growth in 1992, 13.4 percent in 1993, 11.8
percent in 1994, 10.2 percent in 1995, to 9.7 percent in 1998 (See *China Online*, 7 January 2000; and *China Statistical Yearbook 1999*). The aggregate fig-

ures depict a remarkable 25.6 percent growth during the 1996–1999 period (Rawski, 2001). In 1993, for example, the combined volume of Hong Kong and Taiwan foreign direct investment (FDI) accounted for 74.1 percent of China's capital utilization. Further, the average bilateral trade between the Mainland and Hong Kong grew from 14.9 percent in 1980 to 49.3 percent in 1993, and then decreased to 41.6 percent in 1998. Also in 1993, 67.4 percent of the Mainland's export was conducted via re-exports through Hong Kong, while the bulk of the re-exports from Hong Kong to the Mainland originated from Taiwan—hence the significant role Hong Kong played in mediating trade relations between the Mainland and Taiwan. Meanwhile, Mainland China's imports from Hong Kong reached its peak of 46.1 percent in 1997, with only 5.8 percent of these actually produced in Hong Kong and most of the rest produced in Taiwan (see Lin and Lin, 2001). The mutual dependence of trade relations between the Mainland and Hong Kong, and the fact that Hong Kong has been the main entrepôt for the Mainland and the middleman between China and Taiwan, could not have been more evident. With the opening of China's markets to more direct foreign trade, however, Hong Kong's dominance over PRC trade and its role as the middleman are likely to erode (Martin, 2000).

Taiwan, on the other hand, had invested a total of $51.9 billion[2] in the PRC by the end of 2000. The amount goes as high as $100 billion if one also includes investments from Taiwanese businesses via offshore Hong Kong companies, which accounted for 50 percent of Taiwan's cumulative outbound foreign direct investment. Furthermore, by the end of 2000, almost 75 percent of Taiwanese firms had investments in the PRC. Additionally, because of Taiwan's restrictions on imports from the Mainland, it has always had a trade surplus with the Mainland. Total exports, for example, from Taiwan to the Mainland increased from $384.2 million in 1981, to its peak of $22.4 billion in 1997, and to $21.3 billion in 1999, with an average annual growth rate of 37.2 percent. Taiwan's imports from the Mainland, on the other hand, rose from $75.2 million in 1981 to $4.5 billion in 1999, registering an average annual growth rate of 29.7 percent. The trade surplus in 1999, for example, totaled $16.8 billion. Such trade surplus as a ratio of Taiwan's overall global trade surplus increased from 3 percent in 1982 to 266 percent in 1998 (see Sutter, 2002; Master, 2001; and Lin and Lin, 2001). It is evident from the above statistics how much the Greater China economic circle has contributed to the growth of the three economies.

Because of Taiwan's complete ban on investment from China and a near-complete ban on direct shipping from China, as well as other such restrictions, most cross-strait trade takes place through Hong Kong (see Master, 2001). The "three direct links" ("San Tong") of transportation (aviation and shipping), communication, and commerce between the two territories that the Mainland has long been pushing for have yet to come to fruition. A mini-link (Xiao-San-Tong) of a trial shipping route between Taiwan's Kinmen, Matsu, and Penghu islands and the Mainland finally began in early 2001 after much negotiation and delay (see Sutter, 2002). These restrictions clearly violate the WTO principles of

Most Favored Nation and National treatments, and many expect the WTO accession to have a certain impact on the indirect nature of the cross-strait trade.

That said, however, it is important to point out that shipping and aviation rights are not covered by either the PRC or Taiwan's WTO commitments. Traditionally these rights are negotiated bilaterally (see Sutter, 2002). Furthermore, Taiwan could employ the WTO security exemption that provides member nations with broad discretion to use necessary trade and commercial policies to protect their security should situations call for such exemption (see Master 2001). Thus, while the WTO accession and the Greater China formation have meant necessary government concessions on policy and practice, the state retains essential control over *interpretation*, implementation, and enforcement of bilateral and multilateral provisions and agreements.

Although the three governments are not the sole actors engineering the Greater China economic circle—since private initiatives and market forces are integral parts of the increasing interdependence among the territories—each state plays an essential role in brining the collaborations, albeit often indirect, into realization. By purposely designing Shengzhen and Xiaman, two of the original four Special Economic Zones (SEZs) China created in 1980, to be near Hong Kong and Taiwan, respectively, the PRC government has been the most proactive of the three in making the triangular connections a reality (see Gu and Tang, 2002; and Lin and Lin, 2001). The SEZs have now grown from four to more than 400. Furthermore, the PRC government put in effect two important laws to facilitate foreign direct investment (FDI). In 1979, when China adopted its open-door policy, the government passed the "Chinese-Foreign Joint Venture Law" to provide a legal framework to attract FDI. In 1986 the government further promulgated the "Foreign Capital Enterprises Law" to protect foreign investments (see Wei, 2002; and Lin and Lin, 2001). Even though much more conservative and cautious in its approach to the Greater China economic connections, the Taiwanese government played its part in facilitating the process of indirect trade with the Mainland by lifting the Martial Law in 1987 and by ending the "General Mobilization Period for the Suppression of Communist Rebellion" on 30 April 1991. Finally, characterized as "passive" by Lin and Lin (2001:698), Hong Kong government did respond to the Mainland's open door policy by improving transportation links with Shenzhen, Guangzhou, and Xiamen and by upgrading seaport as well as airport facilities to support its entrepôt trade with the Mainland.

Distribution and piracy in Greater China are not only closely related to the resource complementarity among the three territories, they are also affected by relations between the United States and Greater China. The growing economic interdependence among China, Taiwan, and Hong Kong has meant that any bilateral relations between the United States and one of the three Greater China territories will be increasingly difficult to define. By nature, any bilateral relations between any two of the players would involve a third, if not fourth, party. For example, the three largest foreign direct investors in China are Hong Kong/Macau, Taiwan, and the United States (in order of decreasing amounts). The trade balances among the three entities also seem to be related. Over the same period of time (from mid-1980s to mid-1990s), the U.S. trade deficit with China had risen from $1.7 billion to $33.8 billion, while the U.S. trade deficit with Taiwan had dropped from $14.6 to $9.7 billion. The U.S. trade deficit ranking of China rose from the seventeenth in 1986 to the second largest (after Japan) in 1995, while Taiwan fell from the third to the sixth over the same period (Morrison, 1996).

The Greater China Piracy Networks

As mentioned in chapter 1, the Greater China piracy networks intersect and overlap with the legitimate business circles. Paradoxically, the Greater China economic circle is also the Greater China piracy circle. As a shadow economy, piracy network relies as much on preexisting institutions and infrastructure as legitimate businesses do (see more detailed discussion in chapter 6). Just as each territory in the Greater China economic circle plays essential and complementary roles to create the oft-cited economic growth phenomenon in the area, they also play complementary roles in the piracy networks. China's location as a desirable piracy market as well as production and export base, for example, are attributable to its large and relatively cheap labor base, its 1.3 billion plus market size, its long coastal lines and shared borders that provide natural entry, outlet, and connecting points for smugglers, its geopolitical influence, and its uniquely hybrid and ambivalent politico-economic-cultural system.

While piracy level on the Mainland is more of a direct result of its unique market structure and domestic distribution policy and issues, in Hong Kong it has more to do with Hong Kong's location as the entrepôt and the transshipment point for regional and global trade. Since the late 1980s, counterfeit products have been flowing from China into Hong Kong, for resale in the Hong Kong domestic market or for reexport to other markets (see Tackaberry, 1997).

The International Intellectual Property Alliance (IIPA) has named Taiwan the current piracy export and transshipment capital of the world. Even though Taiwan as a market is quite insignificant compared to its powerful Mainland neighbor, its role as a technologically advanced economy and, most important, a rich legitimate content source has made it a crucial link and node on global piracy networks. Thus, its threat to copyright industries lies not in the size of its market, but rather in the various technological, geographical, and commercial advantages that it possesses.

The State in Transition

One can say contradictory things about the modern state; on the one hand it is withering away, but on the other *it is more urgent than ever.* . . . That is how

one can sketch and fill out the image of a state that, like a snake, *is shedding the skin of its classical tasks and developing a new global "skin of tasks."*
                                                    —Ulrich Beck (1994:38; emphasis added)

Treating the national, the regional, and the global as contending sites of power as well as complementary spaces of mutually embedding and embedded processes deepens our understanding of the dynamic relations between the state and globalization. It adds multiple dimensions to a complex issue that has otherwise been overly generalized and simplified. As Beck so eloquently argued in the quote above, it would be a grave mistake to treat the modern state as simply declining, eroding, and withering away. The complex realities of a global informational economy regulated by global trade regimes, of which active state planning and participation is an integral part, call for a multifaceted reading of the state. The cases of the Greater China connections, Taiwan's and PRC's respective WTO accession, and how film distribution and piracy are implicated in these multiple, dynamic, and intersecting processes of globalization—and vice versa—highlight the fast-changing "global skin of tasks" that the state has assumed. The fact that bilateral negotiations and unilateral actions and sanctions remain essential even in a multilateral WTO-regulated world further accentuates the indispensable roles of the state.

Notes

1. China's accession to WTO is based on its status as a developing country, whereas Taiwan's is based on its being a developed country. The difference carries important implications and significance (see Morrison, 1996).
2. All figures are U.S. dollars unless otherwise specified.

4

"VCD Killed the VHS Star"

The VCD is a purely Asian market, and it's driven purely by piracy.
—Steven Metalitz, VP, IIPA (Quoted in Tanzer, 1998)

The Video Compact Disc (VCD) is a little-known quantity in the West, but in the Asia-Pacific region, it is the dominant format for recorded video entertainment. The above quote unmistakably positions VCD with Asia and piracy. In so doing Asia is associated, albeit indirectly, with piracy. While such a claim does have a statistical base, it simplifies an otherwise extremely complex situation with intersecting technological, cultural, economic, and legal contexts and implications. It also brushes over the multifaceted and dynamic local, regional, and global processes that constitute the multiple networks and players of distribution and piracy.

While VCD as a recorded video format is considered obsolete in the West, it lives on in much of East and Southeast Asia and is the best-selling format. Its cheaper prices (some VCD players are sold for less than $40, see *The Economist*, 1999) and digital quality were reasons why VCD stayed on. Rampant VCD piracy (i.e., software) also had a major influence on hardware development and vice versa. The VHS business has more or less been killed off by piracy in which most of the Asian territories have become disc-based markets (*Screen Digest*, 2000).[1]

The VCD development has proved to be one of the most serious and unexpected challenges to the major studios and those transnational electronics makers that hold, determine, and monopolize video and audio entertainment formats and standards. The unexpected VCD rebirth in Asia has not only redrawn the film distribution maps, both legitimate and illegitimate, but also redefined the power relations among various global and local players by reversing the flow of global video technology format and standardization. Even though major transnational electronics corporations still define the global audio-visual entertainment market order, the VCD case has become one of the most fascinating examples of a reterritorialized space in which the state, local manufacturers, and consumers collude to resist and redefine globalization and standardization while transforming and translating a passing, and indeed obsolete, technology into something that fits the local needs.

VCD

Sony and Philips (and later Matsushita and JVC) jointly introduced the VCD technology in 1993 to record video on compact discs. It was cheap, *digital*, convenient, and seemed to be setting the standard. At the time of the introduction of the new format, however, the development of the technologically far superior Digital Videodisc (DVD) was already underway. Even from the beginning, Philips was well aware of the pending arrival of the high-density DVD and the threat it would bring to VCD. The U.S.-based original equipment manufacturers (OEM) decided then not to further develop or produce VCD but rather to wait for DVD. With its greater capacity and a better picture, the DVD standard did replace the VCD three years later (See reports from *The Economist*, 1999, and *Television Digest*, 1994 and 1993, for a brief history of the early development of the VCD technology). Seeing the new format facing a more or less doomed future, Philips and Sony decided to launch VCD in China since it was "a technology that was fit for a poor cousin in laggard developing countries instead of cutting edge economies" (see King, 1999a).

VCD is an extension of the CD-ROM technology, using the compressed MPEG video format and holding about seventy-two minutes of digitized movie. A single movie is thus contained on two or three discs depending on the length of the film. While the VCD image quality is slightly lower than that of the VHS tape, reproduction quality remains unchanged—hence one of the incentives of VCD for pirates. More significant, the equipment is relatively easy to operate and can be switched among CDs, VCDs, and CD-ROMs. In other words, pirates can produce VCDs in the same facilities that manufacture CD-ROMs or audio CDs (see Tanzer, 1998; *The Economist*, 1999; USTR Special 301 Report, 1997). In addition, the cost of reproducing a two-disc film is as low as $.35 and a single disc reproduction line can stamp out 20,000 copies a day (see photo 4.1).

The VCD market in China had achieved the fastest and deepest growth of any new technology in history (see King, 1999a). Several factors explain the unprecedented spread of the VCD technology in China. Given that the production cost is low, and that it is a mature technology, complementary products are widely available. Furthermore, entry barriers to the industry are low and the potential profits are high. This environment facilitated speedy diffusion of the new technology. Other socioeconomic and cultural factors that helped develop the VCD technology in China include the lack of, and thus the demand for, quality entertainment and the ensuing widespread piracy of movies and Karaoke on

Photo 4.1. A VCD Reproduction Line, Tianjing, China (2000)

VCDs (see chapter 6 for more detailed discussion).

When VCD players were introduced in China in 1993, foreign companies' such as JVC, Samsung, and Panasonic manufactured them and they were sold at around $300 per machine. Chinese manufacturers later discovered that manufacturing the players basically meant a conversion of an audio CD player ($70) into a video CD player for about an additional $50. This big profit margin then attracted new manufacturers into the market (King, 1999a). According to a report by *The Economist* (1999), by 1998 China alone had 500 VCD manufacturers.

Sony and Philips have reaped great profit from their decision to export the technology to China as they have tight control over the patent for the VCD chip. They form a monopoly to license the technology to C-Cube Microsystems and Zoran, two U.S.-based chip manufacturers. C-Cube, for example, has 70 percent market share of the chips used in China. Japan, the Netherlands, Korea, and the United States on the whole hold 93 percent of the patents for the technology. At least 10 percent of the manufacturing cost of a VCD player in China goes to foreign patent holders (see King, 1999a).

Table 4.1 documents the remarkable number of VCD units produced in China in the past five years. The production peaked in 1998 with 18.5 million units being produced in one year alone. The overcapacity in the VCD manufacturing market in 1999 led the Chinese government to stop issuing manufacturing licenses. The profit became thinner and the production declined in 2000 and

2001 as the demand for VCD players slowed down (*Asia Pulse*, 2001) while that for DVD increased. In 2001, the State Information Centre estimated that China would export 16 million VCD players and 3 million DVD players (*Asia Pulse,* 2001). Table 4.2 summarizes the user rate of VCD players in urban China. Thirty-six percent of the urban households now own VCD players. With the continued advancement of DVD technology and the lowering of prices, more and more urban households are replacing their VCD players with DVD. The State Information Centre predicted that the VCD players and Super VCD (SVCD)[2] players would be sold mainly to the rural areas while DVD would be sold to urban areas.[3]

While VCD piracy in Asia in general, and in China in particular, has caused revenue losses for Hollywood majors, its impact is more or less contained in Asia. What proves to be more threatening to the United States has been the fast emerging and growing pirated DVD market, as the circulation of pirated DVDs has reached existing U.S. DVD markets worldwide, including that of its own leading market. For example, Mike Ellis, vice president of MPA's Asia-Pacific

Table 4.1. China's VCD Player Production

	1997	1998	1999	2000	2001
Units	15.7 M	18.5M	17.2M	14.5M	1.2M
Revenue	US$1.97B	$1.70B	$1.69B	$1.23B	$874M

Source: Dataques (2001). TableBase™ Accession# 1983464.

Table 4.2. VCD Players in Use per 100 Urban Households in China

Year	VCD players
1998	16.0
1999	24.7
April 1999	21.9
May 1999	22.4
June 1999	22.7
July 1999	23.1
August 1999	23.4
September 1999	23.9
October 1999	24.3
November 1999	24.6
First quarter 2000	34.6
Second quarter 2000	35.7
Third quarter 2000	36.4

Source: *Asia Pulse*, December 19, 2000. TableBase™ Accession# 2716388.

Anti-piracy Operations, pointed out that 4.7 million DVDs were seized in Asia in 2001, accounting for 96 percent of the total worldwide DVD piracy and representing a 154 percent jump from 2000. Furthermore, VCD piracy is still rampant in Asia, with 23.2 million units confiscated in 2001, a 30 percent leap on 2000 (photos 4.2 and 4.3). Ellis estimated that there are 1,500 DVD replication lines in Asia that can copy DVDs at the rate of one every three seconds (Groves, 2002a: 24). Consequently, piracy in DVD format has been particularly damaging to Hollywood majors because of the significance of the global DVD growth in serving the home video business (see also IIPA 2002 Special 301 Report, PRC). In 2002 there were over 5.3 million DVD players in China, and pirated DVDs were selling for $.75 each in Beijing in summer 2002 when I was conducting field research. The price is likely to be even lower outside of major urban areas.

The reversed flow is not just limited to software. In the past two years, large quantities of Chinese-made DVD players have been imported to the United States. A case in point is the impressive growth of Apex DVD players' market share. California-based United Delta Inc., Apex's parent company, is a digital start-up company founded by two Chinese descendents in Canada in 1998.[4] Apex assembles its DVD hardware in China, while using chips and components from the patent holders, the so-called 6C Group: Hitachi, Panasonic, Mitsubishi, Time Warner, Toshiba, and JVC. Around 2,000 patents apply to DVD players, and most of them are owned by the 6C companies.

Photo 4.2. Confiscated Pirated DVDs, Hong Kong Customs (2000)

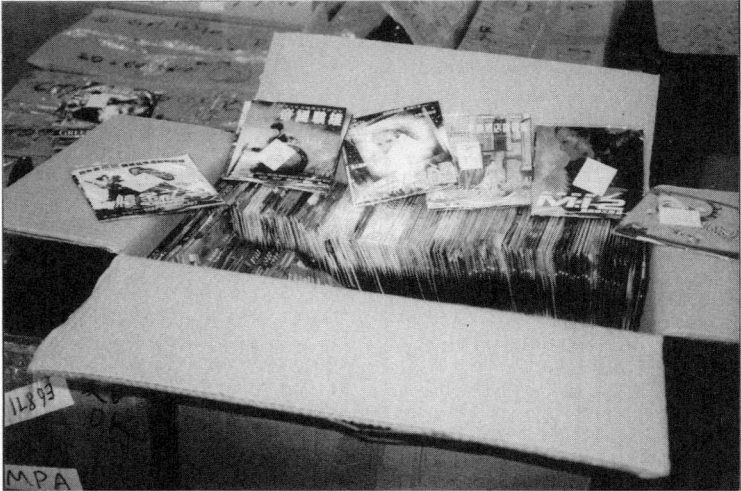

Photo 4.3. Confiscated Pirated VCDs, Hong Kong Customs (2000)

Because Apex's units are equipped with unique features such as the removal of CSS protection and regional encoding and restrictions, Apex players can play DVD movies created anywhere in the world and allow copying of DVDs onto VHS. Additionally, Apex players are the first to support the MP3 secure music format. These features made Apex machines highly appealing to the technologically savvy consumers. With their prices lower than $100, it is not surprising that by 2001 Apex players had captured 20 percent of the U.S. market and overtook Sony and Samsung to become the top seller in the United States. Adding insult to injury, Apex also failed to pay the required licensing fees to Sony, Philips, and Pioneer, the three companies that hold the joint DVD-technology license. Sony Corp. filed a lawsuit in the United States on 26 March 2002 against Apex's infringements of DVD patents. Even though Sony dropped the lawsuit in April, upon United Delta's agreement to pay the higher of licensing fees of $5 per player or 3.5 percent of a player's wholesale price, scores of Chinese DVD manufactures remain defiant of this agreement (see *Zhong Guo Shi Bao*, 8 May 2002; Jones, 20–26 May 2002; and *CDR-Info*, 12 April 2002).

The developments in VCD hardware and software, as demonstrated thus far, are significant and constitute some of the most important factors in optical disc piracy. What follows is a list of issues and cases pertaining to this intricate issue. These issues also apply to the development of the DVD technology.

The Hardware-Software Dynamics

The developments of VCD hardware (players) and software (discs) are closely related. Depending on to whom one addresses the question, it is hard to say if pirated VCDs stimulated the increase in production of the players, or vice versa, or if making such a distinction is even possible since many hardware developers are also involved in software designing and manufacturing. Some pirates believe that because discs feed the VCD machines, pirated VCDs stimulated the growth of the VCD manufacture industry.[5] The so-called bundle deals are a widely practiced promotional activity in China where manufacturers include as many as 100 free VCDs as a bonus to those customers who purchase their machines (personal interview, He Ping, director and consultant, Columbia Pictures Film Production Asia, 6 July 2000, Beijing). Some of these discs are legitimate; most are not.

Overcapacities and Narrow Profit Margin

With the rampant VCD piracy in Asia, one of the strategies deployed by the Hollywood majors is to lower the prices of legitimate VCDs. As a result, however, profit margins for all involved are narrowing (see *Screen Digest*, 2000). To increase profit margins, many authorized replication plants have begun to use spare manufacturing capacity to produce illegal products. Also, with the increasing efficiency of VCD production lines, some of the plants face problems of overcapacity, resulting in overrun productions that end up in either the piracy market (see photos 4.4 and 4.5) or parallel importing gray markets.

The "DVD Version" of VCD

One of the interesting and, to a certain extent, ironic consequences of the DVD development is that it helps raise the quality of pirated VCDs. The best

Photo 4.4. Seized VCD Smuggling Tank, Macau (1999)
Courtesy: Sam Ho

Photo 4.5. A Pirated VCD Stand at a Hong Kong Night Market, December 1999

quality of pirated VCDs is found in those that are replicated from a DVD master
(*Screen Digest*, 2000). Many pirated VCDs boast "DVD version" on the cover
to indicate the high quality of the replication and to attract potential customers.
In major cities, the days of the handheld camcorder "cinema version" are long
gone, as urban consumers are demanding quality in the pirated VCDs they purchase.

The Supply and Demand Imbalance
    Part of the VCD piracy phenomenon is a simple mathematical matter: the
demand for VCDs far surpasses the supply. Both Zhang Hui Guang, vice director of National Anti-Piracy and Pornography Working Committee (NAPWC),
and Jiang Ning Yuan, Managing Director of United East Audio and Video Co.,
Ltd. (UEAV, Warner Bros. Home Video *and* Columbia TriStar Home Video
licensee in China), used the same formula to illustrate this important factor (personal interviews, 6 and 8 June 2000, respectively, Beijing). On separate occa-
sions, they indicated that there were approximately 40 million VCD players in
China. If each comes with a twenty VCD/year demand, there would be a demand of 800 million discs. In 2000, the legal supply of VCDs was 200 million
discs, which leaves 600 million unmet demands. UEAV, for example, releases
ten legal titles a month, which is insufficient for the market. Pirated
goods thus provide an easy solution for the apparent shortage of content supply.

Reversed Flows

Because circulation and flows always involve directions, velocities, and forces, they result in the redefinition of boundaries (e.g., geographical, social, cultural). They also attest to the dynamic relations among various mechanisms of deterritorialization, dis-embedding, and those of reterritorialization and reembedding. The unique popularity and prevalence of VCD players in Asia epitomizes these important processes of reterritorialization, reembedding, and most of all deformation. It is a significant example of the reversed flow of global electronics production. Philips, Sony, and other transnational electronics corporations have been setting and defining the order of international audiovisual technology formats and standards. The VCD phenomenon in Asia is a rare case of defiance over major global corporations. Even though Philips and Sony still hold patents for the VCD technology, pirates and manufacturers, with the indirect blessing of the state *and* consumers, have been able to take advantage of the technology and in turn meet the local businesses' and consumers' interests. In other words, they have actively and reflexively redefined their position vis-à-vis the global economy. To combat VCD piracy, Hollywood majors have had to go back to a technology they had long declared obsolete and produced VCD versions of their films for the Asian markets.

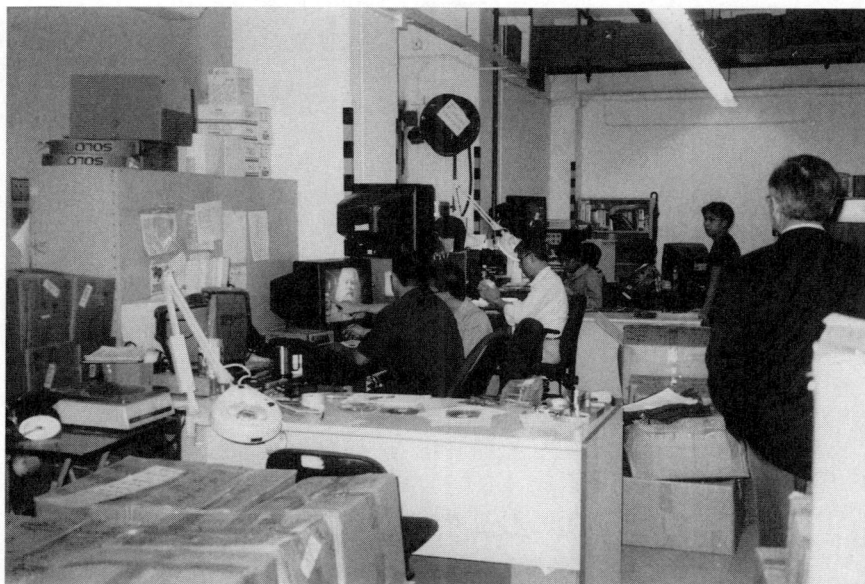

Photo 4.6. A VCD Inspecting Station, Hong Kong Customs

Notes

This chapter's title is inspired by "Chinese Cinema: VCDs Killed the Kung Fu Star." *The Economist*, 20 March 1999, p. 67.

1. Paramount is the only major U.S. studio to still hold out against distributing legitimate VCDs. See *Screen Digest* (2000).

2. The Super Video CD (SVCD) standard is set by the Chinese consumer electronics manufacturers, China National Committee of Standards, and the VCD consortium (Philips, Sony, Matsushita, and JVC). It is a successor for VCD. SVCD contains MPEG-2 video stream and MPEG-1 or MPEG-2 audio stream. See CDR-Info, www.cdrinfo.com/articles/svcd/ and http://www.afterdawn.com (1 December 2002).

3. Digital Video Disc (DVD) technology was introduced in early 1997, using the compressed MPEG-2 video format. It holds six times as much data as VCD. It is more difficult to pirate DVD because of the security chip installed. Even though the production of DVD players has gone up, the growth of the DVD market in China is expected to be slower (King, 1999).

4. Apex is headquartered in Ontario, Canada, and in California. See Apex website www.apexdigitalinc.com/company.asp (1 December 2002).

5. I interviewed VCD lines owners and distributors and they seemed to believe this is the case. Due to the sensitivity of the subject matter, they have requested to remain anonymous.

Part II

Case Studies

5

Film Distribution in Mainland China

Policy

To understand film distribution in China, one may start with the political, ideological, and cultural significance film holds in Chinese society. It informs cultural policies, which in turn shape the cultural environment in general and market structure in particular. Film in China is viewed as one of several existing "cultural markets" and has always been deemed a product of "the political, economic, military, and cultural invasions of the West," thus viewed as carrying with it "a deep colonial branding" from the very beginning.[1] It has therefore always been the government's and the Communist Party's mission to indigenize and nationalize the film industry. After the Communist revolution in 1949, China started building its own "independent national film system" and banned U.S. films entirely in 1950. The protection of the film industry consequently occupies a special priority in China's cultural policies. Although the Chinese government has been embracing market reforms since the open door policies in the late 1970s, the reform has not been extended to the political or cultural arenas. Mao's teachings on art and politics are still influential in shaping current policies and perception:

> In literary and art criticism there are two criteria, the political and the artistic. . .
> . [W]hat is the relationship between the two? . . . We deny not only that there is
> an abstract and absolutely unchangeable political criterion, but also that there is
> an abstract and absolutely unchangeable artistic criterion. . . . *Literature and art
> are subordinate to politics, but in their turn exert a great influence on politics.*[2]

Because art is perceived to be capable of influencing politics while simultaneously viewed as subordinate to politics, it is believed that government regulations and censorship are necessary. The import of foreign films is consequently subject to strict review.[3] Founded in 1979, the China Film Corporation became the country's monopoly film enterprise, regulating film distribution and import/export operations. There are two subsidiaries under the China Film Corporation: China Film Export and Import Corporation controls the import and export of films, while China Film Distribution and Exhibition Bureau in China and its regional subsidiaries own the majority of the cinemas and dictate the contractual terms, play dates, admission prices, and other aspects of film exhibition (see Richardson, 1999; and Wu, 1992).

Figure 5.1 summarizes the regulatory bodies involved in film industry in China, which is a good indication and representation of the complex media regulatory structure in which both the Communist Party and the central government are involved. Two major government organizations govern the operations of media industries in China. The State Administration of Radio, Film, and Television (SARFT) regulates the film (theatrical releasing and distribution), radio, and television sector, while the Ministry of Culture monitors the Home Video import and distribution business (e.g., Deutsche Bank, 2001).

With the import of Warner Bros.' *The Fugitive* in November 1994, China adopted the revenue-sharing system for the first time. Based on the system,

Figure 5.1. Regulatory Bodies Involved in the Chinese Film Industry

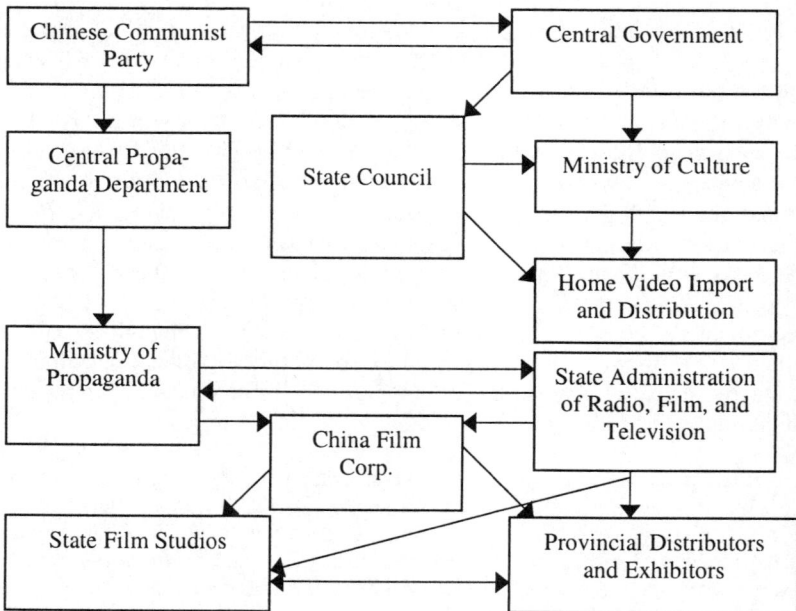

Source: Compiled from Calkins, 1999 and Wu, 1992.

SARFT permitted the import of ten revenue-sharing foreign films a year, those that represent "world cultural achievements and contemporary film art and technologies."[4] Revenue sharing refers to the commercial terms and the industry standard that MPA member companies subscribe to. Under the revenue-sharing system the distributor and the exhibitor negotiate the percentage of the box office receipts each will receive (see MPAA website). According to Wang Yung, Motion Picture Association's legal counsel in China (personal interview, 5 June 2000, Beijing), the specific revenue-sharing agreement between China Film and the major Hollywood studios dictates that the majors receive roughly 15 percent of box office revenue (see also Parkes, 2000). Zhao Jun, deputy director general of the Guangdong provincial film company, provided a more detailed breakdown: for each sold ticket, 46 percent will go to China Film, the monopolistic Chinese import/export distribution office. From the 46 percent, 13 to 17 percent goes to the Hollywood majors depending on the performance of each film while 29 percent to 33 percent of revenue will stay with China Film. The remaining 54 percent would go to local film companies that handle distribution in their respective localities (personal interview, 25 June 2000, Guangzhou). The quota was increased to twenty foreign films a year upon China's accession to the WTO in December 2001 (see Groves, 2001b, and later discussion).

Foreign film import, distribution, and exhibition in China have been important partly because they indirectly subsidize local film distribution. Although the annual quota of foreign films screened is 30 percent to 35 percent of the total films distributed, foreign films normally take 60 percent of the total box office income (see Jones, 2002c; and Wu, 1992). It becomes necessary for China Film to rely on foreign film distribution profits to cover domestic film distribution losses, as it is often difficult to recover local film distribution costs.

The home video (including VCDs and DVDs) import, as mentioned, is controlled through a different channel from the SARFT: the Ministry of Culture.[5] Starting in 1997, China allowed American home video imports.[6] Even though what is recorded on video is also in film, the medium is considered new (as opposed to the older and more ideologically loaded medium of "film"), and the procedures and regulations for approving home videos for domestic distribution as a result are faster and more lenient. Between 1997 and 2000, for example, the Cultural Ministry approved the import of over 800 home video titles (averaging 200 titles a year), compared to ten theatrical releases a year (personal interview, Wang Yung, 5 June 2000). Although the Home Video review process is faster than that of theatrical releases, it is still lengthy. When given a choice between renting a legitimate copy of an older VCD for RMB$2 to RMB$3 (roughly US$.25) and purchasing a pirated copy of a newly released film for roughly RMB$5 to RMB$15 (US$.60 to US$2, depending on the location of the sale), consumers usually choose the latter.[7]

The Market

Although in terms of box office grosses the Chinese film market lags behind many other developed territories, as far as admissions are concerned, it remains one of the largest and predominantly untapped markets in the world (see table 5.1; Thomas and O'Brien, 2001; and later discussion). It has thus become a *potentially* lucrative investment site for foreign capital. Market access in China, however, has been a serious problem for Hollywood majors and was one of the most contentious issues of the bilateral Sino-U.S. WTO accession negotiations.

The market access problem, according to MPAA vice president Bonnie J. K. Richardson, has severely limited the size of U.S.-filmed entertainment exports to China (Richardson, 1999). She estimates that losses due to restrictions in import and distribution of motion pictures cost the U.S. industry at least $80 million annually. Some of these barriers include limitations on foreign film import, government monopoly on import and distribution of foreign films, cinema ownership restriction, and lengthy censorship procedures. While China's WTO accession has further liberalized the Chinese film industry in exhibition and production, theatrical distribution remains inaccessible to foreign investors. Such a strategy attests not only to the centrality of distribution in maintaining a film industry's viability but also to the Chinese government's determination and efforts in protecting the domestic film industry.

Nonetheless, when China first allowed revenue-sharing foreign film imports in 1994, many saw it as allowing the entry of a menacing wolf. With the WTO accession in December 2001 and the ensuing further opening up of the film market, especially in the exhibition and production sectors, critics view the inevitable larger-scaled admission of the Hollywood majors and other transnational capital into the Chinese market as the entry of a pack of wolves (see, for example, Liu and Lee, 2000; Yie, 2001; *China and Africa* website). Such popular rhetoric registers a common fear toward the invasion of foreign capital and influence. It also reflects, albeit indirectly, a state caught in a dilemma of its desire to partake in the global marketplace and the globalization process and its anxiety over the necessary cost involved in such participation. It has been a

Table 5.1. Selected Admissions (in thousands)

	1995	2000	2005*	2010*
China		2,500,000	2,200,000	2,253,975
Hong Kong	26,800	20,700	23,147	25,808
United States		1,262,600	1,420,800	1,493,275

Source: Compiled from Informa Media Group (2001).
* Forecasts

crucial site where issues of policy, cultural politics, and the dynamics between the state and the global intersect and manifest.

To address some of the market access problems, U.S. negotiators focused on three different areas of the Sino-U.S. bilateral negotiations on China's WTO accession: the General Agreement on Trade in Services (GATS) for the market access issues of import and distribution, cinema ownership, and censorship; the General Agreement on Tariffs and Trade (GATT) for heavy taxes and import duties that partially made China one of the least profitable film markets; and Agreement on Trade-Related Aspects of Intellectual Property Rights (TRIPS) for the rampant piracy problem in China (Richardson, 1999). It is not surprising then that the Hollywood majors were eagerly awaiting China's entry into WTO, as China had agreed to make necessary concessions. According to these agreements, China will import up to twenty revenue-sharing films while allowing foreign investors to take a 49 percent share in exhibition projects and undertake joint ventures in video distribution and production (see *Financial Times*, 10 October 2000, and Parkes, 2000).

The WTO Accession and Film Distribution

> To meet the economic globalization and China's WTO accession, China will seize every opportunity possible to expand the radio, TV and film industries.
> —*People's Daily Online* (English Edition), 1 January 2002

> China's national response to global challenge has been to "attack poison with poison"—competing on transnational media giants' terms by organizing state media conglomerates to stimulate "managed competition."
> —Chin-Chuan Lee (2003)[8]

China's earlier effort in gaining entry to the WTO had already brought forth significant changes in its film import and distribution policies, its IPR regulations and enforcement practices, and its relations with the United States. China's accession to the WTO meant further market liberalization. It also marked a defining moment in the development and reconfiguration of China's film industry. The State Council enacted a new set of regulations on the film industry (production, distribution, and exhibition) as early as 1 February 2002. In addition to the increase of revenue-sharing film imports from ten to twenty films a year,[9] China is set to expand the film industry by reforming the exhibition segment (i.e., building multiplexes, establishing exhibition circuits, and updating antiquated cinemas), inviting foreign investors, breaking regional barriers, and establishing multiple distribution channels.

To many Western businesses, the Chinese film industry represents one of the final frontiers where no significant FDI amounts have yet been made (see King, 1999b). Poor current returns on investments as well as many other restrictions have all contributed to this situation. The WTO accession has created unprecedented opportunities for foreign direct investment in the exhibition and production sectors. The fact that the distribution sector is still off limits to foreign firms attests to the centrality of distribution in maintaining control and ensuring viability of a local film industry.

To minimize damages the WTO accession would bring to the local film industry, the Chinese government has embarked on several strategies to protect the domestic film industry. Preventing Hollywood majors from gaining control over theatrical distribution in China is a crucial one, as control over distribution necessarily means control of the time, space, speed, and content of film releasing—which is crucial to the survival, if not success, of any film industry. Further, by placing restrictions on foreign film distribution, China is also hoping to "gain time" for the local industry so it may remain competitive (Brent, 2000:76). With the WTO accession, however, the State Administration of Radio, Film, and Television (SARFT) did concede to break up the China Film monopoly[10] by adding a second distributor for foreign film distribution. The new group will be chaired by Zhu Yongde and based in Shanghai, with the Shanghai Film and TV Group being the largest single shareholder (Groves, 2002c). The other investors in the group include China Film, Changchun Film Group, Xi'an Film Group, E'Mai Film Group, Xiaoxiang Film Group, and the sole exhibition representation, the Chengdu-based Urban Theatre Development Association. Individual stakes are limited to 20 percent to prevent any single stakeholder from dominating the second distribution group (Groves, 2002d). In "The Execution Plan of Film Distribution System Reform" promulgated in February 2002, SARFT further ruled that China Film and the new distributor would each handle ten foreign films during the second group's first year in distribution. To protect the local film industry, both groups would also be required to distribute twenty domestic films each annually (Groves, 2002d).

Thus, by allowing joint ventures only in production and exhibition while still maintaining control and having a majority stake in exhibition, China is preventing Hollywood from controlling the Chinese market in the short term. Such policies work similarly to those of "import substitution" whereby Western companies, in this case film studios and investors, are encouraged to invest and co-produce films within China itself. It is also a form of "technology transfer" that would allow the Chinese film industry to eventually develop on its own and compete with foreign film producers. In other words, even though China has allowed more foreign films to be distributed within China, it provides much better incentives for those who would co-produce with Chinese studios or build exhibition facilities within China (see King, 1999b).

Consequently, the exhibition sector would see much more FDI than its distribution counterpart. China's Ministry of Culture predicted that in 2002 alone at least twenty joint-venture cinemas would open with the new WTO-induced exhibition regulations, whereby foreign investors with at least RMB$10 million (around US$1.2 million) registered capital can own up to 49 percent of stake in cinemas (see Jones, 2002c; and *People's Daily*, 28 January 2002). Two examples that further exemplify U.S. exhibitors and distributors' entry to the post-WTO Chinese exhibition sector include the U.S. IMAX Corp.'s move of its Asia

Pacific headquarter from Singapore to Shanghai on 28 June 2002 (*People's Daily*, 28 June 2002) and Warner Bros. International Theaters' aggressive move to the Chinese market (DiOrio and Groves, 2002).

The latter case is especially significant given that Warner Bros. has always been ahead in investing in the Chinese film market.[11] It is, after all, the first Hollywood major to enter the Chinese market with *The Fugitive* (1994), the first revenue-sharing film distributed in China. Its exhibition arm, Warner Bros. International Theaters, has 1,370 screens in eight countries and is focusing on the post-WTO Chinese market in hopes that the WB studio can release its movies in its own cinemas (see DiOrio and Groves, 2002). Table 5.2 documents two biggest U.S.-backed exhibitors, Warner Bros. International Theaters and United Cinemas International (a joint venture of Universal and Paramount that focuses more on European territories), and their global operations.

These developments are particularly significant given that the Chinese exhibition sector is primarily untapped, especially in terms of overseas exploitation. Table 5.3 shows that the end-2000 screen count in China is an impressive 46,069. This figure, however, is misleading, as only 3,100 (6.7 percent) of these cinemas are located in urban centers where major movie-going audiences are located, and of these urban cinemas only 600 (1.3 percent) show foreign films. Most of these theaters, furthermore, are single screen theaters with antiquated projection and sound systems and uncomfortable seating on cement floors. There are additionally 120,000 mobile projection units for the rural areas. China's WTO accession and its loosening up of exhibition regulations will no

Table 5.2. International Screen Count for UCI and WBI

Territories	No. of Screens	
	UCI	WBI
Australia	0	318
Austria	38	0
Brazil	99	0
China	0	9
Germany	164	0
Ireland	31	0
Italy	42	121
Japan	89	336
Poland	65	0
Portugal	14	80
Spain	186	104
Taiwan	19	60
UK	355	342
Totals	1,102	1,370

Source: *Variety*, 29 July–4 August 2002.

Table 5.3. Exhibition Profile, PRC

Year	Sites	Screens
1993	55,034	76,231
1994	51,354	68,961
1995	45,521	61,769
1996	41,969	59,576
1997	37,158	51,258
1998	35,631	49,113
1999	34,529	47,591
2000	33,425	46,069

Source: Informa Media Group (2001).

doubt create drastic changes in the exhibition sector, with the multiplex market a particular attractive area for foreign investors (Thomas and O'Brien, 2001).

The new "Execution Plan of Film Distribution System Reform" also recommends the formation of at least two competing cinema circuits in each city and provincial area to eliminate the middle layer of inefficient provincial subdistributors (Groves, 2002d). With these competing circuits in place, China Film and the new distributor would be able to deal directly with exhibitors. These reforms are also designed to help eliminate two major hurdles in the film distribution and exhibition systems in China, namely, the multilayered and inefficient operations of regional and provincial distribution companies and the rampant underreporting of box office figures by cinemas and some local distributors (see Groves, 2002c). The distribution structure in China has always been viewed as a major obstacle, as every province has a monopolistic state-run distributor. This means that one has to sign different contracts with different provincial distributors to distribute one's film, thus multiplying unnecessarily complex and bureaucratic relationships (see Palmer, 2000).

Finally, the Chinese government is consolidating state-owned media into integrated media conglomerates to remain competitive. The China Radio, Film, and Television Group, for example, is the latest addition to the recently formed Hunan Radio, TV, and Film Group (2000), Shanghai Radio, TV, and Film Group (2001), China Radio, TV, and Film Group (2001), among others (see Lee 2003). The China Radio, Film, and Television Group was formally established on 6 December 2001 in Beijing and consists of all companies and institutions under the auspices of SARFT that include China Central Television, China National Radio, China Radio International, China Film Group Corporation, China Radio and Television Transmission Network Corporation Limited, and China Radio and Television Website (*People's Daily*, 6 December 2001). The group employs 20,000 staff in total, with fixed assets valued at RMB$21.4 billion (approximately US$2.67 billion). The new trend towards consolidation and state conglomerates is a state strategy in combating the post-WTO Western influence. As of 2002, China has twenty-six press groups, eight radio and television groups, six publishing groups, four circulation groups, and three motion picture groups (Lee, 2003).

Approaching Wolves?

Don't knock on our door too loudly. We know you are there, and we'll let you in as soon as we can.

—Zhu Yongde, President, Shanghai Film Group
(*Variety*, 18–24 March 2002:13)

China's WTO accession will only intensify these adverse effects. *A warning of an approaching wolf eight years ago today translates into warnings of an approaching pack of wolves.*

—Dai Jinhua, film and literary scholar
(*China and Africa* Forum, April 2002, emphasis added)

These two quotes register complex and conflicted sentiments the Chinese intelligentsia have toward the further opening up of the film market in the context of China's WTO accession. The critic's fear of the approaching pack of hungry wolves, or Hollywood majors' impatient demand for further access to the untapped Chinese film market, is contrasted with the film executives' shrewd market calculation and control in dictating whom they shall allow in and when. While the entry of Hollywood majors is perceived to be an inevitable threat, Zhu's comment accentuates the fact that China might reap benefits from the approaching wolves by being cleverly prepared and positioned. A good hunter could very well turn a risky situation into a highly advantageous one by proactively setting up necessary traps as well as incentives for the wolves. There are, after all, valuable assets that a wolf could bring, including the wolf itself.

China's WTO accession *is* an historical moment with profound impacts. Chinese film policy and market access were a central focus of the Sino-U.S. bilateral negotiations on China's WTO accession and are undergoing major changes. As the foregoing discussion illustrated, the trajectory of the Chinese film policy vis-à-vis foreign film imports is thick with ambiguities and contradictions.

As Chin-Chuan Lee (2003) points out, how the Chinese government manages the first five years of its WTO accession will have decisive influence on its future policy landscape. It needs to keep a delicate balance between harnessing new media technology to economic growth and protecting its own ideological power. Its current approach of keeping foreign investment in information infrastructures, service provision, and technological knowledge (i.e., hardware) while protecting the content area (i.e., software) is in line with a perceived policy of dividing the media into hardware and software components where the latter is more ideologically loaded. While this observation is perhaps an overgeneralization, as control over hardware is also essential, it is insightful. In the film policy area, the Chinese government has been more than determined in keeping the area of theatrical distribution inaccessible to foreign investors, an essential strategy in keeping the domestic film industry viable. As the number of revenue-sharing films increase to fifty by 2005, it will be crucial to observe how the distribution sector evolves in the post-WTO China.

Notes

1. See Liu (1999:217). Other cultural markets include cultural entertainment, audio-visual, performance, print, artifacts, cultural tourism, artworks, stamps, and new culture.
2. Talks at the Yenan Forum on Literature and Art (2 May 1942), in *Three Selected Works of Mao Tse-Tung* 69, 86–89 (1967). Cited in Calkins (1999:241). Emphasis added.
3. In 1998–1999, for example, because of the critical stance Disney's *Kuntun* and Columbia's *Seven Years in Tibet* took of China's Tibet policies, both companies were temporarily banned from importing films to China; this gave the other majors an upper hand in getting the allotted ten revenue-sharing film slots.
4. See *China and Africa* site. Also personal interview, Zhang Lihui, General Manager, Warner Home Video, China, 9 June 2000. Zhang was in charge of WB-China's theatrical distribution from 1995 to 1997.
5. See Liu (1999) and the PRC Radio and Television Association (1996) for detailed discussions of regulations and policies.
6. See appendix B for a list of all majors' videos that were given permission for distribution in China between 1997 and June 2000.
7. I interviewed a white-collar engineer in Shanghai who indicated that he and his family would much prefer buying pirated VCDs than renting from Maya, a well-established chain video rental outlet in Shanghai, primarily because of speed. One can easily find pirated VCDs of newly released films while the legitimate VCDs are usually months behind. Personal interview conducted on 18 June 2000, in Shanghai.
8. The page number of this quotation is not available at the time of writing as the book is scheduled to be published in spring 2003.
9. In addition to revenue-sharing films, there are also foreign films whose rights are sold for a flat fee of normally $50,000; very few studios would agree to this arrangement (see King, 1999b).
10. The China Film Import-Export Corporation (CFIEC) has long monopolized foreign film distribution in China.
11. Sony/Columbia TriStar is another one of the majors that has a long-term strategy in place in developing the Chinese film market. Sony's Columbia Pictures Asia, for example, started in April 1998, after Hong Kong's handover to China almost a year prior on 1 July 1997, to become a Special Administrative Region of the People's Republic of China. Its director Barbara Robinson has acquired films (e.g., Zhang Yimou's *The Road Home* and *Happy Times*) while expanding the operation to include development staff in both Beijing and Taipei, and she has started producing films such as Ang Lee's *Crouching Tiger Hidden Dragon*, Tsui Hark's *Time and Tide*, and Feng Xiaogang's *Big Shot's Funeral* (See Palmer, 2000). Contrary to popular belief, Columbia Asia focuses primarily on Asian markets. The U.S. box office returns are viewed only as gravy to a film's success. And Robinson views *CTHD* as "the epitome of collaboration between Hong Kong, Taiwan, and China" since the film uses actors and creative talents from all three territories of Greater China, the spectacular yet still inexpensive locations on the Mainland, and

the directing talent of Ang Lee, a naturalized U.S. citizen from Taiwan (cited in Palmer, 2000).

6

Film Piracy in Mainland China

> It is not difficult to sum up China's principal problem with its overall intellec-
> tual property regime: it is the absence of effective and deterrent *enforcement*
> that will drive the local copyright industries into the ground and continue to
> cause the international community to refer to China ignominiously—based on
> piracy levels of 90 percent and above—as the "piracy capital of the world."
> —IIPA 2001 Special 301 Report: People's Republic of China
> (2001:25, original emphasis)

> What is more astonishing and more valuable is that the Copyright Industries
> have a *surplus balance of trade with every single country in the world.* No
> other American business enterprise can make that statement; particularly in
> view of a $400 billion trade deficit in 2000.
> —Jack Valenti (2001, original emphasis)

Having been designated a "Special 301 Priority Foreign Country"[1] by the United
States Trade Representative (USTR) three times in the past decade (1991, 1994,
and 1996) and subsequently subject to potential trade sanctions for its failure to
contain copyright piracy and to provide market access to the U.S. copyright industries,[2] China has proven to be one of the most challenging markets for the
U.S. copyright industries.[3] With its ever-enticing billion-plus market[4] and a fast-
growing economy, however, China occupies a unique position in the global
economy and, consequently, holds considerable negotiation leverage vis-à-vis
the United States and the international trade regimes.

Meanwhile, the copyright industries in the United States are one of the fast-
est-growing economic segments, and are *the* leading economic sector in foreign
sales and exports.[5] The annual losses due to piracy are estimated at $9 billion in
1999, $8.1 billion in 2000, $8.4 billion in 2001, and $9.21 billion in 2002 (see
USTR 2001 and 2002 "Special 301" Decisions). Of these, $2.1 billion in 1999
(23 percent), $1.08 billion in 2000 (13 percent), $1.5 billion in 2001 (18 per-

cent), and $1.85 billion in 2002 (20 percent) were estimated losses in China alone, the greatest of any single territory. Piracy in China has therefore constituted an especially acute problem in this "information economy," given that the "products" traded globally are often copyrights to intangible entertainment and informational goods. Piracy also has far-reaching implications for theory because it is located at the intersection of the multiple and often-contradictory dynamics of capital, space, time, speed, technology, information, and flows. It is fundamentally about power and control in an increasingly complex and, some would say, de-centered global economy.

Globalization, Technology, and the State: Multiple Networks

> Control societies function with a third generation of machines, with information technology and computers, where the passive danger is noise and *the active, piracy and viral contamination.*
> —Gilles Deleuze (1995:180; emphasis added)

From maritime to cyberspace, from the use of force to digital decryption, piracy has always been around. The difference today is the unprecedented ease, rate, and velocity afforded by the extraordinary developments in digital technology. The same digital technology that makes possible instantaneous global financial transactions also provides optical disc and Internet pirates with the ultimate capacity to copy, distribute, and profit with exceptional quality, speed, and reach. This technological development and the current state of capitalism are inextricably linked. Indeed, Deleuze (1995:180) views this technological development as being deeply rooted in a "mutation of capitalism," a capitalism that is no longer concentrative, proprietorial, or directed toward production as capitalism in the nineteenth century tended to be. It is instead directed toward "metaproduction" that sells services and buys activities. It tends toward "informatization" (Hardt and Negri, 2000:9), information, and markets. Further, with the advancement of digital technology, spatial boundaries are rendered ineffective while speed becomes the ultimate determinant for global success. It is this specific global informational economy that provides *both* the copyright industries and piracy networks the necessary environment to thrive and prosper.

The difference lies partly in the fact that piracy networks can bypass those state and international regulations (albeit those promulgated in a general climate of deregulation) that the legitimate businesses in most cases would have to abide by.[6] Piracy networks move much faster in a smoother environment where they observe fewer legal or trade codes and so hold certain advantages (most important, speed) over legitimate businesses.[7]

That said, however, piracy networks as part of the "shadow" economies are very much part of the formal economy (see Nordstrom, 2000). They operate through and around formal institutions such as the state, its regulatory and enforcement capacities, and its sovereignty. In the case of film piracy in China, for instance, one might ask how pirates and their networks figure in the film distribution system and how they are related to local and central political bodies and relations? What are the relations among the various components of piracy networks (e.g., hardware manufacturers, production line distributors, software retailers) and between the legitimate and the illegitimate distribution networks? Are power relations more or less stable? When the U.S. government, for example, has to resort to repeated annual threats of trade sanctions to keep designated foreign countries in line with intellectual property rights agreements, which side holds the power and why? Are the offenders necessarily powerless? When local enforcement seems to be the key to curb piracy (see the opening IIPA quote), and when state intervention seems to be more critical than ever, is the power of the modern state diminishing as is widely speculated?

These tensions underscore the urgency and the new configurations of the state in a global economy. They also highlight the operations and complex intersections of multiple networks, each with its unique and shifting sets of relations and configurations: global regimes, nation-states, regions, MPAA and MPA, production line distributors, hardware manufacturers, and retailers, consumers, pirates, among others.

The existing theoretical frameworks (e.g., political economy, recent writings of globalization, as mentioned in chapter 1), where the focus tends to be on the dichotomy between the center and the periphery, the local and the global, are inadequate in examining issues of information, technology, and the global economies of space and signs. Sassen (1998:202), for example, points out some of the problems of the recent literature's focus on the "national-global duality," namely, that such duality inevitably leads to propositions about the declining significance of the state in relation to global economic actors. It also leads to emphases on, for instance, industry outputs, instantaneous transmission capacity, and the inability of the state to regulate those outputs, while ignoring the production process involved and the infrastructure necessary for that capacity. A better framework would be to view globalization as conceptually reconstituted "in terms of a transnational geography of centrality with *multiple linkages* and strategic concentrations of material infrastructure" (p. 214, added emphasis). It also points to the need to do case studies, as every site will be a different configuration of linkages. Globalization can thus be seen not as an inevitable condition, but as specific *processes* embedded in and dependent on those linkages and the material infrastructure.

Likewise, it is out of what Latour terms as "double dissatisfactions" regarding social scientists' tendency to define a trajectory or a movement by focusing on oppositions between two notions, micro and macro, agency and system (or individual and structure), that he proposes the Actor Network Theory and the concepts of framing and summing up as a way to pay attention to these two dissatisfactions (1999:17, see also chapter 1). In this sense the social possesses the property of a "*circulating* entity." The network in ANT then is referred to as the "*summing up* of interactions through various kinds of devices, inscriptions, forms and formulae, into a very local, very practical, very tiny locus" (p. 17) where no interaction is not framed (p. 19).

Similarly, Latham (2000:10) views the new global economy as constituted with "multiple networks" shaping diverse and divergent market spaces, rather than simply as a single world market space. Instead of viewing markets as place-based "marketplaces," then, we would understand one that is a network-based "market plexus" (Latham, 2000:10). In this case, while technology- and network-based (as opposed to vertically organized and place-based) global economies and "market plexus" have greatly weakened territorial boundaries, they have multiplied other qualitatively different and more powerful forms of demarcation, be they functional, regulatory, ideological, technological, or otherwise. To create and maintain the networks which define these shifting cartographies requires "a diffuse plurality of agents such as states, international organizations, corporations, experts and individual investors" (Latham, 2000:9). Provided that any given market plexus would have restricted and limited circuits of entry and access that are tied to various conditions, globalization should be viewed not simply as the withering away of boundaries, but their construction; not fewer, but more different sorts of boundaries. Membership in and access to these networks therefore represent a form of power.

Intellectual property rights represent a form of boundary within which the rights owner, not necessarily the creator per se, has exclusive use rights. When combined with entry barriers, IP rights often create a strong monopoly position and formidable market power (see Maskus, 1999). The windowing strategy and the copyright industries' crucial need to control copyright is an effort to maintain such market power in an age where the definitions of boundaries are ever more fluid.

To focus on China, then, is not to endorse a reactionary (re)turn to the "local," one that celebrates an essentialized and fixed locality not touched by global flows. It is instead to view globality and locality, as Hardt and Negri (2000:45) have suggested, as *both* regimes of identity and difference and as "different networks of flows and obstacles in which the local moment or perspective gives priority to the reterritorializing barriers or boundaries and the global moment privileges the mobility of deterritorializing flows." In other words, it becomes dubious at best to maintain that one can somehow reestablish local identities that are outside of the global flows.

It is in this critical framework of the multiple networks that this chapter examines and problematizes film piracy in China as circulating and intersecting networks where the foci are transformations, deformations, and translations (see chapter 1 for more discussion).

Film Piracy in China

China's geographical, technological, economic, and political environments as such have made it not only a desirable *market* for pirated goods but also an appealing *production* and *export base* for makers, distributors, and exporters of such merchandise, with wide-ranging implications and consequences. Its threats to the transnational copyright industries are substantial. When viewed from the perspective of being a lucrative market for pirated goods, the consequence of piracy in China takes the form of revenue losses in one single territory. From the perspective of being a production and *export* base for pirate networks, however, potential losses can be far more immense and damaging.[8]

Although the motion picture industry is not the one that bears the heaviest copyright revenue losses in China (see table 6.1), it is one of the most visible in anti-piracy actions in China (and Asia in general). The Motion Pictures Association (MPA) works closely with Chinese customs in investigating, raiding, and cracking down on pirate factories and smuggling. Table 6.2 is an example of such MPA involvement in 2000 and 2001. In the IIPA reports, MPA is the only foreign organization listed as having participated in similar raids and investigations. From the two tables, one can see that the MPA actions increased 35 percent from 636 raids conducted in 2000 to 983 in 2001, while the piracy rate declined slightly from 90 percent in 2000 to 88 percent in 2001. Note, however, that while the motion picture piracy rate has decreased somewhat, the amount of losses has increased from $120 million in 2000 to $160 million in 2001, partially due to the increasing growth of the new CD-R piracy that was beginning to spread through Asia (see IIPA 2002 Special 301 Report, PRC).

Film piracy in China is embedded in complex and intersecting settings, both internal and external. These factors have provided the necessary soil for piracy to take root. This section explores several specific spatial-temporal contexts: WTO, globalization, and Sino-American relations; technology developments; market conditions (supply and demand imbalance); copyright regulations and enforcement; spatial organization and networks; and finally issues of reception, consumption, and subjectivity.

The USTR Special 301 Episodes

China in some ways represents a nightmare scenario for corporate America, a post-Napster Wild West chaos where any intellectual property can be illegally copied, and commonly is.

—Lisa Movius (*Salon.Com*, 8 July 2002)

In China, the development of a copyright-related legal framework and anti-piracy policies is closely related to the market economy reforms and China's insertion into the global economy. Following Deng Xiaoping's Open Door Policy in the late 1970s, the United States, along with other Western countries, started to pressure China to adopt more protective IP laws.[9] By the early 1990s China had become a lucrative market for foreign investments. The pressure for full protection of foreign rights increased (Jayakar, 1997). It is not a coinci-

Table 6.1. People's Republic of China: Estimated Trade Losses Due to Piracy (in US$millions) and Levels of Piracy: 1995–2001

Industry	1995 Loss/Level	1996 Loss/Level	1997 Loss/Level	1998 Loss/Level	1999 Loss/Level	2000 Loss/Level	2001 Loss/Level
Motion Pictures	124.0/100%	120.0/85%	120.0/75%	120.0/90%	120.0/90%	120.0/90%	**160.0/88%**
Sound Recordings/ Musical Compositions	300.0/54%	176.8/53%	150.0/56%	80.0/56%	70.0/90%	70.0/85%	47.0/90%
Business Software Applications	488.0/96%	507.5/95%	987.9/96%	808.4/95%	437.2/91%	765.2/93%	714.6/93%
Entertainment Software	1,286.0/99%	1,380.0/97%	1,409.4/96%	1,420.1/95%	1,382.5/95%	NA/99%	455.0/92%
Books	125.0/NA	125.0/NA	125.0/NA	125.0/NA	128.0/NA	130.0/NA	130.0/NA
TOTALS	2,323.0	2,309.3	2,792.3	2,553.5	2,137.7	1,085.2	1,506.6

Sources: Compiled from 2002 and 2001 IIPA Special 301 Reports, People's Republic of China (pp. 32 and 26, respectively).

Table 6.2. Administrative Copyright Enforcement Statistics in China (Motion Picture Association), 2000 and 2001

Actions	2000	2001
Number of raids/searches conducted	636	983
Number of administrative cases brought by agency	631	769
Number of defendants found liable	631	769
Ratio of convictions to the number of raids conducted	99%	78%
Ratio of convictions to the number of cases brought	99%	78%
Number of cases resulting in administrative fines	440	501
Total amount of fines levied:		
US$0–$1,000	401	493
$1,001–$5,000	37	4
$5,001–$10,000	2	4
$10,000 and above	0	0
Total amount of restitution ordered in how many cases (e.g., $XXX in Y cases)	N/A	N/A

Source: Compiled from IIPA 2001 and 2002 Special 301: People's Republic of China (pp. 33 and 44, respectively).

dence, then, that the USTR placed China on the Priority Watch List in 1989 and 1990 to "encourage it to commence a law reform process" (1999 Special 301 Report: PRC, p. 2). Responding to the pressure and realizing the need to conform to international standards to be part of the world economy, China in 1990 incorporated international standards and enacted the Copyright Law of the People's Republic of China. But the law was considered incompatible with the Berne Convention and in 1991 USTR named China a Priority Foreign Country. On 30 September 1992, China's Berne-compatible regulations went into effect, and in October 1992 China joined both the Berne Convention and the Universal Copyright Convention. The copyright framework in China was by then comparable to that of other countries (Jayakar, 1997). With a legal framework in place, the copyright industries began to attribute the high level of piracy in China to the lack of enforcement. Before long, more "aggressive and deterrent enforcement" became the focus of anti-piracy campaigns and "the key to reducing piracy in China" (2000 Special 301 Report, p. 26).

With the move toward a global information society, the IP rights regime has also been increasingly globalized through the World Intellectual Property Organization (WIPO), the World Trade Organization (WTO), and Trade-Related Aspects of Intellectual Property Rights (TRIPS). While these multilateral organizations, treaties, and agreements are comprehensive, and seek to ensure that their member-nations provide standardized IPR protections, they rely heavily on state laws to conform to the treaties and agreements to ensure their effectiveness. Concerned transnational copyright holders would still have to work through the state on copyright protection issues. Bilateral and unilateral measures such as trade sanctions and retaliations are thus often deployed to improve the IPR protection. The United States, for example, has relied on multilateral approaches for overall legal and regulation guidelines and directions while using bilateral and unilateral means to ensure the proper *enforcement* on the local level. Special 301 is one such measure.

According to Special 301, created by Congress with the passing of the Omnibus Trade and Competitive Act of 1988 (amending the Trade Act of 1974), the USTR will identify countries that fail to provide adequate and effective intellectual property rights protection and equitable market access to U.S. businesses. Those that are designated "Priority Foreign Countries" are the ones with the greatest adverse impact on U.S. products. They are therefore subject to trade sanctions at the end of an ensuing investigation. "Priority Watch List" and "Watch List" are two other categories that do not involve immediate trade sanctions.[10]

If Special 301 can be considered a retaliatory measure, then the Generalized System of Preferences (GSP) program would be a reward system. GSP is another unilateral trade tool that has been used by the United States to ensure local enforcement of copyright laws. It provides unilateral, nonreciprocal, preferential duty-free entry for over 4,650 articles from roughly 140 beneficiary countries, which is an important incentive for foreign countries to provide effective IPR protection (among other such conditions to provide market access) to U.S. copyright industries. In the case of China, the Most Favored Nation (MFN) status was also used before China's WTO accession as an incentive for China to maintain the proper functioning of its copyright regime (See Jayakar, 1997).

As noted, China was designated the Special 301 "Priority Foreign Country" in 1991, 1994, and 1996 (see table 6.3). And each time a threatened trade war was avoided at the last minute after much painful negotiation and mutual threats. After China was named the "Priority Foreign Country" in 1991, for example, lengthy negotiations ensued resulting in the Memorandum of Understanding on the Protection of Intellectual Property (MOU) in January 1992, two hours before U.S. retaliatory measures were to be implemented (see both IIPA Special 301 1999 Report: PRC, and Neigel, 2000). Similarly in 1994 U.S. Trade Representative Mickey Kantor placed China on the Priority Foreign Country list and threatened $1.08 billion in retaliatory tariffs on Chinese products. The Chinese government retaliated by threatening sanctions against the United States. Once again, a threatened trade war was averted by a last minute signing of the China-

Table 6.3. China's Status under Special 301 Review

Year	Status	Year	Status
1989	PWL	1996	PFC*
1990	PWL	1997	306
1991	PFC	1998	306
1992	WL	1999	306
1993	WL	2000	306
1994	PFC	2001	306
1995	WL	2002	306

Source: compiled from USTR Special 301 Decision reports.
PFC: Priority Foreign Country
PFC*: Priority Foreign Country (subject to 306 Monitoring) [11]
306: 306 Monitoring
PWL: Priority Watch List
WL: Watch List

U.S. Agreement Regarding Intellectual Property Rights (the IPR Agreement) on 26 February 1995. Finally, in 1996 the USTR for a third time placed China on the Priority Foreign Country list and issued a retaliation list, comprising over $2 billion worth of products. China then published its own retaliation list, identical to that of the United States, subjecting U.S. products to 100 percent tariffs. On 17 June 1996, hours after the deadline, the United States and China agreed on a set of announcements and averted yet another threatened trade war. This agreement then subjected China to monitoring of its compliance with the 1995 and 1996 agreements under Section 306 of the U.S. Trade Act. China has remained on the Section 306 Monitoring list ever since.

To a certain extent, the Chinese anti-piracy efforts coincide with the Special 301 agreements and negotiations. The time the USTR first put China on the Priority Watch List in 1989, China founded the National Anti-Pornography Working Committee. The committee changed its name to "The National Anti-Piracy and Pornography Working Committee" (NAPWC) in February 2000. The committee is the leading anti-piracy organization in China with fifteen institutional members from major communication, transportation, cultural, and informational branches of the government.[12] The NAPWC's 2000 Report categorizes China's effort in curbing piracy into four stages: Phase I (1995) saw the establishment of the title verification system: the SID code.[13] Phase II (1996) highlighted assaults on underground optical disc factories. Phase III (1997) focused on curbing smuggling, with the customs offices playing indispensable roles. And finally Phase IV (1998–present) emphasizes international collaboration and inter-regional cooperation.

Globalization, Uneven Economic Development, and WTO

China's WTO accession on 11 December 2001, as mentioned in chapters 3 and 5, has had significant impact on the Chinese film industry. To gain the WTO accession, China amended its copyright laws to make them TRIPS compliant. It also strengthened its law enforcement sectors. The WTO accession's likely effect on piracy, however, is still unclear. Zhong XiongBing, president of Guangdong Freeland Audio and Video, a Paramount and Universal licensee in China, for example, predicted that piracy would decline after China's WTO accession, while the legitimate optical disc market would grow 5 to 15 percent (personal interview, 21 June 2000, Guangzhou). Pioneer Chan, Golden Image Video and Audio International president, on the other hand, believed that pirates would in fact increase their activities, especially prior to China's WTO accession, and would continue afterwards (personal interview, 23 June 2000, Guangzhou).

Given that piracy as a shadow economy works through and around existing institutions and infrastructure, its existence is inextricably linked to the formal economy. The trajectory of piracy growth in China has consequently paralleled that of the formal economy. Clark (2000), for instance, predicted that the production and sale of pirated products would rise within the first five years of China's WTO membership, after which the rate would likely decrease as economic growth is expected, at least theoretically, to provide domestic companies with opportunities to profit from legitimate businesses. Furthermore, the WTO accession and additional economic growth would also be likely to improve China's enforcement efforts as the legal system further develops.[14] At present, however, the piracy problems are closely related to the uneven development of the market reform in China.

As a result of China's open-door economic reform that began in earnest in the late 1970s—with foci on decentralization, marketization, and globalization—local actors, transnational investors, and the state have become important forces in shaping and redefining regional developments in China. The necessary central government decision and favorable policy in setting up Special Economic Zones (SEZs) in coastal provinces, the subsequent concentration of foreign investment in SEZs and other better-developed regions, and important local initiatives and efforts have all contributed to the rapid development of certain areas. These have also led to the rise of uneven development, interregional inequality, and a large number of displaced floating population in the country (see Wei, 2002; and Movius, 2002).

Piracy is very much a by-product of these marketization processes and the accompanying uneven development of both supra- and subregionalism. Movius (2002) points out that piracy is in fact the most classic example of free-swinging capitalism in China's transitional economy, as it operates independently of the formal restructuring directives and thus has the flexibility to accommodate the aforementioned large numbers of dispossessed population. Its existence has relieved China's increasing social unrest and other related problems due to the shrinking social safety net.

Likewise, Clark (2000) views piracy development in China as attributable to the general trends of globalization and market economy. The following is a list of fourteen factors of piracy that he suggests as most relevant to processes of globalization and regionalism:

1. Continued economic liberalization in China that permits domestic companies to produce goods of their choice and distribute where they choose.
2. The establishment of Hong Kong and Taiwan manufacturing facilities in China that includes those of the counterfeiters.
3. The increasing understanding and appreciation of the monetary value associated with IP goods.
4. The global manufacturing trends of simplified production techniques to cut cost, thus creating easily copied products while facilitating both legitimate and illegitimate manufacturing processes.
5. Better-trained skill base and more sophisticated machinery.
6. The increasingly common large-scale licensing deals that result in overrun productions.[15]
7. The further freeing of domestic market and privatization of companies.
8. The increasing consumer spending power.
9. The continued shift of Hong Kong and Taiwan manufacturing to China.
10. The loosening export controls that grant greater access to world markets.
11. The improvements in China's domestic distribution networks in general, and communication and transportation infrastructure in particular.
12. The compliance with and implementation of international trade-related treaties.
13. The explosive growth of the Internet that provides the smallest businesses the opportunity to advertise and sell worldwide.
14. The Asian economic crisis that causes otherwise legitimate manufacturers to turn to counterfeiting to remain viable.

These factors attest to the fact that while the free market economy facilitates the production, distribution, and sale of legitimate products worldwide, it also helps the circulation of illegitimate ones. China's WTO accession will most likely contribute to the further growth of both formal and shadow economies, at least in the foreseeable future. Furthermore, given that the pirated optical disc reproduction and retailing are a major operation in China, this sector employs a significant number of laborers. To enforce IPR regulations, the government has to take some of the social ramifications into consideration and create alternative employment for these laborers lest social problems or unrest should occur. Finally, given that China is a developing country, adhering to IPR reform might raise important social and economic as well as developmental costs. As Maskus

(1999) pointed out, developing economies may experience net welfare losses before they can see the benefits promised from a strengthened IPR environment. The foregoing analysis would mean the linking of trade and IPR (as a segment of the economy) to wider development issues.

Flexible Transborder Networks and Flows

> But the campaign to nail the pirates is akin to getting rid of poisonous mush-rooms: as soon as one is weeded out another appears.
> —Don Groves (*Variety*, 2002b:12)

Even though this is a study of film piracy *in* China, it does not suggest that it is possible to isolate the issue and view it solely *within* China. It would also be seriously remiss not to examine the multileveled and multilayered flows that take place intra- and supranationally. That pirated goods move at such extraordinary speed and efficiency around the globe is an indication of the network power pirates possess. Piracy in China operates in an inextricably complex market plexus (see Latham, 2000) where multiple networks intersect and interact. This section examines and problematizes issues surrounding the ultrafluid and flexible piracy networks in and around China.

Above Ground → Underground → Overseas → Underground in China
    The fluid piracy routes and strategies have reflected a highly sophisticated and flexible spatial organization. Zhang Hui Guang, deputy director of the PRC Office of National Anti-Piracy and Pornography Working Committee (NAPWC), described it best when she summarized the movements of the piracy actions in and around China: it was first driven from aboveground to the underground; then from domestic/underground to overseas; and finally from overseas the goods are smuggled back into domestic underground (personal interview, 6 June 2000, Beijing). These stages and routes demonstrate the working of flexible piracy networks and their connectedness and resourcefulness. These movements also correspond directly to the aforementioned Special 301 actions and the subsequent Chinese anti-piracy offenses.
    After being named a Priority Foreign Country in 1994, China saw the first phase of the "all-out offensive" to contain piracy the following year (NAPWC Report 2000:11). The focus of this phase of action is on regulating the authorized and legal replication plants' aboveground piracy activities. Between 1992 and 1994 there were reportedly nineteen replication plants with forty production lines,[16] with production capacity of 3 million VCDs per year. The aboveground and more or less open piracy activities by legitimate plants were therefore driven underground, which marked the second phase of the anti-piracy offensive as well as the peak of underground piracy in 1996. According to the NAPWC, the second phase of the offensive had successfully forced the pirates to take their facilities and activities overseas, but only to see finished and high-quality prod-

ucts flowing back into China through various channels. The third phase (1997) dealt with such smuggling activities from overseas, while the fourth (1998 through present) involves international collaboration.

Smuggling is no longer restricted to the coastal provinces. The entry points have expanded to include those of inland provinces. A recent hot spot is along the China-Myanmar (formerly Burma) border. Some of the pirated VCDs now enter China through Yunnan province, which borders Myanmar (NAPWC Report, 2000). On 16 May 2000, China seized and destroyed 250,000 VCDs along the Yunnan-Myanmar border, in one of the most important VCD smuggling cases at the time. The discs seized were copies of seventy-five different films, mostly Hollywood movies and a few Hong Kong ones (personal interview with Zhang Hui Guang, 6 June 2000).

Greater China and the Intraregional Flows

The development of VCD technology and of piracy is closely related to the intraregional activities. Even more crucial are the flows among the Chinese Mainland, Hong Kong, Macao, and Taiwan, or what all together are known as Greater China. Hsing (1998) has pointed out that while capital might not be as concerned about national boundaries in the global economy, it is still very much formed by cultural and institutional boundaries. The "Greater China Economic Circle" that has been the center of much scholarly and practical attention is also a "Greater China Piracy Circle." The extraordinary fluidity and volume of piracy flows among the three territories are an indication of not just geographical but cultural proximity. A production line distributor who speaks the same language and understands the customs would be able to sell the equipment much easier than one who does not. A distributor of pirated products would be able to get a better grasp of the local tastes and needs easier than otherwise. The two local conditions in southern China that Hsing (1998:11) cites as having set the platform for interaction with transnational capital are also true for the operation of piracy networks: (1) southern China's connections with the outside world through Hong Kong and (2) the existence of a large pool of qualified labor.

Greater China, however, is not the sole area in which piracy networks operate. It is a common knowledge that the process of piracy involves multiple locations. Currently, one of the popular routes entails a master originated in the United States, a stamper made in Malaysia or Taiwan, replication done in Hong Kong, and distribution first in the PRC, then going for the global markets.[17]

The emergence of Malaysia as a major player in the East and Southeast Asian piracy networks in the late 1990s is closely related to the activities in Greater China. When China and Hong Kong were cracking down on piracy productions and the export of optical media products in the mid- to late 1990s, pirates as well as production facilities moved to nearby Malaysia, an attractive destination for both production and distribution of pirated optical discs (see 2001 Special 301: Malaysia). Over the causeway between Malaysia and Singapore, pirated goods are trafficked to Singapore. Through Malaysia's ports, pirated goods are further sent throughout Asia, Latin America, Europe, New Zealand, Australia, South Africa, and Canada. Between 1999 and 2000 fiscal years, for example, there was a nearly 3300 percent increase of counterfeit products from Malaysia seized by U.S. Customs.

Another example of the Malaysia connection (in addition to the earlier one of *Star Wars Episode I*) is the VCD piracy map presented in figure 6.1 of *The World Is Not Enough*, the James Bond film released in 1999. The film had its world premiere in Kuala Lumpur, Malaysia, on 19 November 1999. Pirated copies were found in India, Pakistan, Thailand, and Hong Kong within a week, and in China within ten days.

Figure 6.1. *The World Is Not Enough*: **Piracy Timeline**

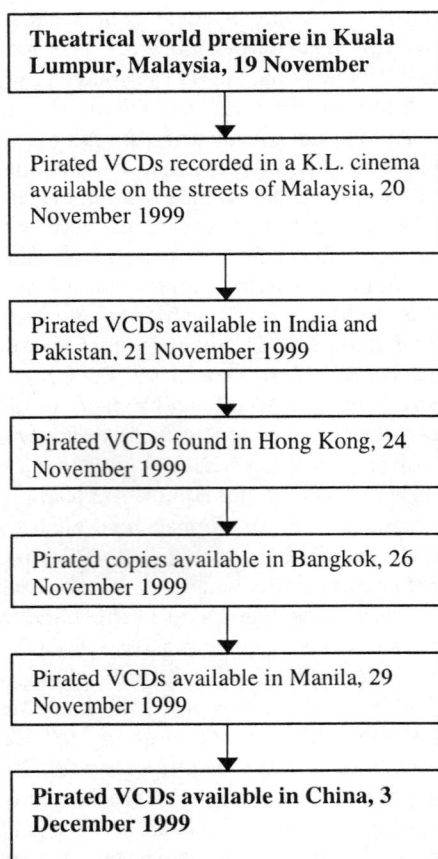

```
┌─────────────────────────────────────────┐
│ Theatrical world premiere in Kuala        │
│ Lumpur, Malaysia, 19 November             │
└─────────────────────────────────────────┘
                    │
                    ▼
┌─────────────────────────────────────────┐
│ Pirated VCDs recorded in a K.L. cinema    │
│ available on the streets of Malaysia, 20  │
│ November 1999                             │
└─────────────────────────────────────────┘
                    │
                    ▼
┌─────────────────────────────────────────┐
│ Pirated VCDs available in India and       │
│ Pakistan, 21 November 1999                │
└─────────────────────────────────────────┘
                    │
                    ▼
┌─────────────────────────────────────────┐
│ Pirated VCDs found in Hong Kong, 24       │
│ November 1999                             │
└─────────────────────────────────────────┘
                    │
                    ▼
┌─────────────────────────────────────────┐
│ Pirated copies available in Bangkok, 26   │
│ November 1999                             │
└─────────────────────────────────────────┘
                    │
                    ▼
┌─────────────────────────────────────────┐
│ Pirated VCDs available in Manila, 29      │
│ November 1999                             │
└─────────────────────────────────────────┘
                    │
                    ▼
┌─────────────────────────────────────────┐
│ Pirated VCDs available in China, 3        │
│ December 1999                             │
└─────────────────────────────────────────┘
```

Source: Compiled from IIPA 2001 Special 301, Malaysia.

If You Can't Beat Them, Recruit Them

To get the best-connected local licensees for distribution, and to convert pirates into legitimate partners, Hollywood majors have been known to work with former pirates for local distribution in China (See *Screen Digest*, 2000). The most notable case is the first of the three Warner Bros. Home Video licensees[18] in China, Xianke. Xianke was the first of two home video piracy "test cases" that MPA brought to the Chinese court in 1994 (see IIPA 1997 Special 301 Recommendation: PRC). The verdict was issued in 1996 for Xianke to compensate MPA for damages of US$14,587, lawyers' fees of US$7,126.46 and court costs of US$11,713.[19] These decisions to recruit former pirates illustrate the majors' strategies in attempting to minimize revenue losses and competition, while taking advantage of the efficiency and sophistication of the piracy networks.

A related issue is the argument that pirated VCDs in fact build up the market for film entertainment. Tim Meade, director of sales and marketing in China for Columbia TriStar Home Video, gave the example of the most successful Columbia video in China to date, *Robocop 3*. It was one of the first group of videos ever released in China and was released before *Robocop 1* and *2* had had a chance to be released legitimately. However, because both *Robocop 1* and *2* had already been distributed by pirates and had established a market, when *Robocop 3* was finally released, there was a built-in demand for it.

The RMB$300,000 Reward and the Family Business Counterstrategy

To induce collaboration from the public, and to encourage cooperation with the police, the PRC government initiated on 18 January 2000, a reward system that included a RMB$300,000 (approximately US$37,000) reward for each seized unauthorized reproduction line (see NAPWC Report, 2000:12). Given the low average income in China, the award is an exorbitant amount of money and has proven to be effective (photos 6.1 and 6.2 are two anti-piracy billboards in Beijing). While the NAPWC reported positive results of the system (personal interview, Zhang Hui Guang, 6 June 2000), the pirates have their own counterstrategies. According to two optical-disc distributors who requested to remain anonymous, the most important counterstrategy is the use of family members in piracy network operations. The family-based businesses involve not only the ownership and managerial operations but also hired hands in the replication plants. The rationale is that only family members would not endanger the lives of their loved ones by tipping off the authorities for the reward. Other methods include frequent change of contact locations and strict secret chain of actions and commands, where one link on the network knows only its immediate contacts.

Photo 6.1. Anti-Piracy Campaign, Beijing.
"When you find counterfeit products and when your legal rights are violated,
call 12315."

Photo 6.2. Anti-Piracy Campaign, Beijing International Airport. "Open your
eyes. Real/Fake. Guarantee consumer interests. Combat counterfeit products.
Protect consumer rights."

Profiles

During my research trip in China I encountered and interviewed a cross section of people on their consumption of pirated movie VCDs. The following are a selected few that represent different backgrounds and preferences. These profiles offer a glimpse of how and why these individuals consume pirated optical media and how, in so doing, they define their positions vis-à-vis the multiple processes of globalization. For privacy and security reasons, they shall remain anonymous.

A Group of Graduate and Undergraduate Students in Beijing

For college students, both undergraduate and graduate, pirated VCDs provide a source of affordable film entertainment. On the college campus that I visited in summer 2000, there was a student-operated online movie and music service with extensive lists of titles. A student committee is put in place to be in charge of the Internet entertainment selections. The extensive film lists include those of the United States, Hong Kong, Taiwan, and Mainland origins. There are also channels featuring documentaries, television series, and traditional theater pieces (e.g., Peking Opera). In the computer lab I visited, there was a projector and a screen onto which the Internet movies could be projected. Most popular among this group of students are U.S. and Hong Kong films. At the time of my visit, the list included some of the newest Hollywood and Hong Kong releases (which indicated that illegitimate copies were used). In addition to these free on-campus services, pirated VCDs for private viewing are a major source for the students' film entertainment. They rarely go to the cinema for movies, as tickets are too expensive. An average student ticket costs RMB$15 (approximately US$2).[20] An average adult ticket costs between RMB$25 and RMB$30 (roughly US$3–4), depending on the film. A ticket for *Titanic* went as high as RMB$80 (about US$10). When a pirated VCD *and* DVD sells in Beijing for about RMB$5–6.5 (about US$.65–.75), the choice is obvious.

A College Professor in Beijing

Professor A is in his late thirties and teaches statistics. For his personal viewing, he prefers U.S. action movies. He often bases his decisions of which pirated VCDs to buy on what he reads in the newspaper or on the Internet regarding the latest and hottest Hollywood releases. When I interviewed him in summer 2000, he was searching for *Mission Impossible 2* and *U571*, both new U.S. releases. He found copies for RMB$10 each for both films. He also buys computer and statistics software from the same pirate source. The legitimate SPSS program, for example, was selling for RMB$12,000 (approximately US$1,500), but the pirated version cost only RMB$8 (roughly US$1). Ditto with *Windows* products. An otherwise RMB$1,700 (around US$200) worth of *Windows 95* was selling in the pirate market for RMB$8 in 2000.[21] Professor A felt that he had no choice but to resort to the pirated copies. He and his classes simply could not afford to purchase the legitimate version. To him, pirated software is indispensable for the development of national higher education.

An Engineer in Shanghai

Mr. B is in his mid-forties and is an upwardly mobile white collar engineer residing in a working-class neighborhood in Shanghai. For his work, he travels to Europe frequently and is quite cosmopolitan. A very reflexive and self-conscious person, he sends his fourteen-year-old daughter to a private English cram school after hours, hoping she will grow up even more cosmopolitan than himself. He tells me proudly that Pudong, a newly developed SEZ in Shanghai, east of Huang Pu River, is "the Manhattan of the East" (see photo 6.3). Mr. Liu also buys pirated VCDs and he loves American movies. When I told him pirated VCDs were selling for RMB$15 each in an area where foreign businesses aggregate, he told me in his neighborhood they were selling for RMB$5 each. His reasons for buying pirated VCDs instead of renting or going to the cinemas are price and speed. Rentals are simply too slow, while going to the cinema is too expensive. For him, he says, to take his family of three to the cinema, he has to also take into account the cab fare, snacks, and ticket expenses, not to mention having to fight the Shanghainese crowd. To him, it is simply not worth it.

A Sojourner Taiwanese Businessman in Shanghai

Mr. C is in his late thirties and is a well-to-do Taiwanese businessman in Shanghai. He owns a real estate marketing company and has a staff of eighty,

Photo 6.3. Pudong: "Manhattan of the East"

both local and those he brought over from Taiwan. He is part of the large foreign business and investor phenomenon in China. He is married to a Beijing woman and has a son. Together they live in one of the most expensive and trendy neighborhoods in Shanghai where many of the expatriate business people aggregate. His new flat is designed by one of the most famous and sought-after interior designers in China. To him, Taiwan and China have already reunified. Look at him, he says; he is the best example. In his spare time, he watches and collects pirated VCDs. When I interviewed him in summer 2000, he owned (and had already watched several times) the pirated *Crouching Tiger, Hidden Dragon* VCD, as the film was first premiered in Asia, months ahead of its U.S. release in December 2000. Mr. C's collection includes films from all three parts of Greater China: the Mainland, Hong Kong, and Taiwan. He also has an impressive collection of American and European art films. A former college film major, he is much more into collecting films and watching a variety of both commercial and independent art films. To him, the price difference between pirated VCDs and the cinema tickets is not an issue. It is rather a matter of choice and the availability of nonmainstream films.

A Peasant Couple and Their Son in a Village in Zhejiang Province
    Mr. and Mrs. D are former peasants turned physical laborers. They and their son live in a small and more or less isolated village in coastal Zhejiang province, in southeast China. They are in their late forties with a teen-age son who is in high school. Mrs. D picks tea leaves for a living and makes around RMB$10 (US$1.25) a day. Mr. D makes minimal wages delivering and pulling big rocks for a local cement factory. With Taiwanese relatives ("overseas connections"), they are still better off than many of their fellow villagers. They love watching Taiwanese and Hong Kong television series on VCD. Their son loves popular culture. He watches Hong Kong and American action movies.

A Street Vendor Pirate in Beijing
    Mr. E is in his thirties and is part of the "floating population" (liudong renkou) in Beijing. He is also a former peasant, from Anhui province in eastern China. He and his wife and their toddler son live in a tiny room in northern Beijing. He makes slightly over RMB$1,000 (around US$120) a month selling pirated VCDs. He sells movies, music, and computer software. His major complaint about selling pirated VCDs is the lack of content, especially those of major Hollywood films. Because most of his clients are recurring customers, he has to accommodate their tastes and demands. He also gives them refunds when they happen to purchase a "cinema version" of VCDs (those shot with a camcorder in the cinema). When asked about the piracy networks and how they operate, he says he only knows the person who delivers the goods to him. According to Mr. E, the police care more about cracking down on pornography than on piracy. But in case of an arrest, he would be sent home without further punishment. And he would always return.

These profiles highlight a complex set of dynamics that involves the economic, the legal, and the cultural. The consumers' and pirates' decisions to consume or sell pirated goods are clearly not attributable to a single factor of greed,
as the copyright industries would have it. They reveal instead a desire and a con-
scious decision to interpret their own realities and to make sense of the fast
changing world around them. These consumption choices are also a sign of the
uneven local and regional developments produced by multiple movements of
capital, images, and people.

Networks, Power, and Reflexivity

Piracy in China is a multifaceted issue involving underlying questions of network, power, and reflexivity. As an integral part of the processes of framing and
overflowing (see chapter 1), these concepts are interrelated and dynamic.

Networks and Boundaries

> To have transformed the social from what was a surface, a territory, a province
> of reality, into a *circulation*, is what I think has been the most useful contribu-
> tion of [the Actor Network Theory].
> —Bruno Latour (1999:19, emphasis added)

Because circulation and flows often involve directions, velocities, and
forces, they result in the redefinition of boundaries (e.g., geographical, social,
cultural). They also attest to the dynamic relations among various mechanisms
of deterritorialization, dis-embedding, and those of reterritorialization and reembedding. In the case of film piracy in China, such entities as global IP right
treaties and agreements, images and products that are moved across borders both
legitimately and illegitimately, international electronic developments and standards, have all gone through various transformation, deformation, and changes
in their framed interactions with local sets of relations and forces. Thus, in this
case, "translation" (of global treaties to national laws; of international electronics formats and standards to local adaptations; of Hollywood imageries and individual consumption), defined as "the process or the work of making two
things that are not the same, equivalent," does involve transformation and
changes (Law, 1999:8).

China's conforming to global IP protection agreements and treaties (e.g.,
the Berne Convention, TRIPS), for example, is an act of translation, but one that
involves lengthy, and framed, processes of negotiations, confrontations, and
debates first among various PRC government branches, and then among the
PRC government, the global trade regimes, and USTR, among others. The end
product is a transformed and reembedded interpretation of international agreements that is contingent upon various levels and layers of local cultural, eco-

nomic, and political codes and specificities. The consumers and producers' media and piracy use is also an act of translation and appropriation generated by evolving circulation. Filtering through individual social, cultural, and political needs and conditions, they give different meanings to these circulating images and signs.

Power as Relations: The Dialectic of Control

All strategies of control employed by superordinate individuals or groups call forth counter-strategies on the part of subordinates.
—Giddens (1987:10–11)

Film piracy in China challenges the way we think about power. It problematizes the loci of power and how they function. The foregoing analysis demonstrates that the state still holds significant power in coordinating, negotiating, and enforcing codes on the circulating entities. The continuous saga of the Sino-American Special 301 negotiations, and the resulting state-pirate tug of war, for example, illustrate some of the most fascinating dynamics and dialectic of control, power, and sovereignty.

So far the existing literature on the state sovereignty vis-à-vis global trade and IP regimes (e.g., Ryan, 1998; National Research Council, 2000) tends more or less to fall into the framework of what Talcott Parsons has critiqued and termed as the "zero-sum" concept of power.[22] Power in this framework is defined in terms of certain mutually exclusive objectives in that one person or one group possesses power to the extent that a second group or person, over whom the power is wielded, would not be able to seize it. To be part of the global economy, or to submit to global trade regimes, then, a state is viewed as giving up sovereignty and hence control over its regulatory, functional, and territorial boundaries.

While it is hard to deny the necessarily hierarchical nature of power (see Giddens, 1977, collected in Cassell, 1993:220) where interests between the powerholders and those subject to that power often clash, power relations are rarely absolute and constant as demonstrated by the Sino-American negotiations and by the state-pirate maneuverings. Parsons's own framework of viewing power as a "non-zero-sum game," and as a "relation from which both sides may gain," instead provides a more adequate conception of power as a "circulating medium" generated within the functional subsystems of the society (Giddens, 1977, collected in Cassell, 1993:213). Power would then have to be viewed within the dynamics of those involved. In this sense power is not absolute; instead, it has to be viewed *in* relations and, indeed, *as* relations.

In such a framework, one is able to examine more adequately the constant negotiations between the United States and China, and the cat and mouse game between pirates and the state. The fact that the United States has to rely on repeated threats of coercive sanctions does indicate an insecure, shallow, and unstable base of power. China's decision not to deter the development of VCD technology could also be read as a resistance to the hegemonic global optical disc standards and practices (e.g., the DVD zoning practices). China's accession to the WTO and its collaboration with other such global regimes or regional alliances are part of its effort in strengthening its power base and negotiation leverage. After all, order is produced by "assemblage" (Lee and Stenner, 1999:100), that parties meet and become "assembled" with others in a manner that would increase the power of all concerned and would yield a new entity that is more powerful or profitable than any participants acting alone.

The crucial question is, then, does the institutional order of the capitalist economy and the state have to be necessarily treated in zero-sum or constant-sum terms? Given that power can be both competitive and collective (Bromely 1999), why could it not be viewed as *both* a constant-sum or zero-sum phenomenon in some aspects and a positive-sum one in others? In the case of both the copyright governance and TRIPS, and the Sino-American negotiations, for example, the state power is indispensable and instrumental not only in implementing and enforcing international agreements, but also in reflexively negotiating and maneuvering its positions vis-à-vis transnational regimes and regional and domestic influences while shaping national information policies.

Film piracy in China brings into play complex relations of power and control. It demonstrates a plurality of strategies, maneuverings, and manipulations that all those involved deploy to acquire and maintain power.

Reflexivity and the Reproduction of Self

> The laborer does not only lie the path of variable capital as producer and exchanger. He/she also lies in that circulation process *as consumer and reproducer of self* (both individually and socially). Once possessed of money the laborer is endowed with all the autonomy that attaches to any market practice.
> —Harvey (1990:110; added emphasis)

> Power relations in social systems can be regarded as relations of autonomy and dependence; but no matter how imbalanced they may be in terms of power, actors in subordinate positions are never wholly dependent, and are often very adept at converting whatever resources they posses into some degree of control over the conditions of reproduction of the system.
> —Giddens (1982), collected in Cassell (1993:243)

While much has been written on audience's reception of legitimately distributed Hollywood products, there has not been much in the study of piracy consumption. Lash (1994:111) focuses his discussion on the aesthetic dimension of reflexivity as he sees the "receding social structure" being displaced by "information and communication structure." This line of theorization is especially relevant to issues of piracy consumption. If, according to Lash (1994:121), life chances are a question of "access to and place in the new information and communication structures," entertainment and information piracy has provided this otherwise unaffordable access to and place in the new information structures. It offers alternative channels of information to those strictly regulated by the state and the copyright industries.

So what is the role of the consumer in the process of film piracy? Is the consumer a greedy participant? A naive victim? A reflexive bricoleur? In Giddens's (1987:10) writing of the "dialectic of control," he views subordinates in relations of power to be possessed of human agency. Given that power presumes the active compliance of others, no matter how great the extent and intensity of control the powerholders possess, the subordinates can always bring strategies of their own. Social actors therefore not only monitor the contexts and ongoing flow of their activities, they also expect others to do the same (Giddens, 1984, in Cassell, 1993). In other words they are reflexive and purposive agents who have reasons for their activities and are aware of others' actions and the context in which these actions take place.

The few sketches I provided of some users and distributors of piracy are people who reflexively and consciously make their decisions to improve their living. It does not have to be at the level of Professor A, who is highly aware of the disparate condition his students and his college would be in if not for the pirated software programs. It is also the peasant couple's and their son's desire to get a glimpse of the world and space outside of the village, be it through Hollywood action movies or Hong Kong and Taiwanese television series. It has provided them with a space of hope or escape. It is Mr. B's desire to get his hands on the latest and best Hollywood movies so that he and his family will not be left out of the globalization bandwagon and so that his daughter will grow up to be an even more sophisticated cosmopolitan. It is certainly the Street Vendor E who sells pirated goods to earn a living in Beijing so that his toddler son will grow up with a better chance of getting an education in the city. And it certainly is Taiwanese Businessman C who desires the diversity of independent art films legitimate stores are unable to offer.

Notes

1. See "Copyright and Trade Issues," International Intellectual Property Alliance website (www.iipa.com/copyrighttrade_issues.html) and later discussion.

2. The copyright industries can be divided into two categories, the "core" copyright industries and the "total" copyright industries. The core industries include those that create copyrighted works as their primary product: the motion picture industry (television, theatrical, and home video); the recording industry (records, tapes, and CDs); the music publishing industry; the book, journal, and newspaper publishing industry; the computer software industry (also includes data processing, business applications, and interactive entertainment software on all platforms); legitimate theater; advertising; and the radio, television, and cable broadcasting industries. The total copyright industries encompassing the above-mentioned core industries as well as portions of other industries which create, distribute, or depend on copyrighted works, for example, retail trade, the doll and toy

industry, and computer manufacturing. See "Copyright Industries in the U.S. Economy —the 2000 Report."

3. See IIPA website for its annual reports of "USTR 'Special 301' Decisions and IIPA Estimated Trade Losses due to Copyright Piracy and Levels of Piracy."

4. By 2015, China will have 1.6 billion people. See Schwarzacher, 2001.

5. According to the "Copyright Industries in the U.S. Economy—the 2000 Report," the real annual growth rate of the core copyright industries has been more than double that of the economy as a whole: between 1977 and 1999, the core copyright industries witnessed an estimated compound annual growth rate of 7.2 percent while the rest of the U.S. economy grew at 3.1 percent. The copyright industries' foreign sales and exports are also larger than almost all other leading industry sectors, including the combined automobile and automobile parts industries and the agricultural sector.

6. Although the "legitimate" transnational corporations (TNCs) do rely on, and indeed celebrate, deregulation to move smoothly in the world market, they require national regulations to ensure proper local protection, which includes laws and regulation (e.g., ban on parallel imports, copyright protections, labor relations), taxes and tariffs, legal entry, among others.

7. This is certainly not to suggest that there are no inherent codes in the language or culture of the techno savvy piracy networks.

8. Culturally and ideologically, China has not been the most receptive to the concept of intellectual property. In addition to the Marxist issues, many Chinese still believe in a cultural adage that justifies the act of stealing books as an acceptable behavior.

9. See Neigel (2000) for a brief history of Copyright Law developments in China.

10. See "Copyright and Trade Issues," IIPA website (www.iipa.com/copyrighttrade_issues.html).

11. 306 monitoring refers to Section 306 of the Trade Act, under which those countries that have had a Priority Foreign Country designation the previous year and have already been subject to a Section 301 trade investigation are monitored. See USTR Special 301 Decisions (IIPA website).

12. The committee consists of the General Office of the State Council, the Publicity Department of the Central Committee of the Communist Party, the Political and Law Committee of the Central Committee of the Communist Party, the Ministry of Public Security, the Ministry of Railways, the Ministry of Communications, the Ministry of Information Industry, the Ministry of Culture, the General Office of Customs, the Civil Aviation Administration of China, the Administration of Broadcasting, Film and Television, the State Administration for Industry and Commerce, the Press and Publication Administration, the Publicity Department of the General Political Department of the People's Liberation Army, the People's Government of Beijing Municipality. See the Working Committee's 2000 Report.

13. According to IIPA 1996 Special 301 Report, PRC, the source identification (SID) code (a title verification code) allows reliable tracing of CD products to the factories that they were produced in.

14. Weak penalties and poor funding of the IP enforcement agencies are two fundamental enforcement problems that currently exist in China.

15. As the 2002 Special 301 Report on PRC points out, in the past several years there were virtually no licensed plants producing more than negligible pirated goods. In 2001, however, approximately 80 percent of both the licensed and unlicensed plants in China produced pirated goods.

16. Personal interview with a production line distributor, who requested to remain anonymous, conducted on 26 May 2000, Hong Kong.

17. Personal interview with Zhong XiongGing, director of Guangdong Freeland, licensee for Paramount and Universal, 21 June 2000, Guangzhou, China. Mike Ellis, director of MPA's Asia-Pacific Anti-Piracy Operations, also confirms this usual route for pirate networks.

18. The three Warner Bros. licensees in China are Xianke, United East Audio and Visual, and Zhonglu-Takara. According to Warner Home Video general manager Zhang Lihui, the reason why Warner uses three licensees instead of one is partly to spread the risk in case one does not do well enough. Personal interview, 9 June 2000, Beijing.

19. There is another more recent case in which in summer 2000 two of the majors were in the process of designating a pirate network to be their licensee. Due to the sensitivity of the subject matter, both the source of the information and the identities of the majors cannot be disclosed.

20. The average pay for a worker in China is RMB$700 a month (roughly US$90).

21. I found copies of newly released *Windows XP* selling for RMB$8 each as well in Beijing, in November 2001.

22. See Giddens's extensive discussion of Talcott Parsons's writings on power (Cassell, 1993:212).

7

Film Distribution in Taiwan

[Vice President] Annette Lu said, by joining WTO, Taiwan will become globalized, not *Mainlandized*.

—*ChinaTimes.Com* headline,
(1 January 2002, emphasis added)

We are tired of calling everybody's attention to the fact that we are not a part of PRC. . . . Unfortunately, we still find ourselves *rejected by the international community*, in the same category as rogue and pariah states such as Iran, Iraq, North Korea, and Cuba. We do not export arms, steal nuclear know-how, lob missiles over other countries, invade our neighbors, persecute scholars and religious worshippers, or violate human rights. *We are isolated simply because of the fact of our proximity to our formidable neighbor across the Taiwan Strait.*

—Tien Hung-mao, foreign minister, Taiwan,
(*Harvard Gazette*, 2001, emphasis added)

On 1 January 2002, Taiwan—or rather, "Chinese Taipei"[1]—formally joined the WTO and became the 144th full member of this global trade regime, only three weeks after the People's Republic of China gained its WTO accession on 11 December 2001. It was a long-awaited "historical moment" that would bring "a significant boost" to Taiwan's international status (Chang Chun-hsiung, Taiwan Premier)[2] on this politically isolated island that calls itself the Republic of China. Only twenty-seven countries in the world currently recognize Taiwan. The number dropped from seventy-eight when the United States terminated diplomatic relations with Taiwan in 1979 while formalizing relations with the Mainland (see ROC Government Information Office, 2002; Ko, 2001; Clifford, 2000; *People's Daily*, 1 June 2001; and *ChinaTimes.Com*, 23 July 2002).[3] Using political pressure, the PRC has since maintained a policy of a "diplomatic blockade" against Taiwan, discouraging other countries from recognizing Taiwan (see Gewertz, 2001).

99

The above two quotes from the vice president and foreign minister of Taiwan, respectively, attest to this deep sense of international political isolation and identity crisis that Taiwan has been struggling with in the past few decades. Deemed a renegade province by the People's Republic of China (PRC), Taiwan has been negotiating issues of its political legitimacy and cultural/ethnic heritage and origin since 1949, not least of which dwells in its name and what it represents. The struggle has deepened and become more visible after the lifting of martial law in 1987 and the subsequent democratization process initiated by the then newly founded opposition party, the Democratic Progressive Party (DPP). It also manifested itself in DPP's effort to retell the history and thus redefine the nation. It is especially significant, then, that this "historical moment" when "Chinese Taipei" finally won its WTO accession took place on the independent-minded DPP clock.

After years as an underground opposition movement, the DPP was founded on 28 September 1986, and became the majority party on 18 March 2000, when Chen ShuiBien was elected president. That outspoken Vice President Annette Lu (Lu Shiou-Lien) felt the need to remind her fellow citizens that joining WTO should not be equated with "mainlandization" signifies a sense of defiance. It also indicates the ultimate compromise Taiwan makes in situating and defining itself vis-à-vis the Mainland and various transnational trade bodies.

A "crisis industry" (see Chen, 1995:9), Taiwanese cinema reflects this overall political and cultural ambiguity in which it is situated. Just like Taiwan has to define itself vis-à-vis the Mainland, the Taiwanese film industry has also been shaped by the cross-strait political conflicts from the beginning and by the cross-strait economic reality in more recent times. Not only are film contents a direct product of this somewhat schizophrenic environment; the market structure itself is also an outcome of volatile political and cultural uncertainties. The powerful piracy networks operating in Greater China are direct products of this complex system of relations (see chapter 8).

The vertically integrated market structure (most notably the convergence between exhibition and video distribution) and the capital flight to the Hong Kong film industry from major Taiwanese exhibitors-cum-distributors (and hence the subsequent missing production link in Taiwan) have fully impacted the Taiwanese film industry. Other factors include the strong VHS and cable markets, Taiwan's reliance on the United States for trade partnership and political support, and the related Special 301- and WTO-induced lifting of foreign film print quota and other related restrictions. While some Taiwanese films (e.g., those directed by Hou Hsiao-Hsien, Edward Yang, and Tsai Ming-Liang) have in the past two decades won an impressive number of international awards, a Taiwanese film industry as such is close to nonexistent (see later discussion).

Industry Structure

Today's film production model [in Taiwan]: Taiwan's capital, Hong Kong's talents (both on and off camera), and Mainland's location.
—Ru-Shou Robert Chen (1995:22)

Even though this chapter is about film distribution in Taiwan, it would not be possible to have an understanding of the issues without situating them in the larger contexts of the local film industry development as well as Taiwan's relations with the Mainland and Hong Kong. Taiwan's film industry was developed in the context of a mixed economy with both state-sponsored and private enterprises, resulting in government-operated studios as well as commercial firms. Regardless of the ownership structure, however, all films were subject to strict government control and censorship until 1987, when martial law was lifted and the censorship process was relaxed (see Lu, 1998, and Yu, 1993). As mentioned, ever since the move of the Nationalist government from the Mainland to Taiwan in 1949, the Taiwanese film industry has been one that is shaped by political reality (i.e., Taiwan's political relationship with the Mainland). Hong Kong, with its strategic location and its status as the transient port where many exiled Mainland Chinese settled, became a place over which both sides of the Taiwan Strait exert influence. The film industries of Taiwan, Hong Kong, and the Mainland have thus been closely linked. Such a connection has become even more direct, frequent, and complex since the early 1990s.

From the start, Taiwan's film industry was relatively disadvantaged compared to its Hong Kong counterpart. After the communist takeover of the Mainland in 1949, most film talents and studios, with their capital and know-how, migrated to Hong Kong (including the Shaw Brothers), creating a better structured and funded film market. To ensure that Hong Kong did not fall under the Mainland influence, the Nationalist government on Taiwan had been funding those Hong Kong filmmakers who were right-leaning and pro-nationalist (see ROC Government Information Office Film Industry Report, 1999). Its own industry was much smaller in scale and scope in comparison. Hong Kong had subsequently become a major supplier of Chinese-language films to meet the demands of the Taiwanese market.

Furthermore, and also for political reasons, the Nationalist government on Taiwan initiated a program to invite mainly Hong Kong filmmakers to produce films in Taiwan (Yu, 1993). This program led to the "take-off" stage of the Taiwan film industry in the 1960s (see GIO report, 1999). It also witnessed the founding of the Grand Movie Company in 1963 by Li Hang-Hsiang, a former director of the Shaw Brothers. In addition, the then newly established Guo-Lian and Lian-Bang Films production companies and the state-funded Central Motion Picture Association played an important role in film production in Taiwan.

The early 1970s marked the "Golden Age" of Taiwanese films with the annual production slate reaching 300 films. Taiwanese films found overseas markets in Hong Kong and Southeast Asia. Also starting in 1973, the Taiwanese film industry came under the auspices of the Government Information Office (GIO), which began programs to support the film industry such as offering low-interest loans and founding the Film Library (see Yu, 1993). The fact that the government viewed film as either a tool of political mobilization and nation-building or as a general form of entertainment (as opposed to art) had significant effects on the national film industry development. The private sector, on the other hand, tended to be shortsighted with instant profit making as its major goal, which created an impoverished and inadequate production environment. With the dominance of major film studios, the Hong Kong film industry, conversely, was building a much sounder groundwork, with major investments in studios and exhibition circuits. It was making high budget films, training and developing a star system, establishing marketing networks, and opening overseas markets (see Lu, 1998). With the loss of the Hong Kong market (attributable to the revival of Cantonese-language films and the subsequent decline of the Mandarin-language fares in Hong Kong), as well as the loss of other overseas markets, the Taiwanese film industry began its own decline. From the mid-1970s and on, Taiwan had lost its competition for overseas markets to Hong Kong, which had by then reached international status and had become the Hollywood of the East (see Chen, 1998; personal interview, Woody Tsung, chief executive, HK Motion Picture Industry Association, 20 December 1999, Hong Kong).

Part of the nativist and "self-discovery" movement in Taiwan, Taiwan New Cinema surfaced in 1982 with the releasing of *In Our Time* (1982, codirected by Edward Yang, Tao Te-chen, Ko I-cheng, and Chang Yi). The movement partially revived the local film industry, which was plagued by a supply-demand dysfunction in the local market and the aforementioned loss of its overseas markets (see Chen, 1998). While some of these films won important international film awards (most notably Hou Hsiao-Hsen's *City of Sadness* with the Golden Lion Best Picture Award at the Venice Film Festival), nevertheless, the domestic market began its worst ever decline in the early 1990s. Locally produced films dropped from eighty-two per year in 1980 to sixteen in 1999 (GIO Film Industry Report, 2000; see also table 7.1 for the more recent numbers).

This decline was closely related to the Hong Kong industry. Taiwan had not only lost its battle for overseas film markets to Hong Kong in the 1970s, but starting in 1984 Taiwan itself had also become the number one export market for Hong Kong films (see Lu, 1998). By then, Hong Kong films were generating one-third of the box office revenue from the domestic market, one-third from the Taiwan market, and the rest from other markets (see Yu, 1993). As a result, Taiwanese exhibitors and distributors began to exert major influence on the increasingly lucrative Hong Kong film industry. By investing in Hong Kong film production, Taiwanese exhibitors and distributors began to affect how and what films were made in Hong Kong. It also caused the subsequent capital flight to Hong Kong and the ultimate abandonment of local production in Taiwan. The resulting vertically integrated market structure proved to be especially damaging

Table 7.1. Domestic, Hong Kong,* and Foreign Films Released in Taiwan 1995–1999

Year	Domestic Films	%	HK Films	%	Other Films	%
1993	28	–	–	–	–	–
1994	29	–	–	–	–	–
1995	27	7%	138	33%	249	60%
1996	18	5%	90	25%	252	70%
1997	29	8%	84	23%	249	69%
1998	22	6%	63	17%	290	77%
1999	16	4%	129	27%	327	69%

Source: Compiled from ROC Government Information Office Film Industry Reports 1999 and 2000.
*Hong Kong films here also include PRC films.

to local film production. These exhibitor-cum-distributors also produce, but they do not produce Taiwanese films. Instead they produce Hong Kong films. The capital flight thus created a production gap in Taiwan's own film industry. The most notable and important players were Long-Shong and Scholar, two of the most dominant forces in local film production, distribution, and exhibition. Both collaborated closely with Hong Kong film companies.[4]

Furthermore, the presence of the triad in the Taiwan film industry has also been widely reported and has discouraged legitimate businesses' willingness to be involved in local film industry. With its quick-buck mentality, the triad element had drawn the Hong Kong film industry into a vicious cycle of cheap imitations, rushed productions, and coerced star and exhibition bookings, which also contributed to the decline of the Hong Kong film industry (personal interview, Simon Huang, marketing director, UIP-Taiwan, 24 July 1999; see also Groves, 2002a). Consequently these cheaply made and low quality Hong Kong films began to lose their appeal to Taiwanese audience around the mid-1990s.

With the opening up of the Taiwanese market to Hollywood films (see later discussion), the same group of exhibitors began to change their exhibition strategies and convert their theaters to screen mainly Hollywood fare, creating an even worse exhibition environment for local films. In fact, as Curtin (2003) has so correctly pointed out, it is the vacuum left by the serious distribution infrastructural problems in Taiwan that caused such a shift of distribution and exhibition strategies and changes in the industry structure. Between 1990 and 1995, the total number of theaters in Taiwan had decreased by 100 (Teng, 1996). The serious capital flight to both Hong Kong and the Mainland resulted in the ultimate collapse of the Taiwanese film industry and the decline of the Hong Kong industry as well. The barely surviving local film production was only sustained to a certain degree by the Government Information Office's Guidance Fund, which was set up in 1990 with a budget of NT$15 million to encourage domestic film productions. The budget was increased to NT$50 million in 1992, to NT$100 million in 1996, and to NT$120 million in 1998. In the past ten years, the fund has supported a total of eighty-eight films, including many award-winning films by Ang Lee, Hou Hsiao-Hsien, and Tsai Ming-Liang.[5]

Often distributors blame these filmmakers for making films that, while high in artistic values, lack entertainment appeal. Woody Tsung, chief executive of the Hong Kong Kowloon and the New Territories Motion Picture Industry Association (MPIA), for example, believes that the existence of the Guidance Fund has contributed to the decline of the industry. The state-sponsored nature of the fund and its review committee has encouraged a certain set of unspoken preferences for specific kinds of contents that may not be commercially viable (personal interview, 20 December 1999, Hong Kong). Filmmakers, critics, and scholars, on the other hand, blame the exhibitors' and distributors' short-sighted, profit-oriented, and monopolistic control of the industry for the decline and near collapse of a once vibrant Taiwanese film industry. While several directors, scholars, and critics have established an alliance to try to collectively strengthen their negotiation position, it has been an uphill battle and struggle without adequate and available exhibition outlets and distribution channels (personal interviews, Professors Ru-Shou Chen and Wenchi Lin, 31 and 22 July 1999, Taipei).

The easing of regulation for the import of Hollywood products in the late 1980s (see later discussion), furthermore, had a detrimental effect on the local industry. Beginning in 1993, the Taiwanese film market was dominated by Hollywood fare (see the GIO Report, 1999). By 1998 locally produced films claimed only .4 percent (four-tenths of a percent) of the total box office revenue (personal interview, Frank J. K. Chen, director, Dept. of Motion Picture Affairs, Government Information Office, 20 July 1999; see also tables 7.1 and 7.2).[6]

Table 7.2. Box Office Revenues in Taipei (NT$), 1995–1999

Year	Domestic Films Box Office/%	HK Films* Box Office/%	Foreign Films Box Office/%
1993	82,741,907 –	– –	1,690,879,035 –
1994	100,430,462 –	– –	1,762,452,492 –
1995	59,305,490 2.3%	227,240,180 9%	2,216,524,610 88.7%
1996	41,235,690 1.4%	198,829,460 6.9%	2,616,030,880 91.7%
1997	24,135,840 0.7%	131,202,840 4.3%	2,892,768,960 95%
1998	13,335,540 0.4%	77,975,200 2.4%	3,116,963,430 97.2%
1999	11,053,275 0.4%	75,345,745 3%	2,441,649,765 96.6%

Source: Compiled from ROC Government Information Office Film Industry Reports 1999 and 2000.
* Hong Kong films here include PRC films.

In addition to the (indirect) Mainland influences and the direct Hong Kong and Hollywood impacts on the Taiwanese film industry, the fact that Taiwan has a strong video market that challenges theatrical releases and the resulting reconfiguration of power dynamics in distribution and exhibition have serious and far reaching implications for the local film industry. The VHS market in Taiwan began in 1976, and the VCR household reached 63.56 percent by 1990 (see Lee, 2000). It dropped slightly to 57.1 percent in 1997 (table 7.3). The video market at the outset was mainly conducted through illegal means where illegitimate copies dominated the market. It was not until the government began regulating the video rental market in 1979 and enacted the Copyright Act to crack down on VHS piracy in 1986 did the video market begin to fall into order.

According to Lee (2000), the emergence of a strong video rental market in Taiwan is attributable to two distribution strategies that led to a convergence of theatrical exhibition and video distribution, which ultimately created a serious market imbalance. For Hollywood majors, theatrical and home video are distributed through different channels. In Taiwan the majors distribute through Xiehe (distributing Universal and Paramount) and Biaozhi (representing Warner, MGM/UA, Disney, and Columbia), two local licensees that in general handle package deals (see later discussion of Deltamac, a newly emerged dominant player in home video distribution). Independent video distributors, conversely, tend to purchase individual titles. To control the timing between theatrical release and video release and to minimize the threat of day and date releasing of

Table 7.3. Selected Facts on Taiwan

Population (1998)	21.9 million
Per capita GNP (1998)	$15,370
Economic growth (1999f)	+4.74%
Economic growth (1998)	+4.83%
Economic growth (1997)	+6.8%
Exchange rate US$1 (1999)	NT$32.4
Exchange rate US$1 (March 1998)	NT$32.9
Exchange rate US$1 (1997)	NT$27.5
Foreign exchange reserves (1998)	$88 billion
Avg. movie ticket price (1998)	$6.80
Video piracy rate (1998)	10%
GDP (1998)	$262.3 billion
Unemployment rate (1998)	3%
Movie screens (1998)	600
TV households (1997)	5.8 million
TV HH penetration (1997)	99.5%
Cable TV penetration (1997)	88%
VCR HH (1997)	57.1%
Video Stores (1998)	1,200
Terrestrial TV networks	5

Source: Taipei Economic and Cultural Office/*The Economist*/MPA. TableBase™ Copyright 2001, Accession# 1875883.

the same title on video and in theater, many independent theatrical distributors buy rights to both theatrical and video releasing. Consequently, many local distributors began to get into exhibition to ensure that their acquired video titles receive theatrical releasing, thus increasing visibility while maximizing profit of these titles.

With a cable TV penetration rate of 88 percent (see table 7.3), Taiwan has a very strong cable market with an exceptionally high number of movie channels. Indeed, the number of movie channels on Taiwan's cable TV is the highest in Asia and higher than that of the U.S. cable television system. With each of these more than ten or so movie channels showing ten movies each a day of Chinese, U.S., European, and Japanese films, there is a critical demand for film content. It is not surprising to find that exhibition and distribution companies such as Long Shong and Scholar also own most of these film channels. In 1995, three movie channels won the top ten spots for the most popular cable television programs: HBO with its Hollywood fare, the Unique Entertainment Channels specializing in Chinese movies, and the Sun Movie Channel that showed 70 percent Chinese films and 30 percent American and Europeans films. These three channels won the second, sixth, and seventh spots, respectively (see Teng, 1996). The same theatrical distributors thus also control video and cable markets. The paradox, however, is that these cable channels compete directly with cinemas for audiences.

Furthermore, Taiwan, along with Korea, was one of the very few Asian markets that were still primarily VHS-based in the late 1990s. As noted, Taiwan has a very vibrant video rental market (as opposed to Hong Kong's mostly VCD-based retail market). VCD and DVD retail markets nonetheless are on the rise. A key factor has to do with different windowing timetables. While there is a six-month VHS rental-to-retail window widely observed in Taiwan, VCDs and DVDs are in general released simultaneously with rental VHS, greatly affecting the VHS rental and retail business. Finally, the VCRs are increasingly used for time shift recording and VHS rentals. They are also used to play children's titles when adults watch VCDs (*Screen Digest*, 1998). These unique life-style choices have all affected the box office performance of theatrical releases in Taiwan.

Policy, Foreign Film Distribution, and U.S.-Taiwan Bilateral Relations

In the merger, deregulation, and globalization climate of the 1990s, the worldwide film markets have also undergone major reconfiguration. Even though Japan remains the most profitable market outside of the United States, other Asian markets have been making headlines in terms of both box office grosses and net profits. Further, the Asian market has been expanding to now include Australia. As a result of the redefinition of the "region," UIP, for example, has its Asian regional office in Australia (personal interview, Simon Huang, marketing manager, UIP-Taiwan, 24 July 1999, Taipei).

For Hollywood majors, Taiwan has become one of the top markets in the world. Table 7.4 shows that Taiwan moved from being the fifteenth market in the early 1980s to a steady position of the number ten market in the mid-1990s. Table 7.5 shows that in 2000 Taiwan remained the tenth most important market in film rentals. In terms of net profit, however, Taiwan occupies one of the top spots for most majors and is the top market for Warner Bros. and Buena Vista.[7] Because Taiwan is a highly concentrated and populated market, distribution incurs lower marketing and promotion expenditures. Thus, while total box office grosses in Taiwan are not the highest, the net profits have been among the top.

Unlike the Hong Kong market where most majors work with a local sub-distributor or a licensee to distribute their films, furthermore, in Taiwan the ma-

Table 7.4. Major Overseas Markets for U.S. Majors (1983–1997, in US$million)

Territory	1983	1984	1985	1986	1995	1996	1997
Japan	102.4(1)	77.0(2)	74.9(2)	102.6(1)	364(1)	270(2)	319(1)
Germany*	66.2(4)	48.0(4)	48.5(4)	64.7(5)	250(2)	310(1)	281(2)
U.K.	49.7(5)	35.0(6)	41.2(5)	49.1(7)	174(4)	168(4)	234(3)
France	81.3(3)	69.5(3)	50.2(3)	98.5(2)	176(3)	187(3)	197(4)
Canada	91.0(2)	111.0(1)	75.5(1)	86.8(3)	110(6)	147(7)	176(5)
Spain	39.4(8)	33.1(7)	24.6(8)	48.2(8)	156(5)	164(5)	168(6)
Australia	44.8(7)	33.0(8)	28.8(7)	27.4(9)	105(7)	153(6)	148(7)
Italy	48.4(6)	40.0(5)	31.0(6)	64.6(6)	90(9)	135(8)	117(8)
Brazil	15.5(10)	11.4(10)	4.9(14)	24.5(10)	94(8)	86(9)	91(9)
Taiwan	10.6(15)	8.0(15)	7.9(11)	12.5(15)	58(10)	80(10)	87(10)

Source: Lee, 2000.
Note: In parentheses are numbers that represent the territories' world rankings.
*The statistics for 1983–1986 were for West Germany.

Table 7.5. Top Ten Overseas Markets for U.S. Majors (2000)

Territory	Rentals (in US$million)	Change
Japan	303	- 14%
U.K.	251	+ 6%
Germany	208	16%
France	168	5%
Spain	157	4%
Australia	122	6%
Mexico	110	+ 13%
Italy	102	even
Brazil	80	+ 8%
Taiwan	70	+ 13%

Source: Motion Picture Association. TableBase™, Copyright 2001, Accession# 2952759.

jors (except for Disney/Buena Vista) have all had a long history working through their own local branch offices.

In general, Hollywood majors' presence in Taiwan can be roughly divided into three major phases: 1946–1970 marks the beginning of the majors' operation in Taiwan; 1970–1990 represents a transitional period for the majors as they suffered business setbacks; and with worldwide deregulation and globalization trends, 1990–present witnesses the dominance of transnational corporations and the majors' oligopoly structure repeated overseas. These three phases reflected and coincided with major film import policy changes in Taiwan (see Lee, 2000):

1. From 1946 to 1970, foreign (mostly American) films dominated the Taiwanese market. Quota was used both as a mechanism through which local film industry was protected, and also as a diplomatic tool to give preferential treatment to American films.
2. From 1970 to 1990, the American government and the majors protested the quota system and other such restrictions, and asked for deregulation. It marked a contentious period for the two governments in regards to film import policy.
3. From 1990 to the present, in addition to meeting the demands from USTR and Special 301, the Taiwanese government made multiple compromises in deregulation and in opening up the film market to gain accession to the WTO.

Back in the 1920s and the 1930s, when Taiwan was under Japanese occupation, the Taiwanese film market's growth had already received international distributors' attention. Paramount and Universal were the first two major studios to set up Taiwanese operations under the jurisdiction of Japanese distribution. Later MGM, UA, and Universal licensed distribution to the Taiwan Film Society (Taiwanese owned), while Paramount, Warner Bros., Fox, and Columbia licensed to Taiwan Film Distribution Society (Japanese owned). On the Mainland, the majors had their distribution offices in Shanghai before World War II. When Taiwan was recovered from Japan in 1945, and with the increasingly chaotic political situation on the Mainland, the majors began to view Taiwan as a possible site to which their distribution offices could relocate. In 1949, when the Mainland was "liberated" by the Chinese Communists, the majors moved their distribution offices to Taiwan. As a result of the Treaty of Friendship, Commerce and Navigation (FCN) between the Republic of China and the United States in 1948, the majors were able to set up distribution offices in Taiwan without having to go through local licensees. MGM was the first major to set up a branch office in Taiwan in the postwar period (personal interview, Simon Huang, UIP, 24 July 1999; Lee, 2000; and Young and Wang, 1996).

To protect the local film industry and to prevent foreign imports from dominating the film market, the Taiwanese government had been in favor of a protectionist policy. In June 1954 the Foreign Film Import Regulation was put into effect, imposing a print quota system and restricting day and date releases in

Taiwan (see tables 7.6 and 7.7). To add a further deterrent to the import of foreign films, the Taiwanese government set up a lengthy censorship process through which all imported films had to be examined (see GIO Report, 2000).

The U.S.-Taiwan trade relations had also had great influence shaping the Taiwanese film policy and the subsequent film import and export structure, especially in the late 1980s and beyond. Taiwan is the sixth-largest trading partner of the United States and the second-largest Asian market for the United States (second to Japan). Its export-oriented economic policy and strategy and its reliance on the U.S. market have created a trade imbalance between the two. During the 1980s, Taiwan's tremendous trade surplus with the United States became an issue and created tension while the U.S. trade deficit with Taiwan soared. The U.S. businesses were demanding greater access to the Taiwanese market. The U.S. government, through threats of retaliation, began to pressure Taiwan to remove import barriers (see Morrison, 1996). In addition to having forced Taiwan to open its market since the 1970s, the United States began to pressure Taiwan to appreciate its currency, as the United States had long viewed the Taiwanese currency—the New Taiwan dollar (NT$)—as undervalued. The appre-

Table 7.6. Foreign Film Import Quota (1954–1970)

Fiscal Year	U.S.	Europe	Japan	Others	Total
1954	349(78%)	59	24	12	444
1960	310(70%)	73	34	27	444
1961	280(67%)	88	34	13	415
1962	260(63%)	108	34	13	415
1963	260(63%)	108	34	18	420
1965	220(60%)	90	34	22	366
1966	188(59%)	77	77	28	25
1967	188(59%)	77	28	25	318
1968	179(59%)	73	27	25	304
1969	170(59%)	69	26	23	288
1970	162(59%)	66	25	22	275

Source: Lee, 2000.

Table 7.7. U.S. and Chinese Distribution Quota (1954–1970)

	1954	1963	1965	1967	1968	1969
United States	277 (79.4%)	230 (88.5%)	190 (86.4%)	161 (85.6%)	152 (84.9%)	136 (80%)
Local	72 (20.6%)	30 (11.5%)	30 (13.6%)	27 (14.4%)	27 (15.1%)	34 (20%)
Total	349	260	220	188	179	170

Source: Lee, 2000.

ciation would weaken Taiwan's export advantage. Given that Taiwan had been one of the most heavily trade-dependent countries and was relying on the United States not only for economic survival but also for political security, Taiwan found itself in a weak bargaining position. Thus the New Taiwan Dollar appreciated more than 40 percent from 1985 to 1987.[8] In 1987 the government further liberated its financial policy and allowed unlimited exporting of foreign currency. The sharp appreciation of the NT dollar, along with other domestic developments, had greatly increased the volume of Taiwan's overseas direct investment. This import-friendly environment also created much incentive for local distributors to acquire distribution rights to foreign films, most significantly those of Hollywood major studios.

Under U.S. pressure, the Taiwanese government lifted most of the film import restrictions in the 1980s and 1990s, most notably the film quota system and print control. The issue of foreign film import quota had created contentious relations among U.S. and Taiwanese governments, distributors, and exhibitors. It was estimated that, for a major release, at least fifteen copies of prints were needed for the Taipei area. The supply and demand imbalance created multiple cases of illegal import of prints (see Tien, 2000). The lifting of the quota system in 1986 nevertheless adversely impacted the local film industry. The loosening of restrictions on the maximum number of print copies allowed, furthermore, changed the foreign film release patterns and strategies in Taiwan. Prior to 1986 the number of print copies was limited to three per film. The government gradually increased the number of prints allowed; it changed the number from thirty-eight to fifty in five months in 1997 and to fifty-eight in 1999 (see tables 7.8 and 7.9). The government further relaxed the restrictions on day and date releases.

Table 7.8. Number of Prints Allowed 1965–1999

Year	Number of Prints Allowed
July 1965	3
November 1984	4
August 1986	4
April 1987	6
January 1988	8
June 1990	12
June 1992	14
January 1994	16
October 1994	24
June 1995	28
June 1996	31
June 1997	38
November 1997	50
May 1999	58

Sources: Government Information Office, 1999; Lee, 2000.

Table 7.9. Foreign Film Day and Date Restrictions 1984–1999

Year	Number of Day and Date Releasing within the Same City
September 1984	4 in Taipei, Kaohsiung, and other cities
February 1991	6 in Taipei and Kaohsiung, 4 in others
October 1994	9 in Taipei and Kaohsiung, 6 in others
June 1995	11 in Taipei and Kaohsiung, 6 in others
August 1997	11 in Taipei and Kaohsiung, 10 in others
November 1997	18 in Taipei and Kaohsiung, 10 in others
August 1997	18 in Taipei and Kaohsiung, 10 in others (nonprofit screenings are not subject to the same restrictions)

Source: Government Information Office, 1999.

It increased from four theaters per given city in 1984 to eleven in August 1997 and eighteen in November 1997. The lifting of this restriction greatly increased the scale of foreign film releases in Taiwan (see GIO Film Industry Reports, 1999, 2000; Lu, 1998; and Yu, 1993).

Such a change in policy had much to do with foreign exchange rates and export-import regulations and environment and was also tied closely to bilateral trade negotiations between the United States and Taiwan. It was also related to Taiwan's effort in gaining accession into global trade bodies such as GATT and, later, WTO. The Special 301 was an especially important bilateral negotiation that had tremendous effect on Taiwanese trade and cultural policies. The U.S. Trade Representative, for example, had been using Taiwan's effort in gaining the WTO accession to urge Taiwan to eliminate its print import quotas and day and date restrictions on imported films, as a day and date restriction necessarily limits the number of screens in a particular city that are allowed to show the same film on the same day (see IIPA Country Report, Taiwan, 1997). On 1 January 2002, all such restrictions were lifted upon Taiwan's formal accession to the WTO. To offset the negative effects such a policy could have on the local film industry, since even more theaters would now prefer to play U.S. films, the GIO has decided to increase the guidance fund to NT$25–30 million matching fund per film (roughly US$730,000–US$880,000, see Huang, 2002).

After the increase of prints allowed into Taiwan in 1997 and the easing of restrictions of day and date releases, we see a sudden increase of active distributors in 1998 from eighteen to sixty-two. With the increase of active distributors the number of films released by each distributor naturally decreased (table 7.10). Subsequently, the changing political and economic environments continue to shape the foreign film distribution landscape in Taiwan.

Such loosening of restrictions of quota, print copies, and day and date releasing has great implications for the major distributors' control of the space and time of releases. Such control has historically afforded them a crucial tool to

112   *Chapter 7*

Table 7.10. Number of Active Distributors, Average Releases per Distributor, and Distributor Rental Revenue in Taiwan, 1996–1999

Year	Number of Distributors	Avg. Releases per Distributor	Distributor Rental Revenue (in US/NT$millions)
1996	18	20.1	96.9/2,662.73
1997	18	19.8	125.0/3,597.10
1998	62	14.2	124.6/4,144.40
1999	–	7.0	–

Sources: Screen Digest (1999 and 2000), TableBase ™ Copyright 2001 Accession# 2088012; and TableBase ™ Copyright 2001 Accession# 2550795.

remain dominant. In continuation with their centralized distribution strategy and joint venture tradition, UIP[9] and Fox/Columbia maintained their respective partnership in distribution in Taiwan in the 1980s and 1990s. In 1999, after ten years of joint operation, Fox and Columbia went their separate ways in Taiwan. Columbia now distributes its films in Taiwan through Buena Vista International –Taiwan (personal interviews, Rudy Tseng, vice president and general manager, Buena Vista International, 3 August 1999; and Josephine Chen, marketing manager, Fox–Taiwan, 20 July 1999, Taipei). Warner Bros. has been distributing its films independently in Taiwan. Disney films were first released through MGM, Fox, Warner, and then Era, a local licensee and a major independent distributor (see later discussion) in 1992; and in 1995 Disney began its Buena Vista Taiwan operation (personal interviews, Rudy Tseng, vice president and general manager, Buena Vista International, 3 August 1999; Simon Huang, marketing manager, UIP-Taiwan, 24 July 1999, Taipei). Albeit a newcomer to worldwide film distribution, Buena Vista has the largest market share in Taiwan and has been a top distributor in general (see table 7.11). Of the twenty-eight Hollywood films that have broken the NT$100 million box office gross record, Buena Vista occupied nine slots (see table 7.12).

As early as the late 1940s, when the majors began to set up branch offices in Taiwan, they adopted a "localization" strategy, recruiting local personnel to operate local distribution businesses. The tradition continues with one of the most interesting cases being Warner Bros.' decision in 1992 to hire Spring International's president Chen Jun-Rong to head Warner Bros.' theatrical distribution in Taiwan. Founded in 1988, Spring was one of the largest local independent distributors of Western films (see table 7.13 and later discussion). To strengthen local operation, Warner Bros. recruited one of its formidable local competitors to head its theatrical distribution. Once Chen became Warner's general manager, he was running two companies simultaneously while incorporating local methods of marketing and promotion for Warner's releases, including the heavy use of newspaper ads (see Lee, 2000).[10] Eric Shih, a former reporter, later replaced Chen.

Table 7.11. Selected Majors' Market Share in Taiwan (1997, in NT$millions)

Company	Capital	Annual Gross	Staff	Market Share
Buena Vista	25	800	12	21.90
Fox	1	750	12	20.53
UIP	1	650	17	17.79
Columbia	1	500	12	13.69

Source: Lee, 2000.

Table 7.12. Box Office Performance (Taipei): Films with Box Office over NT$100 million (Roughly US$3.1 million, at NT$32=US$1)

Rank	Title	Distributor	Release Date	Box Office
1	*Titanic*	Fox	19.12.1997	388,992,700
2	*Jurassic Park*	Universal	17.07.1993	231,210,570
3	*The Lost World*	Universal	21.06.1997	213,165,660
4	*Independence Day*	Fox	12.07.1996	187,755,640
5	*Armageddon*	Buena Vista	24.07.1998	163,847,960
6	*Die Hard 3*	Buena Vista	16.06.1995	158,482,200
7	*Face/Off*	Buena Vista	21.08.1997	147,874,370
8	*Air Force One*	Buena Vista	09.10.1997	144,914,960
9	*Forrest Gump*	Paramount	15.10.1994	133,668,950
10	*Mission Impossible*	Paramount	20.06.1996	133,632,450
11	*Twister*	Universal	18.07.1996	129,155,030
12	*The Rock*	Buena Vista	15.08.1996	128,770,360
13	*The Fifth Element*	Spring	07.06.1997	124,382,570
14	*True Lie*	Universal	12.08.1994	124,339,630
15	*The Ghost*	Paramount	15.12.1990	120,544,260
16	*Speed*	Fox	25.06.1994	119,769,960
17	*Tomorrow Never Dies*	United Artists	24.01.1998	117,996,990
18	*Con Air*	Buena Vista	26.07.1997	117,720,020
19	*Daylight*	Universal	01.02.1997	114,795,130
20	*Saving Private Ryan*	Paramount	25.09.1998	113,040,910
21	*Men in Black*	Columbia	18.07.1997	111,602,960
22	*Terminator 2*	Local	06.07.1991	110,118,080
23	*The Last Emperor*	Local	23.04.1988	107,842,780
24	*Ransom*	Buena Vista	20.12.1996	106,141,840
25	*Mulan*	Buena Vista	11.07.1998	104,534,940
26	*Godzilla*	Columbia	19.06.1998	103,578,130
27	*Deep Impact*	Universal	06.06.1998	102,769,400
28	*Enemy of the State*	Buena Vista	1999	102,000,000*

Source: UIP-Taiwan (Personal Interview, Simon Huang, 24 July 1999).
*Huang estimate.

**Table 7.13. Top Ten Hollywood Film Box Office Grosses (1990–1998)
(NT$millions)**

	1990	1995	1996	1997	1998
No. of top 10 films (majors)	8.0	9.0	9.0	9.0	9.0
Box office grosses	410.8	705.6	1,032.8	1,399.3	9,184.5
Grosses by local distributors	93.0	67.2	81.8	124.4	9.1
Major local distributors	Hongfei, Spring	Spring	Era	Spring	Era

Source: Lee, 2000.

Independent Distribution in Taiwan

Because of the sharp appreciation of the Taiwanese currency and the general climate of deregulation, the 1980s witnessed a rapid growth in local independent distribution. Such growth also coincided with the corresponding revival of American independent production in the 1980s. Tien (2000) divided the development of the local independent distribution of American films into three phrases:

1. 1954–1980: this period marked the beginning of local independent distribution of foreign films. Due to government policies in restricting foreign film import, however, the independent distribution landscape was very limited.
2. 1980–1988: many viewed this decade as the golden era for independent film distribution in Taiwan. The independent sector in the United States, first of all, experienced prosperity in this period, which translated to enthusiastic responses from independent Taiwan distributors. Secondly, the popularity of the VCR had stimulated independent film growth and reception worldwide. And finally, the aforementioned currency appreciation and deregulation encouraged an import-friendly trading environment, which was conducive to film importation and distribution.
3. The late 1980s to present: the third stage has seen a decline in local independent film distribution as the majors enjoyed unprecedented growth and dominance in Taiwan. This decline is clearly shown, among others, in the weak box office performances of independently distributed films.

The number of local independent foreign film distributors, for instance, dropped from its peak of thirty-eight in 1989 to sixteen in 1994; by the late 1990s there were fewer than ten independent distributors in Taiwan. The two remaining powerful players in the late 1990s were Spring International and Era Communications, as shown in table 7.13. Independent distribution in Taiwan is closely linked to the majors. When the majors experienced vigorous growth in the 1990s, most notably in 1998 with an 85 percent box office increase from the previous year, the independents suffered a devastating drop of 93 percent in the same period.

In the early 1980s, when the video market was in complete chaos, Chiu Fu-Sheng entered the market. A media mogul who began in advertising in the 1970s, Chiu founded Era Communications in 1982 and began building his video distribution empire. Era grew to an island-wide distribution network of 1,000 plus licensees. In September 1993, Era partnered with the Shaw Brothers' TVBI Company Limited in Hong Kong and was licensed to distribute TVB programming in Taiwan. The joint-venture cable channel TVB Super Channel (TVBS) became an instant success in Taiwan. Chiu also entered foreign video distribution and represented MGM, RCA/Columbia, Disney, Orion, and Warner home video at one time or another. In 1986 Era began theatrical distribution, buying film rights to U.S. independent films, with the most notable his acquisition of the rights to *Rambo 3* with US$2 million. It grossed NT$89 million (US$2.6 million) in 1988. With other incomes, the gross came to NT$200 million (close to US$6 million, see *TVB.com*, 2002).

Because of its dominance in the video market, Era charged hefty fees from both theaters and video rental stores. Realizing it was hard to get the best playdates, Era further signed a contract with an exhibition circuit for the exhibition of Era films. Additionally, Era began investing in and producing high-profile and high-quality films such as Hou Hsiao-Hsien's award-winning *City of Sadness* (1989), *The Puppet Master* (1993), and Zhang Yi-Mou's award-winning *Raise the Red Lantern* (1991), among others. Era, thus, successfully achieved vertical integration with production, distribution, and exhibition. Chiu is also striving to integrate horizontally with ventures in the Internet, publishing, music/recording labels, and broadcast television. To get the right to broadcast baseball games, he even started his own professional baseball team (personal interviews, Wolf Chen, former Era vice president, summer 1999, spring 2000, 2001, and summer 2002; see also Tien, 2000).

Spring International, on the other hand, was not as diversified as its major rival Era. Chen Jun-Rong founded Spring International in 1988 and made its name distributing *Sex, Lies and Videotape* in 1988 and *When Harry Met Sally* in 1990. The deciding film was *Dances with Wolves* in 1991, which grossed NT$140 million (roughly US$4 million). Spring was also first in running a theme-oriented art film festival in Taiwan in 1997. The popular film festival runs twice a year (see Tien, 2000). Although not horizontally diversified, Spring was still vertically integrated. It was involved in both Chinese language and foreign film distribution. It owned two Spring cinemas in Taipei, had a live theater group, and was involved in production. It also had collaboration plans with Golden Harvest of Hong Kong. Yet its cable movie channel, Sun Movie—after being one of the top ten most popular cable channels for six years (starting in November 1995)—ceased operation in 2001 (*Taipei Times*, 2001).

The independent scene in Taiwan underwent a rapid restructuring as the 1990s drew to an end. Era shifted its focus from film production and distribution to cable and satellite television developments, while Spring slowly shrank its operations. In late 2000, a new independent distributor entered the scene and in less than two years outperformed even some of the majors (see table 7.14). Mata Entertainment is a film distribution company founded by former Era vice president (of theatrical distribution) Wolf Chen in September 2000. Its parent company CMC Group is a publicly traded company and a leading CD-R producer in the world, with a global market share of 32 percent (JP Investment Clinic Web, 2002). Because it is a technology hardware developer and manufacturer, CMC decided to model itself after Sony in integrating content and software into the hardware business. Before the founding of Mata, CMC had already been involved in video distribution through its subsidiary Deltamac (De-Li), the current market leader in home video distribution for all majors except Buena Vista and Paramount. Buena Vista has its own home video division in Taiwan, while Paramount distributes its home video through Xiehe.

CMC founded Deltamac in 1997 because it saw great potential of the VCD and DVD markets in Taiwan. It envisioned that the Taiwanese home video market would soon be dominated by the VCD and DVD formats. Deltamac subsequently made deals with the majors to distribute DVDs and VCDs. Its strategy was to convince the majors that because Deltamac would focus solely on DVD and VCD distribution, it would not compete with the two main video licensees for the majors, Biaozhi and Xiehe. Deltamac's strategy paid off. In 2002 DVDs and VCDs made up 70 percent of the home video market, while Deltamac accounted for 60 percent of the Taiwanese home video market share (personal interview, Wolf Chen, CEO and president, Mata, 30 April 2002, Taipei). Mata, on the other hand, has been distributing around twenty films a year, including

Table 7.14. Top Grossing Distributors in Taiwan, January–June 2002

Distributor	Box Office Gross (in NT$)
Buena Vista	287,210,000
Mata	286,400,000
Fox	142,470,000
Warner Bros.	136,180,000
UIP	132,470,000
Spring	23,800,000
Era	10,060,000

Source: Compiled from Truemovie.com (2002).

those by New Line.[11] In the first half of 2002, Mata was the number two distributor in Taiwan in box office grosses and market share (see table 7.14).

Tables 7.15 and 7.16 summarize major distributors' (both Hollywood majors and independents) box office grosses, net profit, and number of films released in 2000 and 2001. From these tables one can see that although in both years independent distributors imported more films than the majors, their grosses were lower. Further, among the major distributors in 2000, BVI and Columbia TriStar (whose films are also distributed by BVI-Taiwan) were clear market leaders, while in 2001 Universal and Warner Bros. became the top distributors. In 2001, Mata began to show its market power as a major independent distributor in Taiwan, distributing a total of twenty films, the highest of all distributors. It also occupied the fourth position in the market, after BVI, Universal, and Warner Bros. (see table 7.16).

In short, while independent distributors in Taiwan have been distributing more films (54 percent) in 2000 and 2001 than their Hollywood major counterparts had, they consistently performed worse than Hollywood majors. Furthermore, the majors' films were played much longer and had much better exposure in terms of the number of opening screens. Comparatively, the majors also spent in 2001 far more in advertising and publicity than their independent counterparts (76 percent). The majors' films also accounted for 75 percent of the total American film box office grosses and net in Taipei. What is also clear from the two tables is the emergence of Mata in 2001 as a major player in foreign film distribution in Taiwan. It distributed the largest number of films that year and fared fairly well and was placed number four in 2001.

The fast changing landscape of independent distribution in Taiwan continues the decline it started in the late 1980s. Major independent distributors have dwindled down to fewer than a handful, while Mata has appeared as a major force to be reckoned with. Mata is in the process of merging with the leading video distributor, Deltamac, and CMC, their parent company, is a major global information technology producer and manufacturer. Both of these facts have great implications for the future of video and theatrical distribution in Taiwan. To further explore these issues I conducted an in-depth interview with Wolf Chen. The interview is included in chapter 8 and is intended as a roadmap for a better understanding of the independent film distribution landscape in Taiwan.[12]

Full Impact: Warner Village and Exhibition

All the theaters were occupied with Hollywood films, and even if I managed to get one theater, my film may still be pulled off once a big-cast movie is showing.
—Wang Shiao-di, director (*Taipei Times*, 23 November 1999)

With the growth of the Taiwanese market and the deregulation of film imports

Table 7.15. Taipei First Run Box Office (1 January–31 December 2000)

No. of Films Released	Distributor	Weeks in Release	No. of Days for Opening Date	No. of Days Screened	Box Office Opening Weekend (NT$)	Gross Box Office (for the year, NT$)
15 (+2 1999)	BVI	89	244	630	120,168,685	452,781,745
16 (+2 1999)	COL	125	270	878	132,268,135	522,666,580
12	FOX	75	179	529	73,544,995	271,783,795
3	MGM	13	20	84	17,547,485	103,916,770
3	PAR	25	63	178	54,051,140	207,341,530
11	UNI	64	161	449	43,122,660	173,163,645
12 (+1 1999)	WB	81	183	564	88,079,240	290,724,650
Total 156		782	1,959	5,497	711,731,740	2,623,872,050
Total MPA 72		472	1,120	3,312	528,782,340	2,022,378,715
Percentage 46		60	57	60	74	77
Total Independent 84		310	839	2,185	182,949,400	601,493,335
Percentage 54		40	43	40	26	23

Source: Compiled from Mata Entertainment (2002).

Table 7.16. Taipei First Run Box Office (1 January–31 December 2001)

No. of Films Released	Distributor	Weeks in Release	No. of Screens for Opening Date	No. of Days Screened	Advertising and Publicity (NT$M)	Box Office Opening Weekend (NT$)	Gross Box Office (for the year, NT$)	Total Net (NT$)
9	BVI	52	158	282	7,650	65,294,905	243,923,340	217,940,698
12	COL	62	202	411	6,690	53,692,000	162,150,005	152,218,349
9	FOX	56	148	353	5,930	38,622,195	163,871,465	155,054,364
4	MGM	46	56	110	1,610	8,645,160	27,299,665	25,481,987
8	PAR	39	109	229	5,330	49,541,560	168,233,865	155,505,545
11	UNI	76	175	495	11,115	138,054,520	524,426,120	490,882,304
12	WB	81	187	525	11,350	116,847,655	457,782,720	428,380,854
21	MATA	69	234	496	9,418	66,359	207,354,475	192,868,190
15	ERA	64	169	390	5,637	38,509,560	122,565,285	113,985,715
7	L.S.	28	60	144	1,050	7,650,640	28,663,870	26,657,399
17	SPR	82	210	571	NA	35,176,310	149,596,695	139,124,926
17	IND	48	155	384	NA	17,714,831	64,493,365	59,978,829
Total 142		673	1,863	4,390	65,780	569,815,695	2,320,360,870	2,158,079,160
Total MPA 65		382	1,035	2,405	49,675	470,697,995	1,747,687,180	1,625,464,101
Percentage Total 46		57	55	55	76	83	75	75
Independent 77		291	828	1,985	16,105	99,117,700	572,673,690	532,615,059
Percentage 54		43	45	45	24	17	25	25

Source: Compiled from Mata Entertainment (2002).

in the late 1980s and on, Taiwan has become a highly lucrative territory for the majors. The rapid growth of the exhibition sector, especially that of the multiplexes, reflects such changes in the market ecology.

Figure 7.1 illustrates changes of major players in exhibition in the 1980s and 1990s in Taiwan. In the 1980s a few first-run theaters such as Guo Bin (Ambassador), Le Sheng, Shi Shing, and Hao Hua dominated the Taiwanese foreign film (mostly Hollywood films) exhibition sector. With the changing and increasingly lucrative video rental market in the 1980s, however, several major Chinese language film distributors decided to distribute Western films and to move into exhibition to ensure theatrical releases of video titles. The prominent players were Long Shong and Scholar, two major distributor-turned-exhibitors who also invested heavily in Hong Kong film production. With the entry of these distributors as well as Warner Village, the first foreign direct invested theater in Taiwan, exhibition in the 1990s experienced drastic changes. Major players now include four groups, with the first-run luxury theaters still leading the race, and Warner Village following closely behind. Long Shong and Scholar occupy the third position, while a few independent cinemas the fourth (see photo 7.1). In addition to the advantage of having huge screens, the luxury first-run theaters such as Ambassador also own the property on which the theaters are built, thus saving high property rental cost. The net profit as a result is much higher. The newer players such as Warner Village, Scholar, and Long Shong all operate on leased property and therefore incur much higher expenses (personal interview, Simon Huang, marketing manager, UIP-Taiwan, 24 July 1999, Taipei; Tien, 2000). Meanwhile, the emergence of the multiplex in the 1990s changed the exhibition structure in Taiwan. Quan-Qio Movie Town was the first multiplex to appear in Taiwan in 1994, with eight screens plus a surrounding shopping arcade. The other multiscreened theaters built after Quan-Qio came mostly only with screens, without shopping facilities. It was not until 1997 when Warner Village, now a new landmark of Taipei, entered the exhibition sector did the new multiplex-shopping mall structure take hold (See Lee, 2000).

Warner Village, a joint venture between Warner Bros. and the Australian exhibitor Village Roadshow, is the first fully foreign-owned cinema in Taiwan (see photos 7.2 and 7.3). It opened partially in late 1997, and fully on 23 January 1998 (GIO Film Industry Report, 2000). This seventeen-screen multiplex has not only become the top grossing cinema in Taiwan, it has also become a tourist attraction for people outside of Taipei. On average, Warner Village charges NT$20 more for its tickets than its counterparts in Taiwan, but it still attracts the biggest number of viewers creating long ticket lines outside its box office. Even though Warner Village saw its total box office gross at NT$60 million, it lost money in 1998 because of high operation costs (the rent alone to the Taipei City government was NT$19.5 million a year). In 1999 it broke even (personal interview, Simon Huang, UIP-Taiwan, 24 July 1999). And often a single film shown at the multiplex would be the top grossing film in Taipei. The entry of Warner Village into the marketplace thus tipped the balance of power toward exhibitors, especially those that operate multiplexes.

Figure 7.1. Changes in Exhibition Structure, 1980s to 1990s

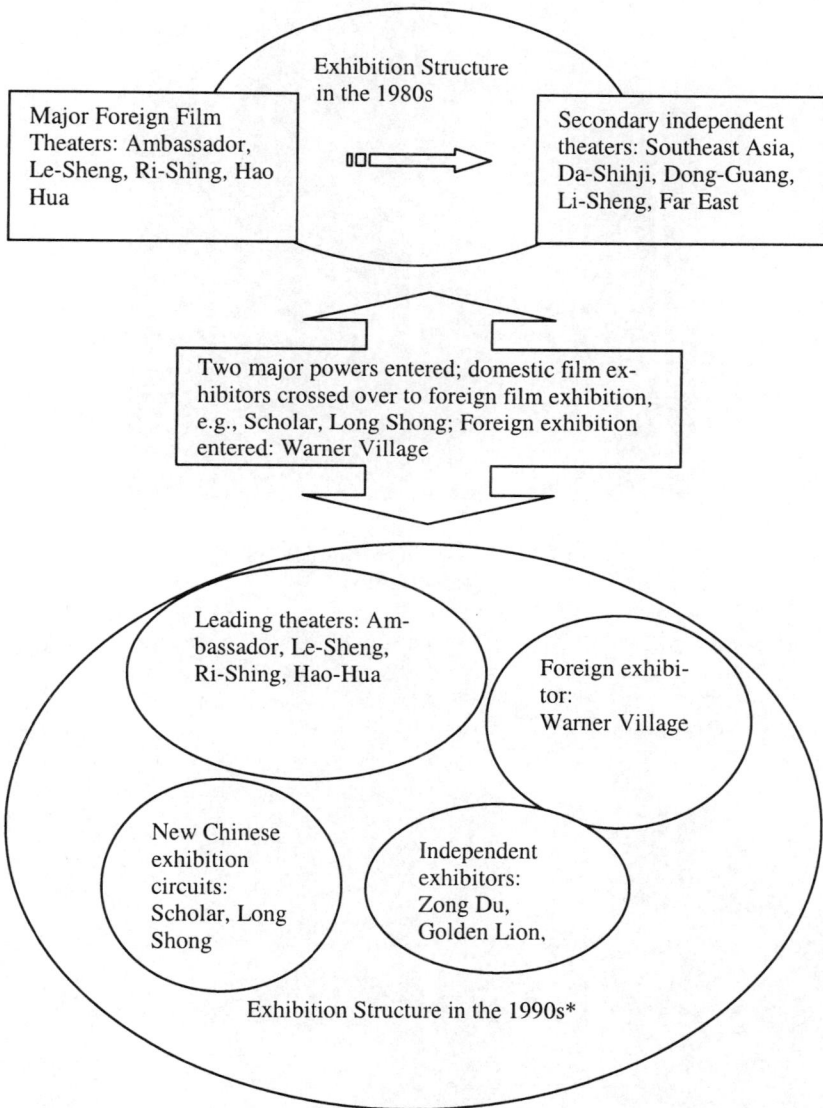

Exhibition Structure
in the 1980s

Major Foreign Film
Theaters: Ambassador,
Le-Sheng, Ri-Shing, Hao
Hua

Secondary independent
theaters: Southeast Asia,
Da-Shihji, Dong-Guang,
Li-Sheng, Far East

Two major powers entered; domestic film exhibitors crossed over to foreign film exhibition,
e.g., Scholar, Long Shong; Foreign exhibition
entered: Warner Village

Leading theaters: Am-
bassador, Le-Sheng,
Ri-Shing, Hao-Hua

Foreign exhibi-
tor:
Warner Village

New Chinese
exhibition
circuits:
Scholar, Long
Shong

Independent
exhibitors:
Zong Du,
Golden Lion,

Exhibition Structure in the 1990s*

Source: Tien, 2000.
* The size of the circles represents the booking and negotiating power each group of exhibitors
possesses.

**Photo 7.1. New World (Xinshijie) Theater,
Taipei (1999)**

Photo 7.2. Warner Village (1), Taipei (2002)

Photo 7.3. Warner Village (2), Taipei (1999)

The lifting of the day and date releasing restriction further strengthened the competition advantage of the multiplexes. With the entry and success of Warner Village, many local exhibitors and investors began building more multiplexes.

Scholar Films, for one, opened Universal Cinema City, and Long Shong opened Broadway Cinema City, both in December 1997. In early 1999 three theaters—Today, Golden Horse, and Phoenix—merged to form the Carnival Cinema City. Warner Village itself has opened three more multiplexes: one in Tai-Chung (central Taiwan), one in Kao-Hsiung (southern Taiwan), and one more in Taipei. By 2000 there were more than a dozen multiplexes in operation in Taiwan (GIO Report, 2000). Because of the increase of multiplexes, and the resulting closing down of smaller venues, the number of theaters has been decreasing. There were fifty-five theaters in Taipei in the mid-1990s, for example, and there were only forty-one theaters as of mid-2002. The actual number of screens, however, has gone up from 122 to 156. Six of these theaters account for 40 percent of the total box office, and all six of them are multiplexes. The paradox with the increase in the number of the screens is that box office grosses in Taipei have fallen since 1998, including a drop from $74.3 million in 2000 to $68.2 million in 2001, an 8 percent decrease in one year alone (see Wu, 2002).

With Taiwan's accession to the WTO, the lifting of all exhibition and distribution related restrictions, and the increasing dominance of the multiplexes, Taiwan's film market will no doubt experience further changes. The power relations between exhibitors and distributors (both majors and independents) promise to be ever more dynamic. Warner Village's pricing and other operation strategies in the three major markets in Taiwan have great implications for the survival of smaller theaters and, consequently, the future of both foreign and local film exhibition and distribution landscapes in Taiwan.

A Dubious Future

The post-1949 Taiwanese film industry was linked, directly and indirectly, to those in Hong Kong and the Mainland. Such complex connections have inevitably shaped the development of the Taiwanese film industry.

A product of unique political and cultural realities of a divided nation, the Taiwanese film industry was never properly supported from the outset. Taiwan's contentious relations with the Mainland, its political isolation in the world, and its economic reliance on the United States, have all had great influence on its film industry and policy. While the Taiwanese film industry did witness two promising (though short-lived) periods with commercial realization in the early 1970s and an artistic, cultural, and ideological reawakening in the 1980s (i.e., Taiwanese new wave), it has been plagued by shortsighted policy makers as well as film producers, exhibitors, and distributors. The Taiwanese government's reliance on the United States for trade partnership and for political security further weakens its ability and willingness in defining a sound national film policy and vision. The combination of a weak local film industry, an import friendly film policy and environment (especially toward the end of the 1990s and beyond), and a strong local demand for Hollywood products (partly a result of the lack of proper exhibition outlets for local films) has translated into a Hollywood-dominated local market that is highly lucrative for the majors.

In short, unlike the IPR issues where strong state intervention is highly welcomed by the copyright industries, in the commercial film sector the opposite is true. The role of the state, or rather, the absence of a strong state presence, in the case of the Taiwanese film industry is accentuated. Unlike Korea where a clear government protectionist policy has helped to revitalize its national industry, in Taiwan the political and the economic concerns have far outweighed those of the cultural. In the near future, Taiwan's film industry will most likely continue to occupy a dubious space in the cultural, political, and economic environments. It is against this backdrop that one must situate the phenomenon of film piracy in Taiwan. Before addressing piracy directly in chapter 9, however, I will present a profile of Wolf Chen, whose career as an independent film distributor mirrors some of the developments of the policy, the market structure, and the local, regional, and global dynamics of the Taiwanese film market.

Notes

1. In deference to Beijing, Taiwan joined the WTO under the name "Separate Customs Territory of Taiwan, Kinmen and Matsu," or "Chinese Taipei" for short, as it has been known in other global bodies. See Landler, 2001.

2. The *Associated Press*, 1 January 2001. See www.nytimes. com (1 January 2002).

3. Most of Taiwan's diplomatic relations are concentrated in Central and South America and the Caribbean: Belize, Costa Rica, the Commonwealth of Dominica, the Dominican Republic, Grenada, El Salvador, Guatemala, Haiti, Honduras, Nicaragua, Panama, Paraguay, St. Christopher and Nevis, and St. Vincent and the Grenadines. Countries in Africa maintaining full diplomatic relations with Taiwan are Burkina Faso, the Republic of Chad, the Republic of Gambia, Liberia, Malawi, Senegal, Swaziland, and the Democratic Republic of São Tomé and Principe. In the Pacific, countries that have full diplomatic relations with the ROC are Tuvalu, the Solomon Islands, the Marshall Islands, and Palau. In Europe, the ROC maintains full diplomatic relations with the Holy See (see GIO, October 2001). Nauru, the small Pacific island country, is the latest one to have broken diplomatic tie with Taiwan on 23 July 2002 (*ChinaTimes.com*, 23 July 2002).

4. Long Shong was founded by Wang Ying-Shong in 1971. When it first started, Long Shong focused on distribution of foreign films. It switched to domestic film distribution in the late 1970s. In the 1980s, Long Shong started its own film production operations and began working with Hong Kong studios and investing in Hong Kong productions. Consequently, Long Shong started to acquire rights to Hong Kong films and saw the need in exhibition ownership. From then on, Long Shong became a vertically integrated major player in the Taiwan film industry. Scholar, on the other hand, was founded by Tsai Song-lin and began its distribution operations in 1982 and its production business from then onwards. Scholar has also been a major independent distributor for Hollywood films in Taiwan, buying films at such major international film markets as Cannes, American Film Market (AFM), and MIFED. Furthermore, Scholar Films was the first Taiwan film production company to be approved to make film on the Mainland (See Lu, 1998; and GOV Film Industry Report, 2000).

5. In 1997 and 1998, the ROC Government Information Office Guidance Fund had given out NT$10 million in subsidies to thirteen films, which included Hou Hsiao-hsien's *Flowers of Shanghai*, Chen Kuo-fu's *The Personals*, and Tsai Ming-liang's *The Hole*, which have all been released in the United States. See ROC Government Information Office Film Industry Report, 2000.

6. Simon Huang, marketing manager, UIP-Taiwan, however, pointed out that the accurate box office revenues for domestic films should be 3 percent. Personal interview conducted in Taipei on 24 July 1999. Personal interview with Frank Chen was conducted on 20 July 1999, in Taipei.

7. Personal interviews, John Alonte, vice president, Warner Bros. International Theatrical Distribution, Asia, 31 May 2000, Hong Kong; Eric Shih, general manager, Warner Bros. Taiwan, 14 July 1999, Taipei; Rudy Tseng, vice president/general manager, Buena Vista Film Co. Ltd, 3 August 1999, Taipei. They pointed out in their interviews that Taiwan was the number one market for their respective studios in terms of net profits.

8. See Liu and Lien (1999) for more discussion on U.S.-Taiwan trade relations since the Taiwan Relations Act.

9. In 1970, Paramount and Universal joined forces in international distribution and formed Cinema International Corporation (CIC). The original contract was a ten–year contract. In 1972, MGM also joined CIC. In 1981 MGM merged with UA and CIC changed its name to UIP (personal interview, Simon Huang, marketing manager, UIP-Taiwan, 24 July 1999).

10. Simon Huang, UIP-Taiwan marketing manager, also confirmed that newspaper advertising is a must-do in Taiwan. TV ads are only necessary when one has enough advertising budget. Most people still resort to newspapers for their entertainment infor-

mation. Furthermore, because major dailies are nationally circulated, it becomes an effective and efficient advertising vehicle.

11. New Line's films were distributed through Zhong-Yi, also a subsidiary of CMC. Since the inception of Mata, however, Zhong-Yi existed only on paper. The actual distribution has been handed over to Mata. Personal interview, Wolf Chen, 30 April 2002, Taipei.

12. Citing reasons of lacking a shared vision for future collaboration, Wolf Chen told me in a telephone interview on 1 April 2003 that Mata would part ways with CMC, its parent company. Mata will cease operation temporarily in summer 2003 to undergo ownership restructuring and other changes. It plans to resume operation after the summer.

8

Wolf Chen: Profile

Wolf Chen has emerged in the past decade and a half as one of the most influential independent distributors in Taiwan. I followed his career closely and interviewed him multiple times in summer 1999 in Taipei, spring 2000 and 2001 in Santa Monica at the American Film Market, and again in April and May 2002 in Taipei. In addition to these face-to-face interviews, we have also talked numerous times over the telephone. A former journalist now in his late thirties, Wolf Chen's career mirrors the independent distribution changes in Taiwan in the past decade. His recent move from his post as the vice president of distribution at Era Communications to that of the CEO and president of Mata Entertainment, the top independent distributor in Taiwan since its inception in 2000, also sheds light on where independent distribution will likely be headed in the near future. In the following interview, conducted in his office in Taipei, on 30 April 2002, we talked about his career moves, his views on Taiwanese distribution landscape and its future, and issues surrounding piracy, Taiwan's WTO accession, as well as the distribution-exhibition dynamics. The interview was conducted in Chinese. I translated it to English.

> *Wang*: Can you tell me a little bit about your background? I know you were a journalist before entering film distribution; how did you get into distribution?
> *Chen*: Because my reporting beat happened to be the film industry, through my work I got to know Mr. Chiu Fu-Shen, founder of Era. He thought that with my knowledge and interest in the film industry I had the potential to become a good producer. He recommended that I get into producing, since there were not that many good producers in Taiwan, and recruited me to produce films for him. It so happened then that Buena Vista chose Era to be its Taiwan licensee to distribute films for them, and Era needed someone to be in charge of the BVI distribution. So Chiu asked me to be in charge of

Photo 8.1. Wolf Chen, CEO and President, Mata Entertainment

the BVI account, thinking that experiences in distribution would be the best training for a producer-to-be, as one would get the necessary knowledge of the market through distribution. So I started then doing theatrical distribution for BVI films in Taiwan. That's how I started my work in distribution.

Wang: So Chiu really discovered you and helped develop and train you. It sounds like he had a vision and a long-term plan for you.

Chen: Yes. I should say he led me into the field and opened the door for me. The way I got to know him was because I was covering film related news, and he was producing *City of Sadness* at the time. The film entered the 1989 Venice Film Festival and won the Best Picture Golden Lion Award. It was an important event. I covered the film fest for my newspaper. Through the process of attending the festival I developed a close bond with the filmmakers. So I started to have conversations with Chiu. I would share with him my thoughts on film, and he would tell me his marketing ideas and plans. He thought that I had very good background and knowledge on film so he actively recruited me.

Wang: Did Chiu produce *City of Sadness* himself?

Chen: Yes, he funded the film and coproduced it with Yang Deng-Kuei.

Wang: Same with *Raise the Red Lantern* and other films?

Chen: Yes, he funded and produced them.

Wang: But you didn't produce any film at Era, did you?

Chen: No, once I joined Era in distribution I was always in distribution.

Wang: Why did you leave Era, since Era and Spring have been the leading independent film distributors in Taiwan since the 1990s?

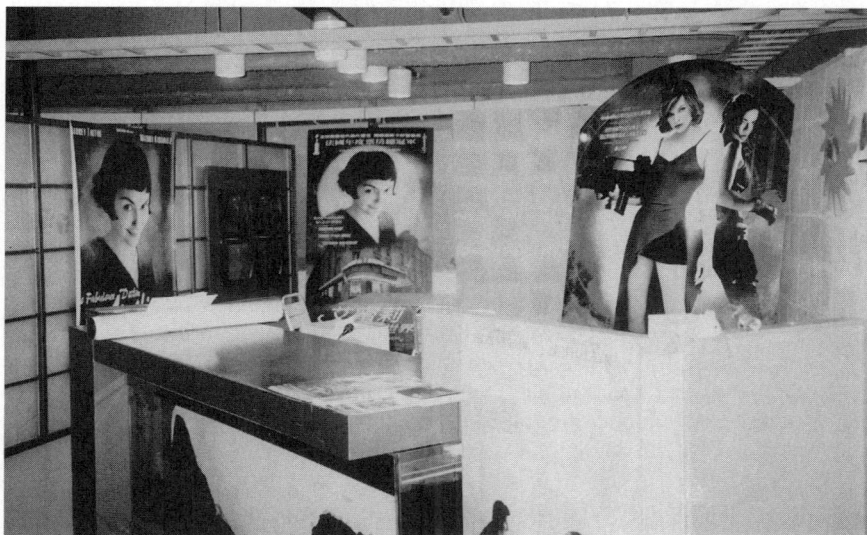

Photo 8.2. Mata Entertainment, Taipei

Chen: Yes, but things have changed. Era in recent years has been focusing much more on cable and satellite television developments and have been investing much more heavily in those areas. Spring, on the other hand, has been shrinking; perhaps it has something to do with the owner's vision and decision. I also thought that my views on distribution started to diverge from those of Era. When opportunity presented itself I decided to join the CMC group. It is a publicly traded company and is one of the world's largest CD-R producers. Since CMC is a hardware developer and manufacturer, the owners decided to model CMC after Sony in integrating the "content" and software part of the business with hardware. I thought that they had the right direction and vision, so I decided to join them and form Mata Entertainment. Mata has in fact become the largest independent film distribution company in Taiwan since it was founded two years ago. It is now leading both in market share and the number of films distributed.

Wang: Really?

Chen: Yes. I think there are only five remaining major distributors in Taiwan: UIP (Universal, Paramount, and MGM), BVI (which also distributes Columbia TriStar), Warner Bros., Fox, and Mata. And up to April this year Mata is the top distributor in terms of market share.

Wang: Higher than BVI?

Chen: Yes. I think it has something to do with the films we distributed such as *The Lord of the Rings*, *Kate & Leopold*, and *Amélie*. They have been doing very well.

Wang: This is pretty incredible. I thought BVI has been the leading distributor in Taiwan (and in the world)?

Chen: Yes, it used to be that BVI, UIP, and Warner would compete for the top market share. But the figure I gave you was only for the first quarter of the year. Come summer, things might be different. Even so, we still think that we will be one of the top distributors in Taiwan this year because we still have *The Lord of the Rings* and other strong films for the end of the year.

Wang: Now, is CMC a Taiwanese company?

Chen: Yes, it is. CMC is very ambitious. In its effort to develop the software and content part of its business, it founded Deltamac, now a leading home video distributor in Taiwan. Deltamac became a publicly traded company last year (IPO). So far, most of the majors' home video products are distributed through Deltamac: Universal, Dreamworks, Fox, Columbia, New Line, and Miramax. Deltamac has over 60 percent of the market share in home video (including DVD and VCD) distribution. It is CMC's goal to form an entertainment group.

Wang: Is CMC itself a publicly traded company?

Chen: Yes it is.

Wang: Does Mata distribute only American indie films?

Chen: Yes. Well, actually we distribute mostly but not exclusively American films. We also distribute French, Korean, Hong Kong, and other films. Because the Taiwanese market is not as receptive to other films as it is to American films, it is harder to promote non-American films such as *Amélie*. It usually requires special strategies in distributing non-American films. We distributed, for example, Wong Kar-Wai's *In the Mood for Love*. The box office gross of that film was good compared to other Chinese-language films. It was not quite good, however, if we compared it to Hollywood films.

Wang: Did you get the right for *In the Mood for Love* directly from Wong? Or did you buy it through Fortissimo, which usually represents Wong's films?

Chen: Yes, we got it directly from Wong Kar-Wai. It is because we have very good relations with Wong. Personally I know him very well. He also likes our distribution network, so he gave us the Taiwan right to this film.

Wang: So did you represent his films when you were at Era?

Chen: No I did not. But I knew him back in the days when I was a reporter. Once he knew I left Era and formed my own distribution company, he decided that Mata would be a good distributor for *In the Mood for Love* given that Mata is a new company with new vision and ideas. It would be good for a special film like *In the Mood for Love*.

Wang: I thought Fortissimo usually represents Wong Kar-Wai's films? So I guess there are different territories?

Chen: Yes, but Wong Kar-Wai normally keeps the Mainland China market and a few other territories that he would manage himself. I think Fortissimo have the rights to European and North American territories, while Wong Kar-Wai keeps the Asian rights.

Wang: Korea films are doing very well these days. How often do you distribute Korean films?

Chen: Korean films usually do well in Japan and Hong Kong. The Taiwanese audience is not as receptive to Korean films. We do have a distribution deal with one of the most important distribution companies, CJ Entertainment, in Korea.

Wang: Why would you distribute Korean films if they have never succeeded in Taiwan?

Chen: I think there is potential given that they are doing so well in other parts of Asia. Most important, CJ gave us an excellent deal in distributing their films. They do not sell us the rights in the form of minimum guarantee deals. They instead invest in the distribution and contribute to the cost of promoting their films. They also see potential in the Taiwanese market and would like to cultivate the market. Taiwan, after all, is a very important market in Asia. CJ has been very successful first in Hong Kong, and later in Japan, they would really like to develop the Taiwan market. Plus Korean television series are doing very well in Mainland China, Hong Kong, Japan, and Taiwan; they think that there is a strong television audience base for Korean programs, which might translate into audience base for Korean films. They also think that the potential is here; the only thing lacking is a good distributor to open the market for them. That is why they have a long-term goal in finding a partner to build the market together.

Wang: I'd like to know a bit more about your operation. What is the structure of Mata?

Chen: There are sixteen people comprising a marketing team, a sales team, and an accounting and finance team, plus administrative people.

Wang: Do you still buy films yourself?

Chen: Yes, in general I do.

Wang: And you go to the three major film markets (Cannes, AFM, and MIFED)?

Chen: Yes. The reason why I am not going to Cannes this year is because we are having a major talk on the Deltamac-Mata merger. One of the reasons for merging with Deltamac is because Deltamac is a publicly traded company and Mata is not. The process of IPO is very complicated. It would simplify the process if we joined Deltamac.

Wang: Is CMC one of the investors in Deltamac? Or does it own Deltamac?

Chen: Deltamac belongs to the CMC Group, and so do we.

Wang: So why is there the need to "merge" if both of you are subsidiaries of the same parent company?

Chen: Because when we go through IPO, the combined capital would be stronger. CMC wants its major subsidiaries to all be publicly traded companies. If we joined Deltamac, it would help Mata to become a publicly traded company, while strengthening the position of Deltamac. In this aspect, CMC has similar ideas as the major Hollywood studios in terms of integration and synergy. It would be much better if home video and theatrical were combined.

Wang: I thought Deltamac distributes most of the majors' video entertainment products?

Chen: Yes, and so do we.

Wang: Would it be fair to say then that the video rental and sell-through markets are pretty much dominated, if not monopolized, by Deltamac?

Chen: Yes, Deltamac is the largest distributor.

Wang: So even BVI does not have its own video distribution?

Chen: No, BVI does have its own home video division, but it is not very successful. Fox, for example, had its own home video entertainment division in Taiwan, but they decided it was not working. It makes more sense to distribute their videos through Deltamac since Deltamac has a much better distribution network in Taiwan, controlling 2,000 stores.

Wang: Is it better than Era?

Chen: Era has been going downhill in film distribution.

Wang: So Paramount and MGM also distribute their video through Deltamac?

Chen: Yes. Era, Jia-Tung, and Xiehe used to be the major video distributors. But they are now almost all on their way out.

Wang: I thought they distributed the majors' videos? Since when did Deltamac start distributing the majors' videos?

Chen: It was five years ago when Deltamac saw that VCD and DVD had great potential in Taiwan. They thought VCD and DVD would one day dominate the home video entertainment market. You know, five years ago not too many people were paying too much attention to DVD. Deltamac grabbed the opportunity and made deals with the majors. Deltamac presented to the majors that they would not be competing with the other video distributors, because all Deltamac wanted was the right to distribute DVD and VCD. Since no other major video distributors would bother to get into VCD and DVD distribution at that time—because the markets were very small—the majors decided to give it a try, given that they had nothing to lose. Today DVDs and VCDs made up 70 percent of the market. The VHS market is now only 30 percent, and it is estimated that it will drop to 20 percent next year, and will disappear all together in the following year.

Wang: But Xiehe and other companies are still in the VHS business?

Chen: Yes they are, but they are having a hard time. Deltamac has established very good VCD and DVD distribution channels. Since the VCD and DVD networks are very well established, and since Xiehe and others are struggling, some of the majors are thinking that they would also give the VHS rights to Deltamac. So Deltamac now represents all formats.

Wang: So the only major that does not distribute through Deltamac is . . .

Chen: Paramount.

Wang: I thought Paramount was part of UIP?

Chen: They left. Well actually, in home video entertainment the group is MCA. But they have gone separate ways in home video distribution.

Wang: But UIP is still in charge of theatrical distribution?

Chen: Yes. But in home video, Universal, Dreamworks, and MGM go through Deltamac in Taiwan. Paramount stays with Xiehe.
Wang: And BVI has its own distribution channel?
Chen: Yes.
Wang: How are they doing?
Chen: They are doing okay. Fox began its own home entertainment division in Taiwan three years ago, but they closed the operation this year. They decided it was not cost-effective to start their own distribution. It would make much better financial sense to go with a local distributor.
Wang: Do they not worry about conflicts of interest and competition if most majors distribute their video through one company?
Chen: Yes, and that's why BVI decided not to do it through Deltamac.
Wang: Deltamac also operates in Hong Kong?
Chen: Yes, it went to Hong Kong two years ago. This year Deltamac set up branch offices in Malaysia and Thailand. Their goal is to have offices throughout Asia.
Wang: They are Taiwan-based?
Chen: Yes. Taiwan is the second-largest home video market in Asia (next to Japan). Since Taiwan is such a strong video market, it is easier for Deltamac to also get rights to the Malaysian and Thai markets. Their goal is also to enter China. Through Deltamac Hong Kong, they hope to get rights to Mainland China.
Wang: How about piracy in Taiwan?
Chen: It's been very serious in Taiwan in the past couple of years. It started two years ago when Taiwan's economy witnessed a downturn and when the stock market fell. They all contributed to the piracy problem. I guess one can say that they were all related as the recession changed consumers' entertainment spending behavior. Pirated VCDs became an alternative.
Wang: It affects theatrical distribution as well.
Chen: Yes. Pirated products come out almost simultaneously with U.S. theatrical releases. The piracy problem in Taiwan is very similar to that in Hong Kong two to three years ago. Hong Kong's piracy problem has lessened quite a bit with its law enforcement efforts. Our government is also paying a lot more attention to this situation. This is especially true given the USTR's pressure on Taiwan to provide adequate IPR protection. I think that starting this year, the government will set up a special police force in charge of piracy related matters. Before, piracy issues were dealt with only when copyrights holders file a complaint, because piracy was not considered a public crime. And we have to present the police with evidence before the police can do anything. This means that we would have to do all of the preliminary work. But I heard now they might treat piracy offences as "public crime." Police can take action as long as it is piracy. It would no longer require the rights holder to file a complaint.[1]
Wang: If piracy is so rampant, why would CMC still be willing to expand your operation?

Chen: Well, these are two separate issues. Actually, the home video market has not grown; it is simply a matter of format shifts.

Wang: Is there still a VCD market or does the DVD format now dominate the home video market?

Chen: There are still VCDs, but the DVD market has been growing with impressive speed. This is especially true when DVD players are getting cheaper. These days one can buy a DVD player for NT$4,000–5,000 (roughly US$120–150). VCD players are even cheaper, at NT$2,000–3,000 (US$60–90). The popularity of VCD in Taiwan has much to do with the prevalence of personal computers. PC in Taiwan is widely spread and most come with a VCD-ROM drive. Unless most PCs now are replaced with those that come with a DVD-ROM drive, VCD will remain a dominant format. Finally, VCD players are getting cheaper and cheaper and are very affordable, although people now have discovered that DVD has much better quality, and that the players are getting cheaper. DVD market is also on its way up.

Wang: I read that as a format, it is much harder to pirate DVD than VCD.

Chen: Yes. So most of the pirated products found in the market are VCD.

Wang: But there are pirated DVD products, yes?

Chen: Yes, but most of them are copies of U.S. DVDs. In other words, pirates replicate existing DVD products from the United States.

Wang: Does it mean that there is no "cinema version" of pirated DVDs?

Chen: Yes, and consequently they are released much more slowly than pirated VCDs.

Wang: How come there is no "cinema version" of DVD?

Chen: Because you can't burn a cinema version. Also it is very costly to burn DVDs. And the "write" function of DVD is not as strong.

Wang: As far as your staff is concerned, do they mostly have backgrounds in business-related fields?

Chen: Well, not really. As a matter of fact, most of my managers came with me from Era. Era now has a new staff.

Wang: Does Era still distribute films?

Chen: Yes, but not as much as it used to, at least in terms of quantity.

Wang: So in general you maintain similar strategies and management arrangements as you did when you were at Era?

Chen: Yes, more or less.

Wang: Did you bring your relations with sellers and other networking connections to Mata?

Chen: Yes.

Wang: Is Mata involved in film production?

Chen: One of the reasons we are merging with Deltamac is because we would like to pave the way for a production arm to exist. Ultimately we would like to be a studio. If we merge with Deltamac we would have more capital and our stock value would increase. We hope in three years we would be able to produce films. We are now making smaller and more scattered and random investments to test the market. So far, CMC has invested in a couple Hong Kong films, including Du Chifeng's (Johnny To) action film *Full Time Killer* (*Chuen Jik Sat Sau*, 2001) last year.

Wang: Has CMC invested in any American films?

Chen: No, not yet, although it is in the plan. Because it would require a lot more capital we would wait until we have gathered enough capital to make formal investments. So far, CMC has only funded Hong Kong films, and Mata has jointly funded *Full Time Killer*.

Wang: Why Hong Kong films? I thought the Hong Kong film industry has also been declining?

Chen: Yes, but Hong Kong films have been doing pretty well in its domestic market. Plus they also perform pretty decently in the Japanese and Korean markets. *Full Time Killer* also starred Takashi Sorimachi, a major Japanese star, with Hong Kong's own Andy Lau. Both actors have good track records in Asia. We funded the film because of its Asian market potential.

Wang: In terms of film production, is your focus on the Asian markets?

Chen: Yes. So far our capital only allows us to focus on regional production, not global. But we do hope to eventually go for the global market.

Wang: I remember during last year's AFM you were talking to comedian Rob Schneider for some sort of cooperation deals? Was it in film production?

Chen: Oh, yes. We were discussing the possibility of funding his films. But we decided that his main appeal was mostly within the United States. He is not widely recognized in either Asia or Europe. We are still interested in possible collaboration with Schneider. If he has a project with global appeal, we would be considering it. But so far we haven't seen it.

Wang: Do you have a list of all the films that Mata has distributed?

Chen: Yes we do. Here it is (see tables 8.1 and 8.2).

Table 8.1. Mata Box Office Grosses 2000 (in NT$)

Title	Opening Date	End Date	Grosses	No. of Prints
Frequency	02.09.2000	10.11.2000	$30,326,145	35
Skulls	09.09.2000	22.09.2000	$1,595,130	28
The Ninth Gate	07.10.2000	27.10.2000	$1,643,945	23
Boiler Room	14.10.2000	27.10.2000	$647,240	18
The Cell	21.10.2000	01.12.2000	$35,415,415	45
In the Mood for Love	28.10.2000	19.01.2001	$12,329,895	16
Watcher	10.11.2000	22.12.2000	$17,286,020	42
*Splendor***	18.11.2000	01.12.2000	$31,850	1
Carnivale	18.11.2000	01.12.2000	$11,230	1
Camouflage	18.11.2000	01.12.2000	$11,840	5
My Best Friend's Wife	18.11.2000	01.12.2000	$13,840	1

Continued on next page

Table 8.1—Continued

Title	Opening Date	End Date	Grosses	No. of Prints
Fanny and			$25,565	1
Elvis	18.11.2000	01.12.2000		
Tumbleweeds	18.11.2000	01.12.2000	$22,795	1
Price of				
*Glory***	18.11.2000	01.12.2000	$11,355	1
Lost Souls	02.12.2000	22.12.2000	$6,662,655	37
The Little				
Nicky	08.12.2000	12.01.2001	$12,735,185	43
TOTAL*			$223,761,780	498

Source: Wolf Chen (2002).
Note: Mata began distribution in Fall 2000, thus this is a partial list as CMC's other subsidiary distributed other films up to September.
* The total here includes grosses from films distributed prior to September.
** From *Splendor* to *Price of Glory* were films shown as part of the week-long Uninhibited Film Festival (Fang Si Ying Zhan).

Table 8.2. Mata Box Office Grosses 2001 (in NT$)

Title	Opening Date	End Date	Grosses	No. of Prints
Blair Witch 2	05.01.2001	23.01.2001	$9,050,525	30
China Strike Force				
(HK)	12.01.2001	08.02.2001	$10,271,455	–
Generation Y Cops				
(HK)	03.02.2001	23.02.2001	$3,548,805	–
Drowning Mona	10.02.2001	23.02.2001	$612,280	20
Nurse Betty	23.02.2001	16.03.2001	$2,487,535	–
Sugar and				
Spice	09.03.2001	23.03.2001	$2,245,035	23
The Wedding				
Planner	23.03.2001	20.04.2001	$7,233,965	38
15 Minutes	13.04.2001	08.06.2001	$37,619,855	–
Dracula 2000	04.05.2001	25.05.2001	$6,950,975	34
The Way of the				
Gun	19.05.2001	01.06.2001	$1,612,685	19
Ai Ni Ai Wo				
(HK)	19.05.2001	01.06.2001	$888,945	3
Town and				
Country	01.06.2001	15.06.2001	$2,297,825	22
Angel Eyes	08.06.2001	06.07.2001	$5,949,895	33
Shaolin Soccer				
(HK)	24.08.2001	28.09.2001	$20,903,485	–
Rush Hour 2	07.09.2001	19.10.2001	$45,314,170	–

Continued on next page

Table 8.2—Continued

Title	Opening Date	End Date	Grosses	No. of Prints
Full Time Killer (HK)	28.09.2001	19.10.2001	$3,054,775	50
Blow	12.10.2001	26.10.2001	$1,423,885	–
Rate Race	02.11.2001	23.11.2001	$6,059,750	38
*The calling/Beautiful Jo/Attack the Gas Station/Tart/No Problem**	03.11.2001	09.11.2001	$83,665	–
Joy and Silent Bob Strike Back	16.11.2001	07.12.2001	$702,650	31
Hardball	30.11.2001	28.12.2001	$6,750,855	40
Heist	07.12.2001	28.12.2001	$3,797,260	38
Spy Game	21.12.2001	01.02.2002	$41,297,090	58
TOTAL			$220,157,365	662

Source: Wolf Chen (2002).
* Films shown at the week-long "Ecstasy Party Film Festival."

Wang: So Mata distributes more than twenty films a year?
Chen: Yes. Ever since Mata was founded in August 2000, we have been distributing more than twenty films a year. Mata was also distributing some of these films on behalf of Zhong Yee.
Wang: I thought Zhong Yee distributed New Line films, that it was New Line's local licensee?
Chen: Yes, and Zhong Yee is also a CMC subsidiary. It does not distribute any longer. It is simply a company that has the contract with New Line. Mata now does all the New Line distribution.
Wang: I know relationships between buyers and sellers are of utmost importance. So what are some of the sellers that you have close working relations with?
Chen: Mostly Miramax. We also have very good relations with Intermedia and Summit. Intermedia is a new German company founded in 2000.
Wang: I guess since Mata is the leading independent distributor in Taiwan, you have advantages in buying films at the film markets? Major sellers would probably prefer to sell films to you?
Chen: Yes.
Wang: Could you take me step by step through the process of distribution of a single film, from acquisition, distribution, to exhibition?
Chen: In terms of box office record, the most successful film we have distributed is *The Lord of the Rings*. But *The Lord of the Rings* is a special case since it was an output deal New Line made with Zhong Yee.

Wang: Could you give me an example of a film that you have acquired yourself?

Chen: Yes, *Amélie* is one example. We bought *Amélie* at Cannes last year. Actually *Amélie* did not compete at Cannes. The director was unhappy with the festival and decided to release the film prior to Cannes, to very good box office grosses, and it received a great buzz. The film, however, did screen at the Cannes market. We went to the screening and loved the film. I bought the film for its potential. We bought the rights to the film from UGC at a reasonable price. Unlike American producers or sellers, UGC did not require that we distribute *Amélie* in any particular way. They didn't care. What was interesting was the involvement of the de facto French Embassy in Taiwan in distributing this film, since one of their goals is to promote French culture. They considered *Amélie* an important French cultural product of recent years. They made the initiative in contacting us regarding collaboration in promoting this film in Taiwan. They also involved Centre National de la Cinématographie (CNC) of France in Taiwan in that effort. CNC donated the prints and advertising (P and A) budget, which is one of their mechanisms in encouraging foreign distributors to distribute French films. They studied our track records in distribution and decided that they would involve in the promotion of *Amélie*. They were much more enthusiastic in distributing this film than UGC, which was not very efficient in the whole process. CNC did most of the monitoring of the process, while pressing UGC for on-time delivery of prints. CNC even provided ten free prints and NT$700,000–800,000 (roughly US$25,000) to cover advertising costs.

Wang: In terms of the actual content or strategies of advertising campaigns, though, how involved was CNC?

Chen: They did not interfere at all. They did try to encourage those French companies or other institutions based in Taiwan that might be interested in being involved in the promotion of the film to contact Mata for possible collaboration or deals. One of the examples is that we made a special screening for a group of French instructors in Taiwan so that they could integrate the film into their teaching, thereby encouraging their students to go see the film. Another example is with French fashion magazines such as *Elle* for cross-promotion deals.

Wang: How did you position the film?

Chen: Usually in Taiwan people perceive French films as art films. But we thought *Amélie* was an accessible film, one that would be accepted by the general public. We thought it was a fantasy film and a drama. So we gave it a Chinese title *Ai-Mi-Li de Yee Xiang Shi Jie* that roughly translated as *Amélie's Fantasy World*. We did a lot of publicity events with the media in early stages to increase the word of mouth effect. We also paid special attention to opinion leaders of women between twenty-five and thirty. We invited celebrities such as Tao Jin-yin, SOS sisters, and Zhang Ching-Fang, who are considered to be the spokespersons for modern young women, to screenings. They all liked the film and recommended it to their viewers and listeners in their respective television and radio shows. Because they really liked the film, they were very enthusiastic about promoting it. Meanwhile, we were very careful about positioning this film in television spots. We did not try to hide the fact that *Amélie* was a French film. We did not package it as a Hollywood film. In fact we emphasized that it was a French film by inviting a French speaker to do the narration for the television spot, thus giving it a French feel. By doing so we also positioned it as a French urban romantic film. I think we created a very successful television campaign.

Wang: How about posters? Did you use the original French posters?

Chen: Yes, in general we used the original French posters with very little modification.

Wang: I'd like to turn to the mainland market now. Does Mata have any plan for development in PRC?

Chen: The Mainland market is quite chaotic. Certainly we are interested in that market, but right now we are still observing. Nothing concrete yet.

Wang: Did you think about entering the market before China gained its WTO accession?

Chen: That was not possible, especially in distribution, as China Film monopolized film distribution in China. It would have been useless for us to enter into the market. In fact, we have purchased the China rights to several films that we acquired, such as *We Were Soldiers*. We have the right of the film to the Chinese market, but will still have to hand over the distribution right to China Film.

Wang: Why would you buy the rights to China then? Establishing relationships? Which company owns the right?

Chen: It was Mel Gibson's Icon. I guess you can say we were building relationships, but most importantly, it was to make the high acquisition price worthwhile. The right to the film was too expensive and we could not negotiate for a lower price. One way to make the price more stomach-able is to include China's rights in the price. This way we were able to close the deal. Thus, if the film does not do well in Taiwan, we could have China as a cross collateral.

Wang: So does Icon do its own international sales?

Chen: Yes. Icon handles most of its overseas sales, while distributing domestically in the United States through Paramount.

Wang: Back to the piracy issues. I overheard you on the phone about Hong Kong producers pirating their own films?

Chen: Yes, it is quite common now. Because when they release a film on video for the local Hong Kong market, chances are it would take a while longer before they could get permission to release the film in China. But the minute the DVD or VCD is released in Hong Kong, pirated copies would appear in China within twenty-four hours. They figure they might as well make the profit themselves. So once the legitimate copies are produced for the Hong Kong market, they are simultaneously released in China. The producers can control the time they want the pirated copies to appear; they can be faster than the pirates.

Wang: How about Hollywood majors? Have they done that?

Chen: No, I have not heard of such instances.

Wang: Has piracy affected your work?

Chen: Oh yes.

Wang: It sounds like you founded Mata at a time when general economy was down and when piracy was rampant?

Chen: Yes. We did begin in a very bad time. Luckily we have been blessed with pretty good products, we have been quite stable. Comparatively speaking, Spring and Era have been doing a lot worse.

Wang: How about anti-piracy actions? Are you actively involved?

Chen: Yes, last month, I think it was on 5 April,[2] we staged a major anti-piracy protest in Taipei. Participants were major exhibitors, distributors, retailers, and artists. Radio stations also stopped playing copyrighted music. They played only instrumentals with public rights for a day. It was a half-day event; we walked from Chiang Kai-Shek Memorial Hall to Sun Yat-Sen Memorial Hall.

Wang: Who organized the event?

Chen: MPA and IFPI (International Federation of the Phonographic Industry) were the major organizers, with participations from other trade organizations such as the exhibitors' association. We took a day off to participate.

Wang: Have you seen any effect of the protest?

Chen: The parade of course was just a signal, so to speak, to let the government know that we were taking actions. Our major request was that piracy be treated as public crime. The legislators are responding favorably and might be able to reach some sort of conclusion this month.

Wang: So your requests mirrored those of the Hong Kong copyright industries a couple years ago when they were lobbying the Legislative Council to elevate piracy to serious crime?

Chen: Yes, and the legislative change in Hong Kong has been quite effective. The piracy rate is only 20 percent of what it used to be before the legislative change.

Wang: Back to distribution. Have you thought about working for a major before?

Chen: There was an opportunity. When Buena Vista International first set up its distribution office in Taiwan, they offered me the job to head their branch office. It was an awkward situation because before Disney started its own distribution operations in Taiwan (i.e., BVI International–Taiwan), its films were distributed through Era and I was in charge. The deal ended during my tenure at Era. Plus I was indebted to Chiu for bringing me in to the business. I told him about the offer and of course he wanted me to stay. What I told BVI was that I would work for them if they could get an okay from Chiu, and they didn't. Chiu told BVI he could accept the fact that Disney/BVI wanted to have its own distribution office in Taiwan, but it would be too much if BVI also wanted to take away Era's staff.

Wang: But if given a choice would you work for a major?

Chen: Certainly it would be much less stressful working for a major. Working as an independent distributor comes with a lot of responsibility and stress. On the other hand, however, working for a major is working for other people. It is not as challenging or interesting as working as an independent. My ultimate goal as an independent distributor is still to revive and stimulate the local film industry.

Wang: Really?

Chen: Oh yes. That is my major goal. As it stands, the local film industry is close to non-existent.

Wang: But having a strong local film industry is not necessarily good for foreign film distributors, no?

Chen: I don't think this is necessarily so. You know, we can always change our focus if there is a strong local film market. We don't always have to distribute only foreign films. The reason why we are distributing western films now is because Asian films are not the dominant format. But once local films regain their popularity we would adjust our focus.

Wang: So you really hope to see a strong local film industry.

Chen: Oh yes. To be honest, we have a pretty well connected distribution network in Taiwan in terms of the links among production, distribution, and exhibition. One of the problems with local films is that there is no demand. Local audience has this preconception that locally made films are too slow with no entertainment value and that they are only made for an art film audience. This preconception is too strong to break. But there are a few young directors in Taiwan such as Zhang Zuo-Ji, Chen Guo-Fu and Yii Zhi-Yan who have new works that are good stories. They are entertaining yet very original. These films are very different from those of Hou Hsiao-Hsien's and Edward Yang's. They don't carry a specific mission or aim to be intellectual or a social criticism. Instead, these filmmakers focus on the story and the story telling techniques. Their films are accessible to the audience. The problem is that today's audience still thinks of these films as similar to the old ones. To change this preconception and to revive the local film industry will take a lot of effort. We will need a steady supply of these films to create a more consistent output. One of the most interesting examples and a possible turning point is *Shuang Tung (Double Vision)* by Chen Guo-Fu.

Wang: It is a Columbia-TriStar co-production, yes?

Chen: Yes. But it is a purely Taiwanese film with a Taiwanese director, writer and cast. And the story is also very Taiwanese. The only Hollywood element in this co-production is the funding source. If this film could have a good box office performance, maybe it would encourage the making of other similar local projects.

Wang: How did Barbara Robinson (of Columbia Asia) find Chen?

Chen: Because they knew each other very well.

Wang: I meant, why would she want to invest in Taiwanese films since there is not that much of a local film industry. I thought they would only look for very accomplished directors with commercially viable projects.

Chen: Well, *Shuang Tung* is a very commercial film.

Wang: With the lifting of the print quota system, wouldn't it be harder for local films to be screened at the cinemas?

Chen: But to be honest with you, the quota system never really made that much sense anyway. As far as the limit for copies is concerned, not all films need that many copies of prints. We had forty copies of *Amélie* for the Taipei area theaters, for example. The limit for prints used to be fifty-eight, but very few films would need all fifty-eight anyway. You also have to understand that an increase of prints means increase of cost for distributors, since prints are expensive. Only really big films require more prints. I think those blockbusters would sometimes take ninety-nine prints. I think *Spider Man* will need 100. You know, in the old days, Jackie Chan's films always required a 100-print release. It really depends on the market.

Wang: How are Mata's relations with the theaters?

Chen: Not bad.

Wang: Wouldn't exhibitors prefer to screen majors' films?

Chen: Sure. But we also have a pretty decent track record. Our performance is as good as the majors, especially this year. Exhibitors actually offer us equal treatment as they would with major distributors. After all, the five most successful distributors I mentioned dominate this market: Warner, BVI (also distributing Columbia), UIP, Fox, and Mata. We are in a good negotiation place with the exhibitors.

Wang: I take that it is better than when you were at Era?

Chen: Yes. We are stronger than Era. I would say that if any theater that did not distribute a Mata film during the first half of this year, they would lose money.

Wang: In Taiwan, which side has the upper hand? Distributors or exhibitors?

Chen: It has been changing slowly. But now it is still a distributors' market.

Wang: What is a typical exhibitor-distributor deal like? In the United States it is in general a 70–30 split.

Chen: In Taiwan, bigger films would have 70–30, and others possibly 60–40 for the first week.

Wang: So the first weekend box office is also the most important for the Taiwan market?

Chen: I think it is the first two weeks.

Wang: How about Warner Village?

Chen: Warner Village is the major force that is changing the market slowly. It has the largest market share, although it also incurs very high cost. But they are slowly changing the ecology of exhibition and distribution in Taiwan.

Wang: How is Mata's relation with Warner Village?

Chen: In general it is pretty good. We do have disagreements over issues of principles, but in general the relationship is good.

Wang: Warner Village has already started another multiplex in Tai-chung?

Chen: Yes in both Tai-chung and Kao-Hsiung. It will open another one in Tai-nan in July, and yet another one in Hsin-Chu end of the year. And one more in Tien-Mu, Taipei. They will likely take 50 percent of the whole exhibition market of Taiwan.

Wang: These are all multiplexes?

Chen: Yes. In fact, in Taichung 85 percent of the exhibition market is occupied by foreign-invested theaters: Warner Village and VCI are two major operations.

Wang: Does Warner Village give Warner Bros. preferential treatments when it comes to playdates and other privileges?

Chen: Yes, there is such a tendency. This is especially so since Warner Bros. and Village Roadshow have been co-producing films. A recent example is Eddie Murphy's *Show Time*, which is a Warner Bros. and Village Roadshow co-production. At the same time *Show Time* was released, Mata was releasing *John Q*, a Denzel Washington film. Warner Village gave *Show Time* more screens and better show times. *Show Time* for example was screened at three screens at Warner Village, while *John Q* only had two. *John Q* had had much better box office performance in the United States and elsewhere. But here Warner Village gave preferential treatment to a Warner-Village Roadshow film. In the end, however, *John Q* still fared better than *Show Time*.

Wang: How is Mata's relationship with the majors' local distribution offices?

Chen: Perhaps because I have very good personal relationship with their general managers, in general we get along very well. We are not really competitive. We often exchange information. Our respective marketing and sales teams also exchange information. I think this actually helps the overall market.

Wang: Do you have similar relationship with other independent distributors?

Chen: Much less so.

Wang: What are some of your major criteria when you buy a film?

Chen: If it would make money. Ha ha.

Wang: Do you consider its genre, cast, et cetera?

Chen: More or less. But to tell you the truth, the market changes so fast that these things might not work. Our risks have become even higher than before. I guess I can say that in the past when one bought a film one could almost have the guarantee that some of the factors would remain unchanged for a couple of years since most of the deals are made on a pre-sale basis and the films would not be released for at least a year or two. In the past, a star would at least have a two-year box office guarantee. Not so anymore. For example, last year if one bought an Arnold Schwarzenegger vehicle, one would have to pay a very high price since he still held box office power (his salary was about $20 million). But one would find out this year that Arnold no longer has the box office power and that they had over-paid for the film. For example, this year Arnold's *Collateral Damage* was released the same time as *Amélie*, but it lost to *Amélie*, a French film without a known cast. These days, audiences are getting smarter. They no longer accept old and traditional films that do not have any originality. There has been tremendous change in the audience's consumption habits. Bruce Willis is in the same boat. He was still a box office guarantee last year and the year before, but no longer. Both his *Bandit* and *Hart's War* failed miserably. Both films did not even get half of *Amélie*'s grosses. Just last year one had to pay around US$1million for both Willis' and Schwarzenegger's films since most of their films were budgeted at over US$50–60 million each.

Wang: Yes, I know. I think *Terminator 3* is the most expensive film ever made, yes?

Chen: Yes. That's why we didn't want to buy *T3*. Actually they were talking to us at the end of last year hoping we would buy *T3* for $3 million because the budget of *T3* was over $200 million. The *Terminator* series was basically a Caralco project. They sold the domestic rights to Warner Bros. They wanted to handle international sales themselves and were asking for a very high price. I think they sold the major international territories to Columbia TriStar. We declined because of the price. The screenplay itself was also quite poor.

Wang: Are most of the deals you make still on minimum guarantee terms?

Chen: Yes.

Wang: How does it work? Let's say you pay $3 million as minimum guarantee.

Chen: So we make further payment if the film grosses over $3 million. We would deduct the $3 million plus cost from the total grosses and then make further division with the seller.

Wang: How much? What is the percentage?

Chen: It depends on the film. Each deal is different. There are 30–70 deals or 50–50 deals.

Wang: So who gets 30 and who gets 70?

Chen: Both are possible.

Wang: So the sellers are better off?

Chen: Yes. But one should also keep in mind that theatrical is not the sole source of income. There is, for example, video.

Wang: I didn't know you do video releasing, too.

Chen: Yes. With most of the films we buy, we usually buy all rights.

Wang: Do you distribute videos yourself or do you sell the rights to others?

Chen: We sell the rights to Deltamac.

Wang: So in the future you will not need to sell the video rights anymore, since Mata and Deltamac will be one company?

Chen: That's correct.

Wang: Will the new company be named Mata or Deltamac?

Chen: We are still discussing details.

Wang: But you will still be in charge of theatrical distribution, yes?

Chen: That's right. Because Mata has been setting pretty decent track record, and the name is pretty much out there, they are evaluating the value of the name and if we should keep it.

Wang: What has been the biggest challenge you face since you left Era and started Mata in the past two years?

Chen: I think the biggest challenge I face has been to reach an understanding with my parent company and investor, CMC.[3] Because they don't know the theatrical distribution business or the film industry, we often have very different ideas of how to run the business. We also speak very different languages. Because CMC is a company focusing on high-tech industry, sometimes the gap between different fields can be very hard to bridge. I think internal communication has been especially crucial. This has therefore been the biggest challenge I have to face. After all, I know the market and the distribution scene very well and can handle most of the challenges that come from the market. That's not a problem. How you convince your boss to agree with your strategies and plans becomes an issue. Other major challenges include the economic slowdown and piracy. But we really can't do much to change these larger contextual environments. All we can do is to fix the surface problems. The roots are much harder to tackle. So we've been trying to shorten the release windows and have release dates as close to those of the United States as possible. This way we can minimize piracy losses.

Wang: When you release films in Taiwan, what kind of strategy do you use? Do you use saturating wide releasing, or do you use platform?

Chen: Platform would only make sense if you have a huge market like that of the United States. Taiwan is a tiny market; it really would not work to do a platform release. There was one exception, which was the Japanese film *The Ring* that was released in Taiwan three years ago. It was mainly because the distributor had no confidence in the film so they started with six screens. The box office performance was exceptionally good, so they added more prints and screens. The box office grosses of the second and third weeks far surpassed those of the first week.

Wang: Who distributed *The Ring*?

Chen: Scholar, which is also in financial problems. They have not released a single film since last year.

Wang: But they still produce films, yes? I know they invested in quite a few Hong Kong films.

Chen: Yes, they did. But they have stopped everything. They still own a few theaters, though.

Wang: How about Long Shong?

Chen: Same thing. The only things still operating are their theaters.

Wang: What happened? How come all of a sudden all these major companies are collapsing?

Chen: I think they are ill adjusted to the new market environment. I think they made wrong judgments of the market. I also think they lack long-term vision.

Wang: Who are the major Chinese-language film distributors?

Chen: Very, very few. That's why many Hong Kong producers ask us to distribute their films, which we are reluctant to. This is especially so this year because we have too many films on our hands. We don't have the energy or personnel to distribute any more films.

Wang: How many films are you talking about?
Chen: Thirty.
Wang: That is a lot.
Chen: Yes. And it is because we bought too many a couple years ago. With its factory and production background, CMC did not have the right understanding of the film market. They thought the more you buy, the lower the distribution cost would be. But this is not true. Not every film has the same price or the same cost in distribution.
Wang: But those decisions really do not have much to do with you, no?
Chen: Well, I have to distribute these films now. That's also why I am not at Cannes this year. We have too many films in stock so we won't be doing major buying at Cannes this year. We are becoming a lot more cautious in selecting and buying films. My staff will only be observing major market trends at Cannes.
Wang: But so far Mata is doing quite well.
Chen: Yes, but it doesn't mean one can relax. The market changes too fast.

Notes

1. Note that the interview was conducted on 30 April 2002, before the BSA anti-piracy campaign and the subsequent student anti-anti-piracy movement took place (see chapter 9). Wolf Chen, like Hank Kwuo and other copyright industry representatives, was quite optimistic about the possible legislative change at this point.

2. The parade took place on 4 April 2002.

3. This challenge of reaching an understanding of a shared vision for distribution, and of bridging the gap of internal communication between Mata and CMC, proves to be insurmountable. In a follow-up phone interview conducted on 1 April 2003, Wolf Chen told me that Mata would terminate its relationship with CMC and would temporarily cease operation in summer 2003 for ownership restructuring. Mata plans to resume operation in the fall. It remains to be seen how this shift will change the landscape of independent distribution in Taiwan. See also chapter 7 (endnote 12).

9

A "Culture of Illegality"?
Piracy in Taiwan

> Besides piratical activity that takes place in Taiwan itself, Taiwanese busi-
> nesses are deeply involved in pirate industries in China, through funding, in-
> vestment, technology transfer, and other facilitation. *Taiwan is a key node in a*
> *web of piracy of entertainment software that engulfs Taiwan, Hong Kong, and*
> *the PRC.*
>   —IIPA Country Report, Taiwan (1996:5, emphasis added)
>
> Taiwan Authorities Permit Massive Transshipment of Pirated Goods Through
> Taiwan: *Taiwan is now arguably the pirate transshipment capital of the world.*
>   —IIPA Country Report, Taiwan (2000:376, emphasis added)

An otherwise invisible country with no political power in, and receiving little
diplomatic recognition from, the global community, Taiwan is nevertheless
viewed as a powerful threat to the global business community. Here, in addition
to recommending the USTR to put Taiwan on the Priority Watch Country list
two years in a row, the 2002 International Intellectual Property Alliance Special
301 Report also goes so far as to brand Taiwan a "culture of illegality."[1] Meanwhile, earlier IIPA reports have likewise prominently positioned Taiwan on the
global piracy map (see later discussion). As the above two quotes demonstrate,
Taiwan's crime has to do with the fact that it is a major node on the Greater
China piracy networks and that it finances and facilitates the networks' regional
as well as global operations. Meanwhile, it is also named the piracy export and
transshipment capital of the world, causing damage to transnational copyright
industries far beyond Taiwan's borders.

Politically isolated and frustrated, Taiwan has nonetheless made great
economic and technological achievements in the recent past. The central role
Taiwan plays on the global piracy networks is closely linked to these conflicting

contexts. Both political and economic realities have meant that the United States is the most influential player in shaping the IP policy in Taiwan, while the geographic location and connections of Taiwan and the business gains pirates receive from piracy trade have stimulated piracy production and export on the island (see also Sun, 1998).

Even though Taiwan as a market is quite insignificant, its role as a technologically advanced economy and as a rich legitimate content source has made it a crucial link on global piracy networks. Its threat to copyright industries lies thus not in the size of the market, but rather in the various technological, geographical, and commercial advantages that it possesses. Just as Hong Kong, the Mainland, and Taiwan each serves an important function in the Greater China economic circle in legitimate business, the so-called resource complementarity (see Lin and Lin, 2001:698, and chapter 3), they also have different yet complementary roles in the underground shadow economy.

The fact that Taiwan is an antithesis to the Mainland in size, power, system, and geopolitical influence, yet occupying a similar position in the global piracy network wielding tremendous influence in disrupting global business order, provides an interesting and important case study of the intricate and conflicting roles of the state in the processes of globalization. The vastly different yet intersecting sets of actors, networks, and dynamic power relations involved in the piracy operations in Taiwan and beyond also beg detailed study in their own right. The transitional period between 2001 and 2002 when Taiwan gained its WTO accession serves as a particularly interesting case study as power relations necessarily fluctuate, with micro- and macro-actors realigning, reattaching, and reconfiguring with different elements and networks, thus producing a highly dynamic scenario for the study of power, technology, the state, and globalization.[2]

Suffice it here to very briefly introduce the multiple events that have come to define, as they unfold, this volatile and highly interesting time. More detailed examination will follow in later sections of this chapter.

As noted, the year 2002 is significant for Taiwan's IPR regulations and law enforcement issues given that the "Separate Customs Territory of Taiwan, Kinmen and Matsu," or "Chinese Taipei" for short, formally became a WTO member on 1 January.[3] A new set of rules is employed governing many aspects of government policies and operations. In the first half of 2002 several highly publicized IPR and piracy events, not unrelated to Taiwan's accession to WTO, tested these new trade, political, and legal environments.

In addition to making multiple concessions in IPR legislation and enforcement to gain entry to WTO in 2001, including the passing of the Optical Disc Law and an amendment to the Copyright Law, Taiwan also made 2002 an Anti-Piracy Action Year (see *AFP,* 2002). After the copyright industries organized a half-day protest on 4 April demanding that the government set up a police task force and that CR infringement be treated as a public crime, the legislators were decidedly sympathetic to their requests (personal interviews, Hank Kwuo, executive director, MPA–Taiwan, 6 May 2002, Taipei; Wolf Chen, CEO and president, Mata, 30 April 2002, Taipei; see also Hung, 2002). Just when copyright owners were eagerly awaiting good news of the possible legislation turn-around, the USTR announced on 30 April that it would place Taiwan once again on the Special 301 Priority Watch List. Along came the widely reported Business Software Alliance's (BSA) 1 May Anti-Piracy Campaign, which created much resistance and defiance from the public and negative reports from the media. With their protests and press conferences, students from six college campuses spontaneously formed an "Anti-Anti-Piracy Alliance" in response to BSA's Anti-Piracy Campaign. The movement quickly gathered speed and won both public and media support and attention, especially those from educators and parents, with rhetoric reminiscent of that from a colonial era, accusing the government of collaborating with foreign powers in oppressing its own people. The government on the one hand finds itself once again unfairly judged by the USTR decision that disregarded its prior anti-piracy efforts and concessions, while on the other hand having to clarify its position vis-à-vis the BSA Anti-Piracy Campaign to an increasingly dissatisfied public.

At issue is not simply which one(s) of these multiple players would gain the upper hand, or if the CR law and enforcement are adequate, or if Taiwan should resort to the TRIPS/WTO dispute settlement mechanism for the USTR decision that was perceived to be unfair. Rather, we witness complex, shifting, and indeed reversible processes of translation among multiple local, regional, and global actors, each shaping and being shaped by intersecting networks; each tries to influence the actions of the others.[4] The constant negotiations and interplay among the actors and networks and the resulting transformation and transfiguration of the situations have created a unique set of power relationships that is never static. What we also witness is a state caught between a rock and a hard place, a state trying to define itself vis-à-vis multiple forces and influences of globalization. The following sections examine these issues, beginning with a brief chronology to summarize piracy development and operations in Taiwan in the past two decades, from which major practical and theoretical issues can be identified.

Brief Chronology

As early as 1985, when IIPA issued its first report on worldwide piracy, Taiwan was the subject. By the end of the 1980s Taiwan's "MTV piracy" had become rampant and reached its highest level in 1988–1989. MTV was something unique to Taiwan where small saloons, "MTVs," offered hip and private audio-visual spaces where young people in crowded urban settings could watch videos, hang out, and, most important, date. Most of the videos shown at MTVs were film as well as music video titles, many of which were unauthorized VHS products.

Table 9.1 summarizes the estimated trade losses due to piracy in Taiwan from 1995 to 2001. As the table demonstrates, the piracy problem improved in the mid-1990s but picked up again toward the end of the decade. As seen in chapter 7, when Taiwan's trade surplus with the United States surged in the early 1980s, the United States perceived the surplus as partially attributable to Taiwan's failure to protect intellectual property rights (IPR), and began to pressure Taiwan to conform to, and implement, international IPR protection measures. As a result, the Taiwan government amended relevant regulations and established the National Anti-Counterfeiting Committee, resulting in the reduction of piracy levels (see Liu and Lien, 1999). Consequently Taiwan was moved from the Priority Watch List in 1992 and 1993 to the Watch List in 1994 and 1995, and was removed from the Special 301 lists altogether in 1996, 1997, until 1998 and 1999 when it was put back on the Watch List. In 2000 and 2001 when piracy activities surged to a high level, Taiwan was again put on the Priority Watch List (see table 9.2).[5]

It is clear that the United States, as the most important trading partner of, and political influence on, Taiwan, has also been the most powerful player shaping Taiwan's copyright policies. When MTV piracy reached its peak in Taiwan by the end of the 1980s, the United States began in earnest negotiating for a new bilateral treaty governing copyright protection (see IIPA Country Report, Taiwan, 1996). Because of various technological developments, the early 1990s saw even larger-scaled piracy activities in Taiwan in pirate CD replication, counterfeit software production, and pirated movies shown on cable channels. The piracy level was so high that in 1992 Taiwan was named a Special 301 Priority Foreign Country and was put under the threat of U.S. trade retaliation.[6] Consequently, Taiwan adopted a new copyright law in May 1992 and signed a broad Memorandum of Understanding (MOU) including wide-ranging IP commitments. Thus, by 1993, Taiwan was dropped from the Priority Foreign Country List to the Priority Watch List. In 1993, Taiwan made further progress by passing its cable law, implementing an export control system, and imposing serious fines and jail terms to convicted pirates. In 1996, right before the USTR made its Special 301 decisions, Taiwan adopted an eighteen-point Action Plan that targeted specifically issues surrounding the Greater China piracy, with four of the eighteen points about the Export Monitoring System instituted in 1993 (see later discussion). As a result, Taiwan was removed from the Watch List and onto Special Mention, and later that year Taiwan was completely removed from the Special 301 lists.

Because of its failure to bring its copyright law into full compliance with TRIPS requirements and adhere to the TRIPS enforcement, however, Taiwan was put back on the Special 301 Watch List by 1998. It was also because of the "leading role of Taiwanese businesses in digital piracy networks spanning 'Greater China' clouds the future prospects in the region for all the copyright industries" that Taiwan was included on the watch list (IIPA Country Report, Taiwan, 1998). Also by 1998, the largest problem in Taiwan was the illegal parallel import of laser discs, most of which were smuggled into Taiwan. Meanwhile, the overproduction of optical media products continued to worsen in 1999, and Taiwan remained on the Special 301 Watch List. In addition, organized crime continued to engage in what was considered to be a low-risk and high-yield piracy enterprise (see also Groves, 2002a).

Table 9.1. IIPA Estimated Trade Losses Due to Copyright Piracy in Taiwan (in US$ Millions) and Levels of Piracy: 1995–2001

Industry	1995 Loss/Level	1996 Loss/Level	1997 Loss/Level	1998 Loss/Level	1999 Loss/Level	2000 Loss/Level	2001 Loss/Level
Motion Pictures	**29.0/15%**	**17.0/10%**	**15.0/10%**	**15.0/10%**	**20.0/20%**	**30.0/30%**	**35.0/30%**
Sound Recordings	5.0/13%	8.0/8%	10.0/12%	55.0/20%	60.0/35%	60.5/40%	51.7/48%
Business Software Applications	115.2/70%	111.7/72%	104.6/63%	112.1/59%	97.6/54%	127.3/53%	197.0/52%
Entertainment Software	105.4/69%	109/69%	102.6/65%	103.2/65%	115.7/68%	319.3/90%	119.4/70%
Books	6.0/NA	5.0/NA	5.0/NA	19.0/NA	21.0/NA	20.0/NA	20.0/NA
TOTAL	260.6	250.7	237.2	304.3	314.3	557.1	333.1

Source: Compiled from IIPA Country Reports—Taiwan (1996–2002).

Table 9.2. USTR Special 301 Decisions: Taiwan 1989–2001

Year	301 Decision
1989	Priority Watch List
1990	Watch List
1991	Watch List
1992	Priority Foreign Country
1993	Priority Watch List
1994	Watch List
1995	Watch List
1996	–
1997	–
1998	Watch List
1999	Watch List
2000	Priority Watch List
2001	Priority Watch List

Sources: Compiled from IIPA Special 301 Decision Reports and IIPA Country Reports (Taiwan).

Finally in 2000 and 2001, Taiwan was elevated to the Special 301 Priority Watch List because of its failure to either implement or enforce comprehensive regulations in controlling and curtailing piracy, even though Taiwan had made multiple anti-piracy efforts in 2000 and 2001 to ameliorate its trade relations with the United States and, more important, to gain accession to WTO. In enforcement, the Intellectual Property Office cooperated with police authorities in 2000 to implement a "K-Plan" to crack down on counterfeit activities. Additionally, Taiwan government required that optical media products such as CD, VCD, DCD, CD-ROM bear source identification (SID) codes for tracking purposes (U.S. Department of State, 2002). On the legislative front, anti-piracy efforts included the Legislative Yuan's passing of the Optical Media Management Statute on 31 October 2001. This so-called OD Law (Optical Disc Law) was promulgated on 14 November 2001. Furthermore, to join the WTO and to ensure that its CR law complies with TRIPS requirements, Taiwan amended its copyright law in November 2001.

From the process described above, one can detect a clear pattern of bilateral IP negotiations between the United States and Taiwan: A power dance of pressure from the United States and the subsequent reluctant compliance from Taiwan. In general the United States would present its copyright industries' complaints to Taiwan. After negative reports and accusations of U.S. imperialism from Taiwanese news media and the Legislative Yuan, exhaustive negotiations would ensue, and Taiwan would finally admit that some aspects of its IP regime were inadequate and needed improvement (see Wang, 1996).

Copyright Law Enforcement:
Unilateral, Bilateral, and Multilateral

Given that there are no international IPR laws per se, only agreements and treaties that require active local government implementation, the role of the state is especially pronounced in the copyright legislative process.

Notwithstanding many political obstacles preventing Taiwan from joining the WTO, including strong opposition from the PRC, Taiwan still made every effort possible in meeting all the requirements, which included revising and updating existing intellectual property laws and enacting new statutes. As early as 1996, Taiwan had in place an intellectual property production regime that complied almost completely with TRIPS (see Young and Wang, 1996).[7] Taiwan further improved its IPR governance in more recent years and gained its WTO accession in November 2001. To understand Taiwan's IPR development, one has to view it in a before and after WTO framework. Such distinction is especially necessary given that only twenty-seven countries in the world recognize Taiwan. Taiwan's accession into WTO means a formal insertion of Taiwan into global trade and legal regimes with great implications for its internal and external IPR management.

The copyright protection and piracy issues in Taiwan were closely related to Taiwan's questionable standing in the global community. Its national identity crisis had no doubt carried great implications for its IPR development. The paradox concerned the fact that because Taiwan was not a member of any international convention granting MFN treatment to all member nations, and had not been a "nation" per se recognized by most other nations, it was not a party to the Paris, Berne, Madrid, Rome, or Washington Conventions. Any granting of MFN with Taiwan would be the product of a bilateral treaty or agreement. As a consequence, before WTO/TRIPS, which requires its members to provide equal IPR protection to all other members, Taiwan's system of IPR protection was based entirely on reciprocity (see Young and Wang, 1996; and Sun, 1998).

The specific U.S.-Taiwan bilateral trade issues (which include IPR) were covered by the bilateral Treaty of Friendship, Commerce, and Navigation of 1946 (the FCN Treaty, see Lo, 1999; and Young and Wang, 1996), through which the United States and the Republic of China had agreed to grant each other MFN treatment for copyrights, patents, and trademarks. While the FCN Treaty was of great importance to the ROC government during the early days of its Taiwan operation when there were few specialized treaties, its usefulness has expired and is therefore outmoded, especially given that most treaties and agreements today are issue specific (see Lo, 1999). To those nations that Taiwan does not have a bilateral treaty with, such as Japan before 1996, their IP works were pirated with impunity in Taiwan, and vice versa (Young and Wang, 1996). As table 9.3 demonstrates, of the 180 plus countries in the world, only eleven had (mostly limited) reciprocal IPR protection agreements with Taiwan (see ROC Ministry of Economic Affairs, Intellectual Property Office report, 2002).[8]

Table 9.3. Countries with Reciprocal IPR Protection Agreements with Taiwan

Country	Effective Date	Specific IP Right Involved
United States	16 July 1993	Copyright
Australia	4 November 1994	Patent, Trademark
Germany	1 June 1995	Patent
Switzerland	1 January 1996	Patent
Japan	1 February 1996	Patent
United States	10 April 1996	Trademark, Patent
France	1 September 1996	Patent, Trademark
Liechtenstein	1 April 1998	Patent
EU	23 July 1998	Trademark
United Kingdom	24 May 2000	Patent
Austria	15 June 2000	Patent, Trademark
New Zealand	19 December 2000	Patent, Trademark
New Zealand	22 December 2000	Copyright
Germany	16 January 2001	Extension on Pharmaceutical Patents
The Netherlands	17 December 2001	Patent

Source: ROC Ministry of Economic Affairs, Intellectual Property Office (2002).

Initially Taiwan did not consider such a lack of participation in international IP regime an inconvenience. In fact, it was used as leverage in deflecting the U.S. demands for Taiwan to comply with international standards. It was not until Taiwanese exports received inadequate and insufficient international IP protection that Taiwan realized that the lack of participation was a major setback to its burgeoning export business. This is especially significant given that Taiwan's information technology, semiconductors, and electronic components, which all need IPR protection, accounted for 35 to 40 percent of its total exports (U.S. Department of State, 2002; Sun, 1998). Consequently, ten years and numerous negotiations later, Taiwan did implement many changes to its IP regime in its effort to reduce piracy. These new programs include the Taiwan Toy Manufacturers' Association Export Monitoring Program, Taiwan's Board of Foreign Trade (BOFT) Trademark Inspection Program, the IP Police in Every Precinct Promise, the Fair Trade Law, the BOFT Software Inspection System, significant amendments to the Trademark, Patent and Copyright Laws, the 1989 U.S.-Taiwan Bilateral Copyright Agreement, and the 1992 Memorandum of Understanding. It was clear then that the U.S. approach in getting paper gains (i.e., getting more rules on the book) was not particularly effective. As Wang (1996) points out, when confronted with these politically difficult choices of taking actions against domestic piracy industries or agreeing to laws that would still be up to further interpretation and implementation, the Taiwanese government would naturally choose the latter. It was also clear that it was Taiwan's own desire in getting protection of its own export products and gaining accession to the WTO that prompted its most sincere efforts in copyright regulation and enforcement. Thus, while the United States may be able to push Taiwan for legislative reform, it is necessarily local self-interests that will prevail (see Sun, 1998).

Taiwan's accession to WTO has certainly changed its isolation status in the international political community. It provides Taiwan with much needed alternatives and flexibility to reenter the global trade arena, as membership to the WTO is not contingent upon UN membership, nor is it based on an independent sovereignty, but rather as a separate customs territory (Sun, 1998). Taiwan's WTO accession also means that it has to comply with TRIPS requirements and will in turn enjoy the benefits of TRIPS.[9]

In Taiwan, the highest IPR policy-making body is the Executive Yuan, under which the Ministry of Economic Affairs (MOEA) is the main organization carrying out IPR policies. On 26 January 1999, the Intellectual Property Office (IPO) was formed under the auspices of MOEA to handle all IPR affairs (see IPO, 2000). Additionally, the National Bureau of Standards grants patents, trademarks, and integrated circuit layout designs. Other offices active in IPR protection issues include the Board of Foreign Trade (BOFT), the Copyright Committee under the Ministry of the Interior (MOI), the Ministry of Justice (MOJ), and the Directorate General of Customs under the Ministry of Finance (MOF) (see National Bureau of Standards, 2002). To the Taiwanese government, such an IPR management structure of independent yet interlinked agencies provides comprehensive coverage while ensuring that each specialized agency is in charge of an area of its expertise. To the U.S. copyright owners and government, however, such structure only invites inefficient and ineffective management in which no one takes full responsibility (personal interview, Justin Lin, former section chief, IPO, 4 June 2002, Boston). They would instead prefer that Taiwan set up a centralized executive authority to integrate resources and intelligence from other agencies, and to streamline its legal procedures (see also Sun, 1998). Targeting this issue, the 2002 IIPA Special 301 Report calls for the establishment of a "permanent enforcement body" headed by a special prosecutor for sustained copyright enforcement (p. 262).

A related issue involves the question of whether copyright infringements should be treated as a public crime, the decision of which would have important repercussions on the Taiwanese copyright regime. At present copyright infringements as such are not considered a public crime. According to Taiwan's Copyright Law, Chapter VII, Article 100, prosecution for copyright offenses shall be instituted or actionable only upon complaint (Copyright Law of the Republic of China, 1999). Thus the copyright owners would have to file a complaint before the police can take legal action and the prosecutor can request a search warrant from the court (personal interview, Wen-Hsiang Lu, deputy director general, IPO, MOEA, 7 May 2002, Taipei). The copyright owners see this as a problem contributing to the difficulties of eradicating piracy in Taiwan. Hank Kwuo, executive director of the Foundation for the Protection of Film and Video Works, Motion Picture Association, for instance, uses his organization as an example to illustrate the problem with current copyright legislation under which offenses are not considered a public crime. He points out that there are more than 1,000 night markets in Taiwan in which the sales of pirated videos are common. When a police officer finds pirated optical discs sold at these night markets, he or she would normally not be able to do anything unless a copyright owner has filed a complaint. With a staff of eleven covering the entire island, for instance, it is impossible for MPA–Taiwan to monitor all piracy sites (personal interview, 6 May 2002, Taipei). If copyright infringements were to be treated as a public crime, the police would then have the authority to take legal actions against pirates while the prosecutor, instead of the court, would have the authority to issue search warrants, thus greatly enhancing the efficiency and effectiveness of copyright enforcement and piracy crackdowns.

One of the issues here is certainly government resources. Treating copyright offenses as a public crime would require the government to apply state resources to the procedures. Furthermore, given that it has been an international trend to decriminalize private criminal offenses, including those of copyright infringement, the Taiwanese government considers it unfair that the U.S. government would pressure it to go against a global legal trend when the United States itself does not treat such offenses as a public crime (*China Times*, 7 May 2002:9; personal interview, Justin Lin, former section chief, IPO, 4 June 2002, Boston). Given the high piracy level in Taiwan, such a change would also imply that law enforcement in Taiwan would have to treat the majority of the population as potential offenders and thus criminals (personal interview, Hank Kwuo, 6 May 2002). On the practical level, it would also further strain the already overworked and understaffed law enforcement personnel, especially in a recession environment in which the government is pressured to streamline its operations.

To the copyright owners, there are other such "procedural hurdles" that "hinder the copyright owners' efforts to protect their works in Taiwan" as the powers of attorneys (2002 IIPA Report:253). Under Taiwan's laws, powers of attorney (hereinafter POA's) and other documentation would have to be issued by the president of a company, not by the company's local manager, officers, or attorneys. Such a requirement creates an inconvenience for copyright industries as it does not comport with the way transnational corporations normally conduct their business. For these corporations, their local attorneys or officers are legally authorized to issue documentation (IIPA Country Report, Taiwan, 1996–2001). Given that a "manager" of a local company is often authorized to execute POA, Taiwan prosecutors' refusal to accept POA by executive vice presidents of a foreign company was thus viewed as unfair, unnecessarily complicated, and costly. The copyright owners refer to TRIPS requirement as their defense, stating that IPR enforcement procedures should not be "unnecessarily complicated or costly or entail unreasonable time limits or unwarranted delays" (Young and Wang, 1996).

Another point of contention between Taiwan and the United States has to do with Taiwan's decision to delay the effective date of the legislation to provide retroactive protection for the full term of protection until Taiwan gains its WTO accession. Furthermore, Taiwan extends a blanket two-year grace period beyond the WTO accession, which in the United States's view amounts to a governmentally sanctioned piracy.[10]

Finally, the fact that organized crime was engaged in piracy networks made the enforcement issues much more complicated. Because piracy is considered a highly lucrative source of revenue yet with much less risk (especially compared to that of narcotics), it has become an area of business many criminal organizations find highly appealing.[11] One of the most noted gangs in Taiwan, Bamboo Gang, for example, has been investing in and profiting heavily from optical media pirate operations in Taiwan (see IIPA Country Report, 1999).[12] A recent trend in Taiwan is criminal organizations' use of students and juveniles (aged 11 to 17) in the distribution of pirated optical media. In 2001, 63 percent of those arrested were juvenile offenders (1,669 out of 2,621 offenders). By using juveniles to distribute pirated products, criminal organizations hope to avoid liability since juveniles are below the statutory age of criminal responsibility. Judges usually reprimand them for their misconduct without imposing criminal penalties. Also, to dodge enforcement, pirate vendors in night markets would use what is called a "conscience vending box" for payment collection. Thus consumers would voluntarily throw money in the box in exchange for pirated optical discs that they have purchased. In the event of a police raid, the (usually juvenile) vendor would simply abscond, abandoning both the goods and the box (see Hung, 2002; 2002 IIPA Special 301 Country Report, Taiwan; and personal interview, Hank Kwuo, 6 May 2002, Taipei).

As illustrated, the local and global dynamics are complex as the state undergoes tremendous transitions and reconfigurations. The trajectory through which Taiwan journeyed in gaining accession into the WTO and its first reluctant and later voluntary involvement in reforming its IP regulation and enforcement attest to its desire to gain recognition in the global community. Having been an outcast for three decades, Taiwan had made its accession into the WTO a top priority in its national policy. As Sun (1998) points out, the irony lies in the fact that instead of being pressured by the United States, Taiwan actively and automatically amended its IP system in order to reenter the global trade regime. Thus, Taiwan has in the past decade or so improved its IPR protection governance. It followed a trajectory that began with much resistance and struggle against a perceived external pressure, namely, a superimposed system from the United States through political measures, and ended with a self-initiated reform by legal means. While Taiwan often finds itself under one kind of pressure or another, the state has, in the process, very consciously selected the course through which it made that compromise, motivated strongly by local self-interests.

Border Control and the State

Taiwan is now arguably the world's worst piracy haven for optical media production for export, as product from Taiwan has been found in 2001 in far away places as Paraguay and Mexico.

—2002 IIPA Special 310 Country Report:254

If one uses the IIPA estimates as the sole criterion to judge which country warrants more monitoring, Taiwan is certainly not one that either has the highest piracy rate or one that witnesses the largest amount of losses. According to the 2002 Special 301 Report (see table 9.4), there are countries that are on the Watch List (one level down from the Priority Watch List) that either saw much greater losses than Taiwan (e.g., Italy), or that the piracy level was much higher (e.g., Bolivia, Colombia, Lithuania, Romania, Malaysia and Thailand), not to mention that there was a 40 percent drop of total estimated losses due to piracy in Taiwan from 2000 to 2001 (from $553.7 million to $333.1 million). So why is Taiwan on the Priority Watch List (or South Korea, for that matter)? What are other criteria if piracy level and losses are not the only consideration? Perhaps the following case and statistics would shed some light on the situation.

On 16 November 2001, the LA law enforcement authority seized the largest amount of counterfeit software in U.S. history, valued at $100 million. The police noted that it was from "a 'well-funded syndicate' operating in Taiwan, and that the bust was like 'intercepting a drug cart'" (IIPA Special 301 Country Report–Taiwan, 2002:252). Meanwhile, by 2000 IIPA had listed Taiwan as one of the world's worst pirate exporters of optical media (see IIPA Country Reports, Taiwan, 1996–2001). Taiwan also topped the 1999 U.S. piracy list as the territory that exported the largest volume of pirated products to the United States (*Taiwan Economic News*, 20 April 2000). Taiwan in 1999 accounted for 43 percent of the total value of pirated products exported to the United States, up 490 percent from the previous year, and was the largest source of counterfeited CDs and DVDs. The U.S. Customs Service seized counterfeit goods from Taiwan with a total value of $42.37 million (USTR Trade Summary, 2001). Mainland China (16 percent), South Korea (4 percent), Hong Kong (3 percent), and Singapore (2 percent) constituted the rest of the top five exporters of pirated goods to the United States. It is perhaps not surprising then that the top three exporters of counterfeit products to the United States are on the Priority Watch List (Taiwan and South Korea) and on 306 Monitoring List (China), while one of the 306 Monitoring countries (Paraguay) is in fact a destination for pirated products exported from Taiwan (see above quote).

Such a scale and scope of cross-border piracy is clearly related to the over-capacity of optical media production in Taiwan. Currently it is estimated that there are at least sixty-one optical media production plants in Taiwan with over 1,187 replication lines that include ninety-three DVD lines, 229 VCD/CD lines, and 865 CD-R lines. The total production capacity of these plants is 1.127 billion, while the legitimate domestic demand is about 40 million for its 22.4 million people (see 2002 IIPA Special 301 Country Report). Taiwan's overcapacity in pirated optical disc production and its subsequent cross-border trade of such goods (i.e., perceived weak border control) consequently becomes a target for the copyright industries.

What is not listed on the IIPA report, but what is very likely an important factor affecting who is put on the list, therefore, is a country's capacity in pro-

Table 9.4. IIPA 2002 "Special 301" Recommendations
IIPA 2000–2001 Estimated Trade Losses Due to Copyright Piracy (in US$millions) and 2000–2001 Estimated Levels of Copyright Piracy

| | Motion Pictures | | | | Records & Music | | | | Entertainment Software* | | | | Total Losses | |
	Loss 2001	Loss 2000	Video Piracy Level 2001	Video Piracy Level 2000	Loss 2001	Loss 2000	Piracy Level 2001	Piracy Level 2000	Loss 2001	Loss 2000	Piracy Level 2001	Piracy Level 2000	2001	2000
Priority Foreign Country														
Ukraine (GSP)	40.0	40.0	80%	99%	170.0	200.0	85%	95%	NA	NA	NA	NA	210.0	263.7
306 Monitoring														
Paraguay	2.0	2.0	80%	80%	253.6	200.0	99%	90%	NA	9.7	NA	99%	270.1	223.2
China	160.0	120.0	88%	90%	47.3	70.0	90%	93%	455.0	NA	92%	99%	1507.0	1085.1
Priority Watch List*														
Indonesia	27.5	25.0	90%	90%	67.9	21.6	87%	56%	NA	NA	NA	99%	174.6	134.3
Philippines (OCR)	28.0	25.0	80%	70%	23.9	1.4	36%	33%	NA	41.0	99%	98%	120.1	133.2
South Korea	25.0	20.0	25%	20%	4.0	7.0	14%	19%	487.7	157.0	63%	90%	685.9	400.2
Taiwan (OCR)	**35.0**	**30.0**	**30%**	**30%**	**51.7**	**60.5**	**48%**	**44%**	**119.4**	**319.3**	**70%**	**90%**	**333.1**	**553.7**
Watch List*														
Bolivia	2.0	2.0	100%	100%	15.0	15.0	85%	85%	NA	1.5	NA	NA	25.5	26.8
Colombia (OCR)	40.0	40.0	90%	90%	73.0	60.0	65%	60%	NA	39.0	NA	85%	153.3	177.2
Italy	140.0	140.0	20%	20%	40.0	50.0	23%	25%	NA	NA	74%	65%	488.5	540.5
Lithuania	1.5	1.5	NA	80%	7.0	7.0	85%	85%	NA	3.5	NA	98%	11.0	12.0
Malaysia (OCR)	40.0	41.0	80%	80%	148.9	15.6	70%	65%	56.4	NA	93%	98%	316.5	140.0

Source: International Intellectual Property Alliance.
*These are partial listings for comparative purposes.

ducing and exporting pirated products. Thus, while many countries in South America or East Europe saw much worse piracy losses, selected Asian countries are the ones that often top the priority watch list. Not surprisingly, those that are caught smuggling pirated goods into the United States are more likely to be put on the list.

Centrally located in the heart of the Asia-Pacific region, both Taiwan and Hong Kong are important transshipment ports for international goods. To control piracy activities and piracy levels in these two territories necessarily means the controlling of the respective borders. The Hong Kong authority proved to be much more cooperative in this matter, as they have enacted a more effective border monitoring system than has its neighbor Taiwan. The United States has in fact used Hong Kong as a model for its treatment of copyright infringement as serious crime, and for its more effective border control. Moreover, unlike Hong Kong Customs, Taiwan Customs does not have judicial power. Thus when the Customs personnel come upon pirated goods, they would have to refer such goods to industry representatives for verification and formal complaint before legal actions can be taken. To Hank Kwuo, such inefficiency attributes to difficulties perceived in Taiwan's border control (personal interview, 6 May 2002, Taipei).

Under U.S. pressure, Taiwan finally instituted the Export Monitoring System (hereinafter EMS) in 1993. The issue is one of strengthening Taiwan's border control. In 1993, it was monitoring mostly pirated products flowing out of Taiwan, rather than flowing through Taiwan, as Taiwan was mainly a production and export base at that point. Many of its pirate products do not stop just at the Mainland or other Asian markets; they continue to flow to South America, Europe, even Africa. By the end of the 1990s, Taiwan had become a major transshipment point for pirated goods flowing through Taiwan from multiple sources to the rest of the world.

The goal of this first-of-its-kind inspection and monitoring system was thus to remove pirated products from its source before they are exported. The result, however, has not been satisfactory. Taiwan cites reasons that the EMS process has hurt domestic industries, as administrative delays have made it difficult for time-sensitive products to compete with products manufactured elsewhere. More important, it was the general indifference from businesses that rendered the system ineffective and costly (see Sun, 1998).

The problem, according to copyright industries, of ineffective border control is not one of legislation, as the tools are present. The issue, rather, has been enforcement (or lack thereof). EMS, for example, has been in place to control transborder flows of pirated goods. But the tools provided by the EMS were not used effectively. Meanwhile, to avoid inspection or detection under the EMS, pirates have increased and expanded their "maze of transshipment points" (IIPA Country Report, Taiwan, 1999:1). Consequently, the United States has been pressuring Taiwan into adopting the Hong Kong legislation's approach in having extraterritorial reach to deter regional trade of pirate products, as Hong Kong enforcement has enacted new criminal offenses against pirate networks whose operations cross the territory's border.

Anti-Anti-Piracy as New Nationalist Cause: A Different May Fourth Movement and a State Caught in Between

As the Taiwanese government was still basking in the afterglow of a successful, albeit hard-won, WTO accession, in May 2002 Taiwanese college students were beginning a revolution all of their own, the anti-anti-piracy movement, hoping to rewrite the market order for IPR-related products and services.

Like many college students worldwide, Taiwanese college students are part of underground global Internet piracy networks, both directly and indirectly. They are involved in the production, dissemination, and consumption of various unauthorized copyright products and services. Some do it for fun. Some do it for profit. More do it because it is free. But on 4 May 2002, many became nationalistic.

My visit to college campuses in Taipei in April and May of 2002 was an eye-opening experience. Most students, both graduate and undergraduate, were very open about their use of unauthorized Internet or other optical media products, although many of them shun DVDs and VCDs. They prefer to watch, listen to, or play on their computer, or to "burn" their own CD-R from files downloaded from the Internet, be it movies, music, software, or games. Those who sell VCDs or burn CD-R on campuses are quite often connected to organized pirate groups. They would come with catalogues of products. When I asked different students in different classes where I could go to find pirated DVDs or VCDs, more than once, someone would tell me to talk to them directly and they could get me anything I wanted. A few students did onsite demonstrations on their lap top computers of downloaded films, boasting better-than-DVD quality. They also cited websites where they downloaded free movies, and other sites for subtitles for recently released foreign films. *Amélie*, for example, was very popular among Taiwanese college students in spring 2002. When the pirated version was first made available on the Internet, it was the original French version without Chinese subtitles. Not to worry, students told me. Go to another site and one would get, free of charge, a file of the Chinese subtitles of *Amélie*. Apparently college students themselves provided some of these "post-production" services. One of the students I talked to was involved in subtitle production and translation.

What is interesting is the fact that many of these people who are involved in the production and dissemination of pirated materials on the Internet are affiliated with educational institutions, corporations, and government agencies, where they would have access to servers and other necessary hardware for such operation.[13] It is no wonder then that the 2002 IIPA Country Report specifically calls for "legalized use of copyrighted materials by government, business and schools" (p. 263).

Many of these students turned patriotic and nationalistic in response to the government's decision to crack down on piracy. On 1 May, Justice Minister Chen Ting-nan announced the government's determination to safeguard IPR and to begin on that day a crackdown on software piracy with participation from all of the twenty district prosecutors' offices (*AFP*, 1 May 2002), a decision made in response to both Business Software Alliance's anti-piracy campaign and the USTR's 30 April decision to keep Taiwan on the Special 301 Priority Country List. The BSA picked 1 May as the day to begin their anti-piracy crackdown after two months of "grace period" that was meant for public awareness and education, during which they would collect evidence without filing complaints (personal interview, Jill Chu, IPO, 6 May 2002, Taipei; Randy Ma, marketing manager, BSA-Beijing, 20 May 2002, Beijing). The government's crackdown on 1 May was intended to strengthen enforcement in support of BSA's campaign. What both the BSA and the Ministry of Justice did not expect was the grassroots backlash that they witnessed after the launch of the campaign.

Students from six campuses who formed the Anti-Anti-Piracy Alliance gathered on 4 May at the gate of National Taiwan University and staged their protest against "American imperialism." It was not a coincidence that the students picked 4 May as the date to stage their demonstration. In 1919 the original "May Fourth Movement" marked a historical moment in Chinese intellectual history. Mainly a student movement, it started as a protest against the Versailles Treaty, which gave the Liaotung Peninsula in Shangtung Province to the Japanese. The student movement later grew into a literary movement and a nationwide rebellion against imperialism and conservatism. On 4 May 2002, the students viewed themselves as continuing the spirit of their predecessors when they shouted such slogans as "Building a New May Fourth," and "Taiwan Says No to Being an American Dog" (*China Times*, 7 May 2002:15; *Taipei Times Online*, 7 May 2002). They also opposed the possible legislative change to treat noncommercial copyright offenses as public crime, citing that intellectual property rights are private rights and that IPR violations should therefore be treated only as civil offenses. In a later press conference on 7 May, the Anti-Anti-Piracy Alliance further accused the Ministry of Justice as "serving as an American Imperialists' debt collector" (*China Times*, 7 May 2002:9), because the justice minister signed a large purchase contract with Microsoft and Symantec on 30 April to buy legitimate software products to set an example, while promising to begin the campaign by cracking down on government agencies, schools, and businesses (Tai, 2002; *AFP*, 2002).

While Microsoft may have seemed to be the immediate beneficiary of the anti-piracy campaign, it eventually found itself serving as the center of a public relations nightmare (Lu, 2002). The real beneficiary turned out to be Linux with its open-code tradition and its software alternatives such as "Chinese 2000" and "Kai Office." The Department of Education of Taipei City, for example, switched its budget originally set for Microsoft software purchase to that for Linux's teacher training workshops (see *Taipei Times*, 7 May 2002; Tai, 2002).

Thus from the copyright industries' anti-piracy parade on 4 April, the USTR Special 301 announcement on 30 April, the BSA Anti-Piracy Campaign on 1 May, to the student anti-anti-piracy protest on 4 May and beyond, within a month one witnessed dramatic events unfold in which situations changed with remarkable speed and unpredictability. Actors and networks of various sizes (from micro to macro) and origins (global, regional, local) changed hands and

A *"Culture of Illegality"?* 163

affected one another's actions. The center of these actions is no doubt the state, as it holds the crucial function of regulating market order through regulations, law enforcement, and policies. Although currently Taiwanese laws are fully compliant with TRIPS requirements, it does not mean that the work is done. The United States, for instance, still demands that the Taiwanese government strengthen its border control, the copyright industries ask the state to build up its anti-piracy efforts and further amend its laws, the public wants the government to take a firmer stand against the "American imperialists" while protecting local interests, and the criminal organizations are becoming increasingly sophisticated in dodging the anti-piracy tactics. On the surface it might seem that the Taiwanese government is indeed powerless amid pressures from the global trade regime, industries, foreign government, its own constituency, and threats from piracy. A deeper examination, however, suggests otherwise.

As noted, the state holds a key role in shaping its IPR environment. It is an area where strong state intervention is desirable. While Taiwan has made multiple concessions, it makes them selectively with its own interest in mind, be it political, commercial, or cultural. The government has been actively defining its IPR governance with local characteristics. It has been, as the above case demonstrated, in constant dialogue with its industries as well as various constituencies. It is a dynamic process in which the consumers use the media, both new and traditional, to make their demands heard, and in which the state, while many times frustrated and powerless, negotiates its position vis-à-vis multiple other forces.

Technology and the Market

The prevalence of CD-R and Internet piracy within Taiwan and Taiwan's extraordinary capacity in exporting pirated optical media that boast both quantity and quality reflect a unique market reality accentuated by Taiwan's advanced technological development and its status as a major legitimate content source.[14] Furthermore, Taiwan is a major supplier of illegal masters and stampers used in pirate VCD replication in China, usually transported through Hong Kong. A stamper is the end product of the VCD mastering process, containing all the data that is replicated onto the VCDs themselves. It is thus a crucial element in the replication process. Because a stamper is a 0.3mm thin nickel plate, it is easily transportable (see IIPA reports).

That Taiwan is a major territory for Hollywood majors also makes it a rich source country of legitimate contents. It is not uncommon to find "overrun" production where legitimate replication plants make unauthorized reproductions off the authorized master (personal interview, Hank Kwuo, executive director, MPA–Taiwan, 6 May 2002, Taipei). Some of these overrun reproductions become parallel import products to other territories, while others become pirated goods.

In addition to finished products, Taiwan has also been one of the leading source countries for raw materials. Both the PRC and Hong Kong play essential roles on these networks. For example, chips and other components would be sent via Hong Kong to China for assembly and packaging, where finished products would then be exported throughout Asia, Latin America, and other parts of the world, a process and route not unlike those of legitimate businesses. Just like film production (as well as other businesses), the Greater China area functions as an integrated network, where the formula often involves Taiwanese capital and know-how, Hong Kong talents and connections, and the Mainland location and labor.

In short, by continually funding pirate operations throughout Greater China, and by exporting much of what is replicated to the rest of the world, Taiwan has served as one of the most important source countries of piracy in the world. Taiwan's crucial position on the global piracy networks in general, and on the Greater China piracy web in particular, has much to do with its powerful position as a rich source country, an advanced technology provider, a crucial financial backer and investor, a convenient port location where border control is difficult, and an export-oriented economy. A weak local film industry also creates a strong market and demand for Hollywood films, thus providing a rich source of legitimate contents and the potential for piracy and parallel import.

Dynamic Power Relations

There are of course macro-actors and micro-actors, but the difference between them is brought about by power relations and the constructions of networks that will *elude analysis* if we presume *a priori* that macro-actors are bigger than or superior to micro-actors.
—Callon and Latour (1981:280, original emphasis)

What Callon and Latour are arguing here is not that all actors have the same size or that they have the same weight or power. Instead they view micro-macro relations as dynamic and not necessarily evolutionary. The key here is how macro-actors are macro because they are able to translate other actors' wills into a single will, thus constituting a macro-order. This enrollment of other actors becomes powerful because of the integrated forces on which it can rely. Thus, by enrolling other actors and by associating with and attaching to different networks, a micro actor can also grow to macro-sized, and vice versa. Such dynamic power relations and translation processes have great implications for the issues at hand.

In the case of Taiwan, for example, we see how Taiwan, as an isolated micro-actor with almost no political power in the realm of international politics, was able to attach and align itself flexibly with regional players (including its arch rival Mainland China), global trade regimes, and transnational technological sectors, while negotiating its relations with pirate organizations and maneuvering its legislative structure to meet local needs and external demands. Also powerless and a micro-actor, Taiwanese college students successfully enrolled and associated themselves with educator, parent, and media networks and translated their wills into a single will.

The supposedly powerful macro-actors in this case, the U.S. government, transnational copyright conglomerates and their powerful associations, for example, found themselves in a much-unexpected position of frustration and vulnerability. Their networks, while powerful, are not flexible. Meanwhile, by flexibly attaching, aligning, associating, and dissociating with diverse networks and elements, pirate networks of various lengths and sizes are ever more resilient. As a consequence, the piracy networks in Taiwan become a leakage point on the legitimate distribution networks, through which multiple intersecting networks and their relations transmute, transform, and transfigure.

This is certainly not to suggest that power relations in this case are necessarily or completely reversed, or that the state maintains its sovereignty in a world regulated by global trade regimes and dominated by transnational corporations. Quite the contrary, the role of the state is highly problematized in a post-WTO global order, while its sovereignty in the traditional sense has declined. A weak state, for instance, is more likely to find itself subjected to all sorts of pressures as the above case indicated. While Taiwan is now a full member of the WTO and has complied fully with TRIPS requirements and standards, for example, its IPR and trade practices and relations with the United States are still dictated by bilateral trade negotiations and are subjected to unilateral trade sanctions and threats. Instead of resorting to the TRIPS dispute settlement mechanism for the U.S. Special 301 decision that was perceived to be unfair, the Taiwanese government still chose to submit to such judgment and its requirements. What the above scenario does suggest, however, is the dynamic and self-reflexive nature of such submission and compromises. It also highlights the crucial and increasingly urgent role the state plays in these processes of globalization and translation/reterritorialization.

Notes

1. So claimed IIPA 2002 Special 301 Report—Taiwan (p. 255) in one of the report's headings.

2. See Callon and Latour (1981) on the dynamic relations between micro- and macro-actors and their complex relations with networks.

3. WTO approved Taiwan's accession on 11 November 2001 in Doha, Qatar, while Taiwan's Legislative Yuan ratified the accession on 17 November 2001. Taiwan officially became a WTO member on 1 January 2002.

4. See also Callon and Latour's (1981) writing on "translation" in the context of social theory and methodology.

5. "Special 301" is part of the investigative and consultation proceedings under Sections 301–310 of the Trade Act. In addition to a "priority watch list" and a "watch list" for countries whose acts, policies and practices that meet some of the "priority foreign

country" criteria. To extend the monitoring process to a year-round basis, in 1993 the USTR also initiated a program of "immediate action plans" and "out-of-cycle" reviews. In 1994 the USTR further created "special mention" on countries that have emerging problems or need to make improvement on IP protection and was meant to serve as a warning citation. In 1995 the USTR again expanded the "out-of-cycle" review category to identify specific countries with specific deadlines by which they would need to resolve specific problems (see Sun, 1997).

6. A country that is named as a U.S. Special 301 Priority Foreign Country would need to complete consultations with the United States in six months or face trade sanctions. See *AFP*, 2002.

7. TRIPS consists of seven chapters including General Provisions and Basic Principles, Standards, Enforcement, Acquisition, Maintenance of Intellectual Property Rights, Dispute Prevention and Settlement, Transitional Arrangements, Institutional Arrangements, and Final Provisions. See WTO website. Also see National Bureau of Standards (2002).

8. According to National Bureau of Standards of Taiwan (2002), however, only six countries or territories had reciprocal copyright relations with Taiwan: the United States, United Kingdom, Switzerland, and Hong Kong had full reciprocal copyright relations with Taiwan, while Spain and Korea granted limited reciprocal protection of Taiwanese nationals residing in these countries.

9. In terms of copyright related issues, Article 9 of TRIPS provides that WTO signatories shall be bound by the entire Berne Convention (except Article 6bis). Furthermore, TRIPS reaffirms principles of national treatment and MFA treatment. Taiwan's accession into WTO therefore automatically ensures its full benefits (National Bureau of Standards, 2002).

10. Another issue is the retroactive protection of the back catalogue of U.S. copyrighted works. The TRIPS Articles 9 and 14.6, which incorporated Berne Convention's Article 18, dictates that its member countries should afford protection of preexisting works whose term of protection has not expired in the country of origin, as they should still benefit from the full term of protection, set at minimum fifty years.

11. In 2002, a raid in Taiwan also uncovered pirated DVDs with a weapons arsenal and cocaine (Groves, 2002a).

12. One of the cases cited by the IIPA Country Report on Taiwan (2001) to show that the Taiwanese government failed to enforce copyright laws and regulations and shut down known commercial pirate plants is that of Digi Gold. Digi Gold is an optical disc manufacturer that has the full range of production capabilities of mastering, replicating, and printing. Its daily production capacity is 30 stampers, 60,000 VCDs, and 30,000 DVDs. Its full annual capacity is estimated at 10,800 DVD/VCD stampers, 21.6 million VCDs, and 10.8 million DVDs.

13. Multiple interviews with both graduate and undergraduate students, conducted in April and May 2002, in Taipei.

14. Much of Taiwan's piracy capacity is tied to its sophisticated technology sector and economy. When I was doing field research in China and Hong Kong, for instance, many people told me that pirated products from Taiwan stood out from others because of their exceptional quality in packaging and subtitling.

10

The Hong Kong Connection: Distribution, Piracy, and Parallel Import

Hong Kong's position as a free port between the Mainland and the West has made it an ideal location for distribution. A land of intermediaries, Hong Kong is a crucial node on multiple intersecting networks where flows of products and capital, both legitimate and illegitimate, overlap and interchange. Thus, while distribution and piracy issues in China are tied directly to the size of the market, the state-run monopolized distribution system, and the overall market supply and demand imbalance problems, in Hong Kong they have more to do with Hong Kong's cultural, economic, and geographic location as the jumping off point to the Mainland.

This chapter examines three forms of film circulation in Hong Kong: authorized distribution, unauthorized distribution (piracy), and the in-between area of parallel importing (the gray market).[1] Piracy and parallel importing challenge the geographical divisions of the market order, upon which the functioning of legitimate distribution depends.

Distribution

With video piracy on the up-swing—estimated to have hit 50 percent in 1999, up from 5 percent in the early 1990s—and 1999 box office of $115 million down 40 percent from a 1992 peak—Hong Kong is an up-and-down territory and thus ideal for distant Hollywood majors to rely on a local distrib with hometown savvy.

—*Variety Deal Memo* (2000:6)

This quote highlights a recent trend of the Hong Kong film market: its unstable box office performance and high piracy rate have contributed to most Hollywood majors' decisions to distribute films through either local licensees or joint ventures with local distributors. What it fails to mention is the fact that the vertically integrated Hong Kong market, where a handful of local distributors control most exhibition circuits, makes distributing through local licensees a necessity. In addition, Hong Kong's small market size does not justify the high overhead costs for majors' branch office operations in Hong Kong.

A city-state with a population of 6.73 million people, Hong Kong's strategic importance lies not in its size, but in the multiple locations it occupies. From the start, this former British colony with no national hinterland had been a place where decision makers controlling global capital exchange congregated. Through their control of capital exchange, prominent British and American firms located in Hong Kong formed direct links to leading global metropolises, most notably London and New York. Western merchants had also used Hong Kong as their base for trading in Asia, and especially with China. Consequently Hong Kong rose to be a trade and financial center, with its ties reaching two major groups: Asian countries and developed countries outside of Asia (see Meyer, 2002).

Hong Kong's trade continued to soar in more recent times, maintaining the two aforementioned trends from the nineteenth century: high levels of exchange with developed countries in North America and western Europe, and with other countries in Asia (Meyer, 2002). According to the Hong Kong Trade Development Council (October 2001), Hong Kong at present has the second-highest per capita holding of foreign currency and is the most service-oriented economy in the world. It is also the world's fourth-largest foreign exchange reserves holding, the world's busiest airport in international cargoes, the world's busiest container port, and the largest source of outward foreign direct investment (FDI) and the top foreign direct investment recipient in Asia, all of which have great implications for distribution and piracy.

A former British colony, Hong Kong was returned to the Mainland on 1 July 1997. Pursuant to the Sino-British Joint Declaration of 1984, Hong Kong will maintain its previous capitalist system for fifty years (see, for example, Tackaberry, 1997). After Hong Kong's handover to Mainland China on 1 July 1997, when it became the Hong Kong Special Administration Region (HKSAR), its fate has been inextricably linked to that of the Mainland. Hong Kong is not only the Mainland's largest foreign investment source but also the most important entrepôt as approximately 40 percent of Mainland China's foreign trade is handled through Hong Kong.[2] Furthermore, 96 percent of Hong Kong's total re-exports either originated from or were destined for the Mainland. Chinese Mainland is one of the leading investors in Hong Kong (see chapter 3 for the Greater China economic circle connections).

Given these impressive global and regional achievements and the unique geographical and cultural location of Hong Kong, it is no wonder that Hong Kong is the regional base for many transnational corporations, including the Hollywood majors, to manage their businesses in the Asia Pacific region, particularly in Mainland China. Based on a government survey, for instance, there were 3,001 regional operations of overseas companies in Hong Kong as of June 2000, an increase of 20.5 percent from a year before.

The Film Market

Named "Hollywood of the East," (Stokes and Hoover, 1999:17), Hong Kong tops the world's per capita film production record. It is the second-largest film exporter (second to the United States) and the third in the world in the number of films produced per year (after India and the United States); its film industry, however, has been declining since the second half of the 1990s. In 1999, for example, the overall Hong Kong box office was off 40 percent from 1992, with the decline in the Chinese film segment reaching 70 percent (*Deal Memo*, 2000). A combination of factors has contributed to this decline: economic crisis in Asia in 1997 and 1998, the turnover of Hong Kong to the Mainland and the ensuing exodus of Hong Kong film talents to Hollywood and elsewhere, falling production standards and heavy reliance on formulaic genres, mass-produced low budget films, infrastructural problems of distribution and exhibition, and optical disc piracy (see, for example, *The Economist*, 1999; Thomas and O'Brien, 2001; Curtin, 2003).

With the economic recovery of 1999 and 2000, the film industry has been slowly recovering (see Hong Kong Government Information Office, 2001). Table 10.1, for example, illustrates the decline and recovery of local film production. In 2000, there was a close to 50-percent increase in local film production, from ninety-five pictures produced in 1999 to an impressive 141 in 2000. Table 10.2 shows the overall box office performance for 1995–2000. The total box office income began its decline in 1996 with a 12-percent drop from 1995. The year 1998 witnessed another 17-percent drop from 1997. In 2000 the box office performance began to pick up, albeit with an insignificant 1-percent growth.[3]

As noted, Hong Kong was a territory where locally produced films dominated box office performance. Local films had always been more popular than Hollywood products and, until the mid-1990s, had between 50 percent and 70 percent of the market share (see Li, 1996). In 1990, for example, eight of the top ten films were Hong Kong made. In 2000, only five were locally produced (see tables 10.3 and 10.4).

Table 10.1. Released by Origin

Year	Hong Kong	International	Total
1997	94	373	467
1998	92	374	466
1999	95	293	388
2000	141	278	419

Source: Informa Media Group (Thomas and O'Brien, 2001), and TableBase™, Accession# 1576296.

Table 10.2. Box Office Performance 1995–2000

	Total (US$millions)	Ticket Price (US$)
1995	172.0	6.43
1996	151.0	6.79
1997	149.0	5.53
1998	124.0	5.75
1999	112.5	5.68
2000 (estimated)	117.5	5.70

Source: Motion Picture Industry Association; *Variety Deal Memo*. See Informa Media Group (Thomas and O'Brien, 2001).

Table 10.3. Top Ten Films in Hong Kong 1990 Box Office

Title	Origin	Gross (HK$)
All for the Winner	H.K.	$41,326,156.00
God of Gamblers II	H.K.	$40,342,758.00
Ghost	U.S.	$34,048,941.00
Front Page	H.K.	$26,348,460.00
Pretty Woman	U.S.	$25,162,625.00
Heart into Hearts	H.K.	$23,275,483.00
A Terra-Cotta Warrior	H.K.	$20,991,782.00
Chinese Ghost Story II	H.K.	$20,784,824.00
Her Fatal Ways	H.K.	$20,476,919.00
The Fun The Luck and The Tycoon	H.K.	$20,292,057.00

Source: Compiled from *Movie World Hong Kong* (www.movieworld.com.hk).

Table 10.4. Top Ten Films in Hong Kong 2000 Box Office

Title	Origin	Distributor
Mission Impossible 2	U.S.	Panasia/UIP
Toy Story 2	U.S.	Intercontinental
Needing You	H.K.	China Star
Tokyo Raiders	H.K.	Golden Harvest
Dinosaur	U.S.	Intercontinental
Summer Holiday	H.K.	Golden Harvest
The Duel	H.K.	China Star
Stuart Little	U.S.	Col. TriStar (HK)
Healing Hearts	H.K.	Star East
Shanghai Noon	U.S.	Intercontinental

Source: Hong Kong, Kowloon and New Territories Motion Picture Industry Assn. TableBase™ (2001) Accession# 2748672.

Given that Hong Kong is a small market, and that foreign film exhibition in Hong Kong is dominated by four major circuits owned by three to four major distributors (see later discussion), the most cost-effective way of operation would be for the majors to work with these sub-distributors and exclusive licensees (personal interview, John Hsu, director of finance and business affairs, Intercontinental, 12 June 2000). On the other hand, however, because of Hong Kong's strategic and geographical importance, even though several majors do not have their local distribution offices, they do have their regional headquarters located in Hong Kong. Buena Vista International (Disney) is one such example.

The importance of having regional offices in a global network constitutes an effort in spatial and temporal control and management. Centrally located in Asia with fairly relaxed regulations, Hong Kong has become a popular location where the majors set up their Asian regional offices. Joe Yan, executive director of sales, Buena Vista International Asia Pacific Region, pointed out that one could take films in and out of Hong Kong without having to go through customs, whereas in Taiwan and elsewhere film import policies are much stricter (personal interview, 20 December 1999, Hong Kong). Warner Bros. regional office, for example, supervises nine territories in Asia, excluding Japan and Australia (personal interview, John Alonte, vice president, Warner Bros. International Theatrical Distribution, 31 May 2000).[4] Located in the same time zone with local distribution offices, it is much easier for the regional office to monitor and check-balance strategies and make last-minute changes if necessary. It is also easier to localize staff and to make sure that other matters are localized efficiently. Furthermore, it is crucial that the regional office serves as a channel between the head and local offices (personal interviews, Joe Yan and John Alonte).

Twentieth Century Fox also has its Asian regional office in Hong Kong with a staff of six: senior vice president, vice president for regional marketing, director of finance, and three assistants. The regional office oversees thirteen territories in Asia: Australia, China, Hong Kong, India, Indonesia, Japan, Korea, Malaysia, New Zealand, Philippines, Singapore, Taiwan, and Thailand. Fox is unique in that its Asian regional office also oversees Australia and Japan. Paul Hanneman, senior vice president, said that the reason why Fox Asia has jurisdiction over Japan is partly because he was Fox-Japan's general manager before becoming the regional head. It was natural for him to continue overseeing Japan once he was promoted to head theatrical distribution in Asia (personal interview, 22 December 1999, Hong Kong; see also Fox Asia site). Given that Japan is the largest market in box office grosses outside of the United States, most other majors run the territory directly from Los Angeles.[5]

Not all majors' regional offices are located in Hong Kong. UIP, for example, has its regional office in Australia. Columbia TriStar, on the other hand, has been restructuring to get rid of the middle layer and functions without an Asian regional office. One of the rationales for eliminating the middle layer of regional office has to do with the new trend in global film distribution: the shortening of release windows and preference for global day and date releasing. Because of

technology and piracy, the windowing strategy has faced unprecedented challenge. The decision-making process has consequently become more centralized.
It is deemed more important that local distributors communicate directly with
home offices in Los Angeles, instead of going through a regional office (personal interview, Li Chow, general manager, Edko Columbia TriStar Films, 2
June 2000, Hong Kong).

Hong Kong ranks about twenty-five among Hollywood studios' export
markets, and is one of the bigger territories where the majors rely on local distributors to distribute films (*Deal Memo*, 2000). Hong Kong's vertically integrated industry structure (especially in distribution and exhibition) contributes to
this phenomenon. The extremely high overhead cost entailed in setting up a
branch office in Hong Kong is yet another factor discouraging the majors from
doing so. The limited space, both geographically and in terms of exhibition, also
makes it difficult to book films in Hong Kong. It makes financial sense therefore
to work with a partner, local or otherwise. Fox and Columbia, for example, used
to have a joint venture in Hong Kong, until Columbia decided to join
BVI/Disney in a number of territories in 1999, including Taiwan (personal interview, Paul Hanneman, senior VP, Fox Asia, 22 December 1999, Hong Kong).

Vertical Integration

We're already late to the party. . . . The other two leading chains in Hong
Kong, Edko and Intercontinental, already have distribution. But I think the
compelling argument [is that] *we wanted more control over the success of our
cinemas* and to bring films to Hong Kong that perhaps might not otherwise be
here.

—Donald Meyer, Director, Lark International Holdings
(*The Hollywood Reporter*, 19 April 2002, emphasis added)

The landscape of foreign film distribution and exhibition comprises of three
major distributors controlling most of the theaters in Hong Kong: Edko, Intercontinental, and Panasia/Golden Harvest.[6] The most recent addition to the distribution-cum-exhibition club is Lark International Holdings, parent company of
the United Artists (UA) and Cityplaza cinema circuits in Hong Kong, and the
Studio City chain in China. Realizing the economic necessity and viability of
having a distribution component and to remain competitive, Lark International
opened its own film distribution arm Lark Films Distribution in February 2002
(see Chung, 2002). Even though Lark Films Distribution acquires a modest scale
of eight to ten independent films a year, Lark International's decision to jump on
the distribution-cum-exhibition bandwagon is significant. Its main goal in film
acquisitions is to build a film library that "could be used for counter programming or to fill in a time slot when [another] quality film isn't available" (Bob
Vallone, UA general manager, quoted in Chung, 2002). Because UA is the top
exhibitor in Hong Kong with thirty-seven screens (see table 10.5), Lark's move
in adding a distribution arm will affect the existing market structure. Such a ver-

tically integrated distribution-exhibition structure has great implications for not only independent distributors in Hong Kong but also those majors that are not affiliated with one of the local distributor-cum-exhibitors.

In most cases Hollywood films are released on three major circuits: the Broadway Circuit (owned by Edko, a major local distribution and production company); United Artists (affiliated with Media Asia, [7] a major film production[8] and distribution company); and the Golden Village/Village Roadshow Circuit associated with the distribution company Panasia, which is a subsidiary of Golden Harvest (Thomas and O'Brien, 2001; personal interview, Andrew Wong, principal, Wong and Choy Architecture Ltd., 30 May 2000, Hong Kong).[9] In addition, Intercontinental, a major distributor and producer, also owns several cinemas in Hong Kong. Table 10.6 lists the major circuits and their relationships with local distributors and Hollywood majors.

Table 10.5. Top Exhibitors by Screen (2000)

1.	UA Cinemas	37
2.	Broadway Edko	31
3.	Newport/Empire	19
4.	China Chem	18
5.	Golden Village	14
6.	AMC	11
7.	Golden Harvest	10
8.	Sil Metropole	9

Source: MPIA; Informa Media Group (2001).

Table 10.6. Major HK Exhibition-Distribution Connections

Exhibition Circuits	Owned by/Affiliated with (Local Distributors)	Hollywood Majors
Broadway	Edko	Columbia TriStar (Sony); Fox; MGM
United Artists	Media Asia Lark Film Distribution	Miramax (Disney)
Golden Village/Village Roadshow	Golden Harvest/Panasia	UIP (Universal and Paramount)
Empress Theatre 1 and 2; London Classics; Miramar Cinema 1 and 2	Intercontinental	Buena Vista (Disney)

Source: Compiled from Thomas and O'Brien (2001); Chung 2002; personal interview with Sam Ho, assistant director, Motion Picture Association Asia/Pacific Anti-Piracy Operations, December 1999, January and May through July, 2000, and summer 2002; Andrew Wong, principal, Wong and Choy Architecture Ltd., 30 May 2000.

For a long time Warner Bros. and Twentieth Century Fox were the only two majors that had their own local distribution offices in Hong Kong, and hence with no specific relations with any of the four major exhibition circuits in Hong Kong.[10] They often found themselves in situations in which they had to fight for good playdates with other majors that were affiliated with a local distributor-cum-exhibitor. Fox decided to shut down its Hong Kong distribution office and entered a joint venture with Edko in March 2002 (Kan, 2002; Adler, 2002; *The Hollywood Reporter* 19 March 2002). Warner Bros. is currently the only remaining major with a local distribution office in Hong Kong.

Additionally, table 10.7 lists the market share of major distributors in Hong Kong in 2000. It is important to note that the table is somewhat misleading as several distributors are listed as working independently of one another or as having their own domestic distribution facility, while in fact they have formed a partnership with local sub-distributors. For example, Columbia TriStar has a joint venture in distribution with Edko. They work closely not only in distribution but also production. A case in point is the record-breaking *Crouching Tiger Hidden Dragon (CTHD)*, a coproduction between Columbia TriStar and Edko (along with five other international production companies, see photo 10.1). CJ Entertainment, a major Korean distributor and producer, also has local arrangements with Edko (personal interview, Bill Kong, executive director, Edko Films Ltd., 27 June 2000). Another example is Golden Harvest, Panasia, and UIP. While Panasia and UIP are listed as a separate entity from Golden Harvest, Panasia is a subsidiary of Golden Harvest. Meanwhile, Media Asia has special arrangements with Miramax (Disney). Additionally, MGM films are released through Fox in Hong Kong, which are now distributed through Edko. Needless

Table 10.7. Distributor Market Share* (2000)

Company	Market Share (Percentage)
Intercontinental	17.2
Golden Harvest	10.9 [+UIP=19.8]
Newport	10.2
Panasia/UIP	8.9
EDKO**	7.5 [+Columbia TriStar=12.5]
Twentieth Century Fox	5.7
China Star	5.0
Columbia TriStar	5.0
Warner Bros.	4.5
CJ Entertainment	2.8
Others	22.3

Source: Showbizdata; Informa Media Group (Thomas and O'Brien, 2001).
*Based on films that reached top ten.
** Because this is based on records from 2000, Fox was still distributing its own films. Market share for Edko is expected to go up with new Edko-Fox joint venture deal in place.

Photo 10.1. A *Crouching Tiger Hidden Dragon*
Poster at a Hong Kong Subway Station

to say, the result of having a distributor-cum-exhibitor dominated market is that the profit-sharing terms weighed heavily in favor of distributors. Not only do distributors normally get 60 percent of proceeds, they also determine the terms of playdates. Additionally, production companies usually pick up advertising costs (see Li, 1996). It is clear that other than Newport, which distributes domestic films, the top three distributors are major Hollywood film distributors: Intercontinental (Disney), Golden Harvest/Panasia (UIP), and Edko (Columbia Tri Star, Fox, and MGM). Table 10.8 lists the breakdown of Hollywood majors' presence in Hong Kong and their respective distribution arrangements.

Piracy

As noted, piracy in Hong Kong has to do with Hong Kong's location as the transshipment point for regional and global trade. Since the late 1980s, counter-

Table 10.8. Majors' Local Distribution Arrangements

Majors	Local Distribution Arrangements
Twentieth Century Fox (also distributes MGM films)	Edko/Broadway Cinema Circuit Asia Regional Office located in HK
Columbia TriStar (Sony)	Edko/Broadway Cinema Circuit No Asian Regional Office
Warner Bros.	Warner Bros.—HK Asia Regional Office located in HK
UIP (Paramount and Universal)	Panasia, a subsidiary of Golden Harvest, with Golden Harvest and Golden Village Circuit Asian Regional Office located in Singapore
Buena Vista International (Disney)	Intercontinental/Empress, London Classics, and Miramar Cinemas; Asia Regional Office located in HK

Source: Compiled from personal interviews with Sam Ho, multiple interviews in 1999 and 2000, Paul Hanneman, Senior VP, 20th Century Fox International, Asia/Pacific Regional Office, 22 December 1999; and Andrew Wong, 30 May 2000; See also Thomas and O'Brien, 2001).

feit products have been flowing from China into Hong Kong, for resale in the Hong Kong domestic market or for re-export to other markets (see Tackaberry, 1997). Such flows have become multidirectional and much more varied. This section examines piracy development in Hong Kong from 1995, when VCD first arrived in Hong Kong to 2000, when the Hong Kong Legislative Council (LegCo) passed the Organized and Serious Crimes Ordinance (OSCO).

In general, piracy in Hong Kong is an integral part of piracy on the Mainland. In 1995 Hong Kong first appeared in the International Intellectual Property Alliance's Special 301 recommendations, which named Hong Kong a destination and an entrepôt for the increased flood of pirated material first from the Mainland and later from other territories (see IIPA Special 301 Recommendation, 1996). The year 1995 also marks a very special date in the history of video piracy in Asia: it was the year the pirated video compact disc (VCD) arrived in Hong Kong, which redefined power relations among various players in the region, and in global electronics and entertainment sectors.

By 1996, the piracy traffic between the Mainland and Hong Kong had increased to so significant a degree that it was described as a piracy "flow" turning into a "flood" (IIPA Special 301 Recommendation, 1997), which caused USTR to place Hong Kong on the Special 301 Watch List. By then it was clear that pirated VCDs from locations other than the Mainland were passing through Hong Kong for export elsewhere in Asia. Therefore, by 1996, VCD piracy in Hong Kong had gone beyond a simple "Chinese border enforcement problem" (IIPA 1997) and become a much more complex issue. The portability of the VCD reproduction lines and the close geographical locations of Hong Kong and China have all contributed to the rampancy of piracy in the region. When the Chinese government on the Mainland curbed piracy, many of the pirates and their equipments relocated elsewhere (see Morr, 1999). The outlying islands of the HKSAR, for example, are recognized as the jumping off point for the coast of Guangdong Province of the Mainland. With the crackdown of pirate VCD production in Hong Kong in the late 1990s, the replication lines themselves were remigrating back to the Mainland and elsewhere, thus reversing the already reversed journey (see, for example, IIPA Special 301 Country Report, Hong Kong, 1999). Compared to the linear trajectories through which legitimate and authorized products circulate, the illegitimate and pirate routes are far more circular, reversible, and fluid.

Thus, because of the serious crackdown in China on piracy, in 1997 the flow of pirated goods was completely reversed. Many of the production bases and facilities were moved to Hong Kong, Macao, and other Asian locations. By 1997, Hong Kong had become an export base and was exporting pirated goods back into the Mainland. Consequently, in addition to being the transshipment point and the entrepôt for Chinese and other goods, Hong Kong was now exporting these pirated goods back into the world's largest market, China. Such reversed flows had caused damage to transnational corporations' profit margins in China. By 1997 the piracy issue in Hong Kong was consequently viewed as the "number one problem between the United States and Hong Kong" (IIPA 1998). In 1997 the losses to the U.S. motion picture industry in Hong Kong were estimated at $20 million, a 100 percent increase from 1995 (see table 10.9). While piracy level remains constant from 1997 to 1998, the year 1998 witnessed a 50 percent increase in the motion picture profit losses from $20 million in 1997 to $30 million in 1998.

VCD piracy became even more widespread in Hong Kong because of the crackdown on the Mainland in 1995 and 1996. Table 10.10 demonstrates that in Hong Kong there was a significant increase in the number of raided VCDs compared to those of the VHS. In 1997, the number of seized pirated VCDs was almost eight times that of the VHS. In China alone the number of VCDs seized was 220-fold that of the VHS, while in Hong Kong it was 2,874,076 to zero. In 2000, the world's total optical disc manufacturing capacity was 16 billion units, of which Southeast Asia accounted for one-quarter (Fuller, 2000). In terms of excess capacity Hong Kong has been the biggest individual producer. The legitimate demand on the island was 300 million units whereas the production capability was estimated at 2 billion units, far surpassing the legitimate demand.[11]

Table 10.9. Estimated Motion Pictures Trade Losses Due to Piracy (in US$millions) and Levels of Piracy: 1995–1998, Hong Kong

1995 Loss	Level	1996 Loss	Level	1997 Loss	Level	1998 Loss	Level
10.0 (Special Mention)	4%	15.0	15%	20.0 (Priority Watch List)	20%	30.0 (Watch List)	20%

Source: Complied from multiple USTR Special 301 Recommendation Reports and Country Reports.

Table 10.10. 1997 Asian Piracy Raids

	Video Tapes Seized	VCDs Seized
Australia	2,965	3,706
China	39,400	868,500
Hong Kong	0	2,874,076
India	67,740	13,201
Indonesia	1,086	26,981
Japan	65,552	0
Malaysia	150,158	838,285
New Zealand	2,578	0
Pakistan	79,451	1,047
Philippines	55,416	4,405
Singapore	0	14,155
South Korea	112,250	0
Taiwan	7,075	316
Thailand	20,240	16,906
Asian Total	603,911	4,661,578
1996 Asian Total	2,211,508	N/a
1996 World Total	4,619,458	N/a

Source: Motion Picture Association; TableBase™ (2001) Accession# 1488260.

On the legislative front, the handover of Hong Kong to China in 1997 had significant impact on piracy. Due to the change of the Hong Kong status from a British Crown Colony to that of PRC's Hong Kong Special Administration Region (HKSAR), the Hong Kong Legislative Council (LegCo) was rushing against the clock trying to update the antiquated 1956 British law before the handover on 1 July.[12]

Thus, on 27 June 1997, just days before the handover, the enactment of a localized Copyright Ordinance to govern copyright matters in the HKSAR went into effect, changing the legal landscape of the anti-piracy effort in the post-handover Hong Kong. It brought Hong Kong closer to the full compliance with the requirements of the TRIPS Agreement, the new WIPO Copyright Treaty (WCT), and WIPO Performances and Phonograms Treaty (WPPT) (see USTR Special 301 Country Report, Hong Kong, 1998). In the same year and immediately following the handover, the new HKSAR also implemented additional reforms under the Import and Export Ordinance to require disclosure and licensing of import and export of optical media manufacturing facilities.

As a result of the newly implemented Copyright Ordinance, 1998 witnessed progress in anti-piracy efforts. With the passing of the new law, the HKSAR effectively deployed a new legal weapon. Because of its status as a producer and exporter of pirated goods, however, Hong Kong still remained on the Watch List in 1998. Furthermore, while there had been progress in the legal front of the piracy problem, the piracy situation was deteriorating. To bring the issue to the public's attention, on 17 March 1999, all Hong Kong cinemas were closed for one day. This cinema blackout was accompanied by an "anti-piracy march," a protest of local copyright industries and celebrities, with actor Jackie Chan being the most visible participant. As part of their plea to the Legislative Council (LegCo), the copyright industries asked for an amendment to the Organized and Serious Crimes Ordinance (OSCO), that serious copyright offenses be included in Schedule I of the OSOC (see "Joint Appeal to Members of the Legislative Council, HKSAR," 1999).

One way to ensure that local or national anti-piracy policies are consistent with those of international standards is through local legislation process. Local law implementation of international treaties or agreements is an interesting indication of the complex working of the globalization process. It illustrates the intricate relations among the state, transnational trade and legal regimes, and transnational corporations. On 12 January 2000, Hong Kong's Legislative Council passed a bill that placed copyright offenses under the territory's Organized and Serious Crimes Ordinance (OSCO), a very significant progress for copyright owners (see Mok, 2000; personal attendance of LegCo sessions, December 1999 and January 2000; personal interview, Michael C. Ellis, vice president and director, Motion Picture Association Asia/Pacific Anti-Piracy Operation, 1 June 2000, Hong Kong). As a result of OSCO, manufacturers of pirated goods face heavier penalties that include a maximum fine of HK$50,000 (US$6,400) or four years' imprisonment per each disc seized, plus the confiscation of assets. Before the OSCO amendment, the maximum sanction was a total fine of HK$500,000 (US$64,000) or a total of two years' imprisonment (Mok, 2000). Backers of the amendment are local and international copyright owners' trade organizations such as Motion Picture Industry Association (MPIA) of Hong Kong, Kowloon, and the New Territories, the International Federation of the Phonographic Industry (IFPI)–Hong Kong Group, Software Publishers Association, Business Software Alliance, Hong Kong Optical Disc Manufacturers Association, Interactive Digital Software Association, and Motion Picture Association (see An Open Letter and Appeal to LegCo, 1999). The most vocal opponent of the move was Optical Disc Manufacturing and Technologies Association (ODMTA) with sixty active members (personal attendance of LegCo sessions, December 1999; personal interviews, Mike Ellis and Sam Ho, MPA, 1 June 2000; and Ricky Fung, CEO, IFPI-Hong Kong Group, 26 May 2000). They argued that the amendment unfairly targeted the CD plants and urged LegCo to exempt the CD manufacturing sector from the amendment or grant the CD plants a grace period (Joint Appeal to LegCo, 1999; personal attendance of LegCo sessions, December 1999). They also advocated the set up of a "copyright registry" that would handle issues of copyright verification process (An Open Letter to the LegCo, December, 1999).

The passing of the bill was a welcome legal development to the copyright industries as they had long been lobbying the HKSAR government to update and change what they perceived to be inadequate regulation and law enforcement measures. The USTR, for instance, had always viewed the inadequacy of penalty levels as the principal shortcoming of the Hong Kong IPR enforcement

Table 10.11. VCD Piracy Development in Hong Kong

Year	Events
1995	VCD arrives; Special Mention Status; Flow—PRC to HK in Bulk; HK as destination, market, and transshipment location.
1996	VCD takes over; Hong Kong itself becomes producer; there are other production sources outside of the Mainland, including Hong Kong.
1997	Explosive growth of digital piracy; reversing the flow; Priority Watch List. The problem of import piracy has turned into one of production and export piracy, including to the Mainland.
1998	A producer, distributor, retailer, and exporter of pirated goods; Watch List; Hong Kong adopts new regulations and anti-piracy strategies that show results.
1999	Blackout day; Watch List; because of the anti-piracy efforts the Hong Kong government initiated, 1999 was the last year that Hong Kong was placed on the USTR Special 301 Watch List; subsequent annul USTR Special 301 Decisions and Country Reports did not include Hong Kong.
2000	OSCO Hong Kong Legislative Council (LegCo) passes a bill that places copyright offenses under the territory's Organized and Serious Crimes Ordinance (OSCO), an important legal step for the copyright owners.

Source: Compiled from IIPA country reports.

regime (USTR Special 301 Decisions, 1996). Even though in 1996 Hong Kong adopted amendments to its copyright law, the government failed to achieve two key objectives: bringing Hong Kong's law into full compliance with the TRIPS Agreement and ensuring that Hong Kong would return to China with an updated copyright law. Both are keys in understanding the process of legislation developments in Hong Kong, one global, the other local (see table 10.11).

Finally, judging from the phases of piracy rate, movements, and directions in Hong Kong, they are also tied to the overall economic developments in the region. The problem was exacerbated by the Asian economic collapse in the second half of the 1990s. Many formerly legitimate optical disc manufacturers started moonlighting at night after regular hours of operations (see Tanzer, 1998).

Parallel Import

Contrary to authorized distribution and illegitimate piracy, parallel import is a gray and murky site situated between the legal and the illegal, the authorized and the unauthorized, and between distribution and piracy. It refers to the flow of those products manufactured in a designated and authorized geographic area with the contractual consent of the copyright owner into a different and unauthorized geographic area (see Morr, 1999). It occurs when "an authentic branded product comes into the domestic market through marketing channels that rival the product's authorized channels" (Weigand, 1991:53, cited in Ang 2000:509). In other words, parallel imports are genuine products that do not involve unauthorized product alterations and should not be confused with counterfeiting. It is thus not the production (or rather the reproduction) part of the process that invites questioning, given that it is legitimate and beyond legal reprimand. Rather, it is the *circulation* of these genuine products that creates a challenge to the geographical divisions of the market order (see, for example, Davison, 1997). Ultimately, these goods may be reimported back into the copyright owners' own domestic market.

Parallel importers provide an alternative supply of products to retailers, importers, and ultimately consumers. The challenge to exclusive licensees is market competition, as parallel importers are able to undercut prices offered by copyright owners and exclusive licensees due to currency differences and low promotional costs. Because the licensed product is imported into an unauthorized market, even though the products are legally reproduced, the act of importing constitutes an infringement on the exclusive geographic domain. Its other label of the "gray market imports" reflects such murkiness in what parallel import implicates.

Like piracy, parallel importing disrupts the spatial security, geographic monopolies, and temporal management of transnational media corporations' global operations and strategies. Parallel importing can be especially detrimental to the film industry, given that the global profits of film distribution rely mostly on the success of the spatial and temporal control of the release windows. The fact that these rights are sold along geographical and product lines adds to the urgency of maintaining a stable geographic market order.

In Hong Kong, parallel import was not banned until the new copyright law took effect. On 27 June 1997, a few days before the handover of Hong Kong to China, Hong Kong's LegCo enacted the Copyright Ordinance of 1997 (see Morr, 1999) that bans parallel importing. Violation of the parallel importing ban entails four years of imprisonment and a HK$50,000 fine (approximately US$6,400, see Burpee, 1997a; Morr, 1999). The Copyright Ordinance was the first change in Hong Kong's copyright law since the 1956 Copyright Act, passed under rule by the United Kingdom. The difference between the 1956 Copyright Act and the 1997 Copyright Ordinance regarding parallel importing is that the 1956 Act excluded it from the definition of infringing copy, whereas the Copyright Ordinance alters this exclusion. With the Ordinance, once a parallel importer produces a work in any area, the Hong Kong licensee can take criminal action against such an offense within the first eighteen months of the product's first production date, after which the licensee can only file a civil proceeding (Morr, 1999). Part of the general copyright regulation reform in Hong Kong, the parallel importing ban is also directly related to the urgency to update the antiquated colonial British laws for the handover of Hong Kong to Chinese rule in 1997 (see, for example, Burpee, 1997a and b; Burpee and McClure, 1996).

The enactment of such a ban caused heated debates and resentment among different groups. In general, those who support the ban are those whose profits are protected by the parallel importing ban, namely, copyright owners and their local licensees, since such a ban facilitates geographical divisions. Those who oppose the ban are local retailers, consumers, as well as parallel importers, who would gain from a *code-free environment of circulation*. An authorized licensee usually incurs high expenditures in promotion that includes pre-sales advertising and post-sales service, as well as other distribution costs. Parallel importers, like their pirate counterparts, normally reap the profit from the legitimate distributors. For the authorized licensees, consequently, the main argument favoring the ban is that parallel importing squeezes their profit margin. The retailers and consumers, on the other hand, criticize authorized licensees' monopolized control of the market, unfair competition, and limited selection and supply (see table 10.12).

Parallel importing put the copyright owners and their exclusive licensees squarely at odds with retailers and consumers. Those who support the ban argue that parallel importers take advantage of the difference in currency rates and in labor costs, thereby providing consumers with competitively priced merchandise. By further taking advantage of the exclusive local licensees' distribution networks and their marketing and advertising campaigns, parallel importers

Table 10.12. Parallel Importing Ban: Pros and Cons

Proponents	Opponents
Copyright Owners; Licensees	Retailers; Consumers; Parallel Importers
Arguments for Parallel Importing Ban	**Arguments against Parallel Importing Ban**
Unfair competition	Fair competition
Profit margin at risk and squeezed	Consumer choice
P.I. disrupts windowing strategies	Price reduction
Better quality control of product	Increased speed
Local industries need protection	Increased selections
Incentive for investment in local production	Ban would cause inefficiency
Development of local culture	Ban would cause protectionism
	Ban would cause decreased supply
	Ban would limit access
	Ban would lead to monopolies
	Ban would limit international repertoire
	Ban would hurt retailers
	Ban would hurt public as well as author interest

Source: Compiled from Morr, 1999; Burpee 1997a and b; Burppee and McClure, 1996; Davison, 1997; and personal interview with Andrew Wong, 30 May 2000.

squeeze the exclusive licensees and copyright owners' profit margin and put their business at risk. Conversely, those who are opposed to the ban cite negative effects of protectionism and monopolies. To them, such a ban creates unfair competition. Parallel importers also take a pro-consumer stand with arguments of selection, price, efficiency, diversity, access, and better supply that parallel importing can provide.

The new parallel import ban has no doubt caused much resistance from retailers in Hong Kong. Before the current ban, parallel imported goods accounted for one-third to one-half of stock of such major retailers as HMV, Tower, and the local chain KPS (see Morr, 1999, Burpee, 1997a). It is obvious that with the ban on parallel importing, retailers suffer from limited sources of supplies. With the Asian economic crisis, the rampant piracy rate, the current ban on parallel importing, and the resulting monopolies, many retailers believe they would likely be put out of business (see Ang, 2000; Burpee, 1997b).

That the Copyright Ordinance of 1997 treats piracy and parallel importing as a single problem invites further concern among retailers. To them it works as a disincentive to the international entertainment product trade (see Morr, 1999). Keith Cahoon, managing director of Tower Records Far East, for example, points out that "equating parallel imports with piracy is completely outrageous. When we're talking about major labels, [revenues] end up in the same pocket. It's just a matter of territories" (quoted in Burpee and McClure, 1996, p. 2).

His comment touches on one of the most crucial issues in the parallel importing ban in Hong Kong: It is precisely the "matter of territories" that matters. With the handover of Hong Kong to the Mainland, the already porous coastal lines along the Mainland will become even harder to control. Hong Kong's proximity to the Mainland has become a major concern for international copyright holders. Furthermore, with the heavy traffic and extensive volume of import, export, re-import, and re-export between the two territories, it will be "difficult to differentiate between parallel imports and pirated goods at the border" (Ricky Fung, International Federation of the Phonographic Industry, quoted in Burpee, 1997b). The real problem with parallel importing, in that case, lies in the fact that the low production and labor costs in Mainland China make for an ideal situation for parallel importing. Products earmarked for sale on the Mainland, for example, are re-exported or re-imported back to Hong Kong at a much lower price than their local counterparts can offer, thereby creating vast profit for parallel importers while hurting exclusive licensees (see Burpee, 1997b; Burpee and McClure, 1996).[13]

Flexible Spaces

Mol and Law (1994:658) differentiate between network and fluid space in that networks consist of a series of elements with well-defined relations, while in a fluid space one finds "variation without boundaries and transformation without discontinuity." If legitimate distribution consists of what one might term "network," then piracy networks are much more fluid and flexible than their authorized counterparts.

Figure 10.1 is a preliminary map of the three forms of film distribution in Hong Kong: legitimate/authorized distribution, illegitimate distribution (piracy), and the gray market import (parallel importing). I use dotted lines to represent both the piracy and parallel importing networks and to signify the smoother and more or less codeless environment they operate in.[14] The shapes I chose to represent the three networks are indicative of the movements and fluidity of these networks.

As illustrated, with their porous (network) boundaries, multiple directions, exit and entry points, piracy and parallel importing networks are far more adaptive than their legitimate and authorized counterpart. Memberships to the legitimate and formal networks, on the other hand, are much better defined with clearly demarcated and exclusive boundaries. The operations of such networks tend to be centralized and fixed. It is also clear from the map that all three networks are defined by their proximity and affinity to the Mainland and its 1.3 billion strong market. The fact that China is now a WTO member has made it an even more open and attractive market. Finally, because not all networks are equal, as each comes with a unique set of relations and configurations with various intensities, the different natures and forms of these networks have great implications for their respective operations and the ensuing strength. Comparatively speaking, then, piracy networks and, to a lesser extent, parallel importing operate in fluid spaces. In a global information economy, it is such a flexible and

Figure 10.1. Map of Piracy, Parallel Import, and Distribution in Hong Kong

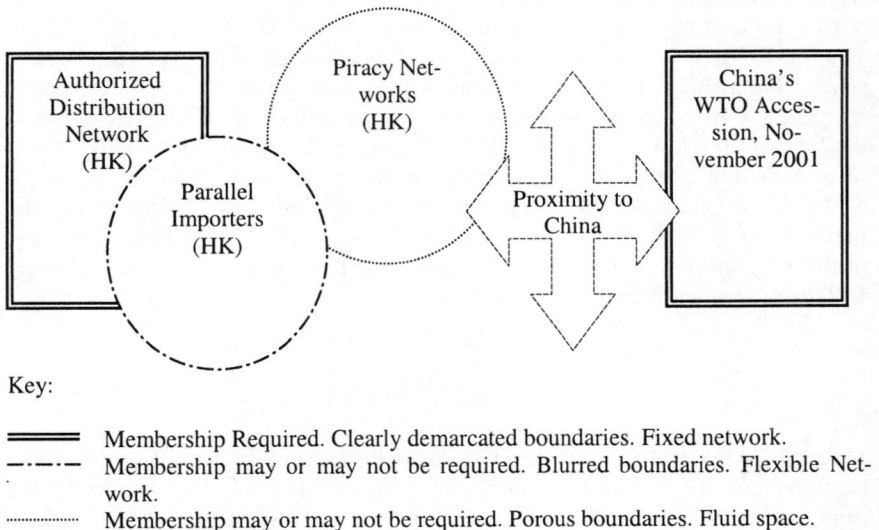

Key:

━━━━━ Membership Required. Clearly demarcated boundaries. Fixed network.
─·─·─ Membership may or may not be required. Blurred boundaries. Flexible Network.
············ Membership may or may not be required. Porous boundaries. Fluid space.

adaptable fluidity that affords them these competitive advantages and disrupts the spatial security of the Hollywood majors (as well as other such transnational players).

Notes

1. Like other major transnational corporations with headquarters in Hong Kong, the fact that Hong Kong is the "gateway to China" (personal interview, Bill Kong, executive director, Edko Films, 27 June 2000, Hong Kong) is very significant.

2. Hong Kong's major export markets are the Chinese Mainland, the United States, and the EU. They made up 37.2 percent, 21.8 percent, and 14.4 percent, respectively, of Hong Kong's total exports in the seven-month period to July 2001. See Hong Kong Trade Development Council, 2001.

3. Note that because the currency exchange rate between Hong Kong and the United States remained unchanged, the decreases in ticket prices shown in table 10.2 are actual lowered prices.

4. Warner Bros. Asia, for example, began in the early 1990s. Prior to that Warner worked with local licensees.

5. Paul Hanneman's background is finance.

6. Personal interview, Andrew Wong, Principal, Wong and Choy Architecture Ltd., 30 May 2000. Wong is one of the first and best-known cinema architects and he designed several of the multiplexes in Hong Kong.

7. Note that Media Asia is affiliated with UA and distribute Miramax films in Hong Kong, but its market share is not as high as the other major distributors. It is nevertheless a very important player in both local and global distribution and production.

8. The past several years also witnessed a reverse flow of filmic products. In addition to *CTHD* and Bill Kong's Edko, Media Asia is another one of the integrated and multifaceted production, distribution, library, and distribution studios that are actively seeking to distribution its productions overseas. Personal interview, Thomas Chung, February 2000, American Film Market, Santa Monica.

9. Domestic films are in general released on four chains: Empire Circuit, Newport Circuit, Gala Film Distribution, and Big Mandarin Cinema Circuit (Thomas and O'Brien, 2001).

10. Personal interviews, John P. Alonte, vice president, Warner Bros. International Theatrical Distribution Asia, 31 May 2000; Paul W. Hanneman, senior vice president, Twentieth Century Fox International Asia/Pacific Regional Office, and Sandra Low, Marketing Manager, Twentieth Century Fox Hong Kong, 22 December 1999. See also *Screen Digest*, 1998, TableBase 2001, Accession# 1576296.

11. The large-scale pirated optical discs produced in Asia are not limited to circulating only within Asia. Latin America, for example, has been a popular destination for these pirated optical discs. One of the more common routes includes transshipment within Southeast Asia, flight to Miami, brought through Panama to Paraguay for packaging, and then finally distribution in Brazil (see Fuller, 2000, and Tanzer, 1998).

12. Furthermore, its design legislation was written in 1949 while its trademarks legislation was based on a U.K. statute that was written in 1938 (see Tackaberry, 1997).

13. A potential problem lies in the discrepancy between the copyright ordinance of 1997 and the Intellectual Property (WTO Amendments) Ordinance of 1996. The improved border control provisions of these amendments do not apply to parallel importing.

Instead there is a two-tiered border control system with separate procedures for parallel importing and for pirated goods (see IIPA Special 301 Country Report, Hong Kong, 1997).

14. It is important to note here that while there are still rules that pirates and parallel importers would have to abide by, they are much more flexible than the formal laws and regulations that their legitimate counterparts would have to follow.

11

Framing Piracy:
On Piracy, Distribution, and the State

So far I have attempted to map the patterns of transnational copyright governance and the issues of film piracy, the role of the state and its relations with transnational trade and legal regimes, global film distribution and Hollywood's struggle to maintain control of property and the market, and the impacts of digital technologies on the spatial and temporal logic of the market.

The unique popularity and prevalence of VCD players in Asia attest to important processes of reterritorialization, reembedding, and, most of all, translation. Philips, Sony, and other major transnational electronics corporations have been setting and defining the order of international optical media (i.e., CD, CD-R, VCD, and DVD) formats and standards. The VCD phenomenon in Asia constitutes a rare case of defiance toward major global corporations. Pirates and manufacturers, with the indirect blessing of the state *and* consumers, were able to turn a soon-to-be-obsolete technology around to their advantage and meet the local businesses' and consumers' interests, while actively and reflexively defining their position vis-à-vis the global economy.[1] To combat VCD piracy, Hollywood majors had to go back to a format they had long declared obsolete and produce VCD versions of their films for the Asian markets. VCD in Asia thus serves as an important example of a reversed flow of electronics standards while defining a new global order according to local needs and interests.[2]

The windowing strategies long practiced by Hollywood, as well as the policing and classification of regional DVD zones by MPAA and the DVD Copy Control Association (DVD CCA) to prevent foreign DVD markets from stepping out of line, have proven to be ineffective.[3] Through the aid of digital technology and the operations in a more or less code-free environment, piracy networks have managed to undermine and challenge the copyright industries' critical attempts to command space and control time. Therefore, while Hollywood products are dominant in the global popular cultural landscape, it is increasingly difficult for the majors to control the distribution of these products.[4]

Ultimately the unprecedented focus on piracy and copyright attests to a global economy in which the control and command of space through time via digital technologies is of utmost importance and in which distribution networks are pivotal in maintaining transnational operations and market extension. As copyright industries are becoming increasingly the leading economic sector in the West, what are being traded in many cases are precisely intellectual property *rights*, or more precisely *bundles of rights*.[5] What ensures the proper functioning of the global information economy then is copyright protection. Piracy consequently becomes a major, if not *the* major, threat to the copyright industries.

Furthermore, contrary to international real property trade laws' institutionalizing government *withdrawal from* markets, international IP treaties and agreements institutionalize government *intervention into* markets (Ryan, 1998). As the Greater China cases show, transnational legal and trade regimes such as WIPO, WTO, and GATT rely heavily on state laws to conform to the respective treaties and agreements to ensure their effectiveness. Hence, the dynamic relations between the global and the national become extremely intricate. The various unilateral (e.g., sanctions), bilateral (e.g., USTR and Special 301), and multilateral (e.g., WIPO, TRIPS) anti-piracy strategies currently practiced further attest to the complexity and difficulty of copyright protection on the "local" level.

The dialectic here is also that even though the "global grid," albeit partial and strategic, seems to be cutting across the North-South divide, as Sassen (2000) has rightly suggested, transnational copyright protection regimes are very much operating along the North-South divide where the North maintains that the weak copyright laws and anti-piracy enforcement in the South have caused most of the North's copyright industries' profit losses, and where the North demands that the South comply with the copyright protection regulations and agreements authored mostly by the North and in its interests.

Finally, the increasing emphasis on copyright protection points to the pivotal role digital technologies play in global trade. The rapidly changing spatiotemporal dynamics and configurations afforded by these technologies have radically changed the nature of "property" and market, the balance of power, and the relations and means of production, distribution, and reception/consumption. The economic, technological, and conceptual separation of content from the medium thus has implications not only for piracy but also for theory (Boyle, 1996). These configurations and changes accentuate the urgent need for a new theoretical framework and a shifting paradigm, as existing theories are insufficient in examining these increasingly complex issues. By taking into account not only the fixed and the enduring but also the processes and the variable, a process- and network-oriented spatial theoretical and methodological framework is more adequate. It provides an encompassing and timely tool for examining the complexity of, and interconnections among, issues of distribution, copyright, piracy, the state, and globalization.

The Networks

Contexts too flow locally through networks, be these geography, medicine, statistics, economics, or even sociology. . . . Each locus can be seen as framing and summing up.

—Bruno Latour (1999:18)

Viewed in the contexts of networks and of framing and summing up, film piracy and distribution in Greater China represent the intersection and transformation/deformation of various circulating entities. Because of the constantly shifting alliances and connections among piracy networks, the state, manufacturers, consumers, distributors, and a complex group of other relations, they also represent different topological possibilities (see Law, 1999). The circulating nature of capital and digital technologies further accelerates the rate of realignments and changes in the topology.

The Actor Network Theory is a conceptual way of mapping that is not pregiven. It addresses the links and the connections on and between networks, and how actors both define and are defined by the networks. Given that circulation and flows always involve directions, velocities, and forces, they result in the redefinition of boundaries (e.g., geographical, social, cultural). They also attest to the dynamic relations among various mechanisms of deterritorialization, disembedding, and those of reterritorialization and reembedding. It is thus important to consider Latour's definition of "network" as a concept that designates "a series of transformations—translations, transductions," as opposed to the word "network" now popularized in the world of information technology, where it means "transport *without* deformation" (1999:15).

In the case of film piracy and distribution in Greater China, then, such entities as global IPR treaties and agreements; images and products that are moved across borders legitimately and illegitimately; international electronic developments and standards; and the distributor and exhibitor dynamics have all gone through various transformations, deformations, and changes in their framed interactions with local sets of relations and forces. Figure 11.1 represents an initial effort to map some of the movements and circulations of these networks of film distribution and piracy in Greater China. With their divergent political and economic systems, their different positions vis-à-vis global trade regimes, the complex and contested relations among them, and shared cultural traditions, Mainland China, Taiwan, and Hong Kong offer us a fascinating glimpse into an important area in which power relations are shifting and dynamics are in formation. The three different forms of state governance also greatly shape the processes of globalization and regionalization.

Figure 11.1 is a preliminary attempt to conceptualize how different networks constitute and redefine different spaces in the case of film piracy and distribution in Greater China.

Figure 11.1. Map of Intersecting and Circulating Networks

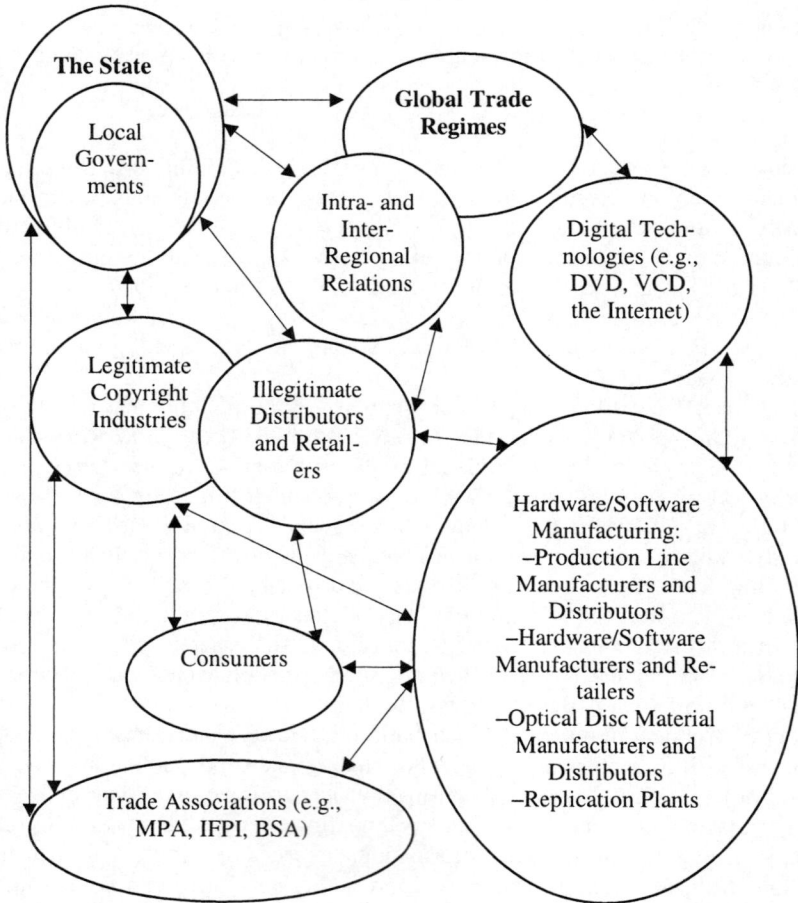

As the map illustrates, piracy and distribution involve complex, interrelated, and dynamic relations among different networks and actors, as well as multiple structures of power. Both piracy and distribution, for example, operate within multiple contexts of law, trade, technology, and the state. Consumers likewise deal with nonhuman objects (e.g., VCDs) that present different meanings. Through these objects, the consumers reinterpret their *already transnational* economic and cultural realities. The study of piracy and distribution helps us understand how, through transnational networks, people make decisions and meanings of the world, selecting and translating signs and objects that make sense to them. It is also about how different actors live in relation to other actors and networks, and how they live through different spaces created by the interaction and intersection of various networks. One such example is that various spaces of reterritorialized Hollywood culture are not simply reproduced, they are instead actively translated and reinterpreted by different actors and networks such as pirates, local distributors, the state, and consumers.

As the foregoing analysis suggests, while there are relatively entrenched structures of domination and subordination, these power relations are never static. The different roles of the transnational trade regimes, the state, technology, transnational copyright industries, and various market forces, and the interrelated *and* disjunctured relations among them, have been ambiguous and paradoxical at best. I hope what I have done with this pursuit is what Callon and Latour (1981:301) have described in their 1981 work:

> For the sociologist then the question of method boils down to knowing where to place oneself. Like Hobbes himself, he or she sits just at the point where the contract is made, just where forces are translated, and the difference between the technical and the social is fought out, just where the irreversible becomes reversible and where the chreods reverse their slopes. There, only a tiny amount of energy is necessary to drag a maximum of information about its growth from the newborn monster.

This book touches only the surface of this complex, fascinating, and fast-changing cross-section of the multiple and contradictory processes of globalization.

Notes

1. Perhaps piracy and reflexivity are best explained in the sort of power that Hardt and Negri (2000:363) see as intrinsic to circulation and mixture. They view this power as part and parcel of what Marx defines as "liberation" as opposed to "emancipation." Emancipation is simply the entry of new nations and peoples into the "imperial society of control," whereas liberation denotes the "destruction of boundaries and patterns of forced migration, the reappropriation of space, and the power of the multitude to determine the global circulation and mixture of individuals and populations." By reflexively consuming pirated goods, the consumers are claiming the power to circulate. By participating in the process, they are in their own way engaging in the formation of a new global culture and a global consciousness.

2. It is important to note here that pirated film content, while varied, remains largely Hollywood oriented.

3. These rights are linked to territory, more precisely demography of marketing, which transcends borders, yet at the same time reimposes them. Furthermore, through the production of DVD players that overwrite the zoning restriction (which most Asian players are), hardware manufacturers work with pirates in increasing the consumers' selections.

4. Although some of the pirates and optical disc manufacturers I interviewed believed that Hollywood majors benefited from piracy because it opened new markets the majors could incorporate.

5. In the post-Fordist environment of flexible production, outsourcing, and vertical disintegration, and in the recent waves of conglomerate merger frenzy, what becomes "core" of the culture and information industries, in Lash and Urry's views (1994), is the exchange of finance by a given firm for not just intellectual property rights but for also "a bundle of" IP rights (p. 135). By "a bundle of rights" they mean that increasingly a number of firms would share these rights, which often come under the heading of "copyright." The typical use of IP rights in the information and culture industries is to "copy" and sell intellectual property. Therefore, the main production process in culture and information industries is the "copying of already acquired intellectual property" (p. 135). The protection of copyright becomes indispensable to the information and culture industries.

Appendix A

Notes on Methodology and List of Interviews

On Methodology

This project took a three-prong approach, including in-depth interviews, field observations, and library/archival research, to examine the issues at hand. The multimethod strategy is advantageous as it provides for more valid results than a single method strategy (see, for example, Jensen and Jankowski, 1991).

Zelditch (1970) constructed a typology, which suggests that participant observation is best suited for case studies and life histories, while interviewing is an efficient and best form for studies of organizations. To truly understand a complex and sensitive issue such as global film distribution and piracy, it seems crucial that one not only conduct a thorough library and archival research but also in-depth, qualitative observation and interviewing of the organizations, places, and people involved.

1. In-Depth Interviewing. The following are some of the localities and individuals where and with whom in-depth interviews were conducted.

   - Film Markets: International film sellers and buyers were interviewed at American Film Market in Santa Monica in February and March, 2000 and 2001.
   - Hong Kong and Taiwan: Local as well as Hollywood film distributors, government policy makers, anti-piracy personnel, and local filmmakers and scholars were interviewed.
   - Mainland China: In-depth interviews were conducted with government policy makers in Beijing; film distributors, VCD/DVD plant owners, and anti-piracy personnel in Beijing, Tianjin, Shanghai, and Guangzhou; street pirates in Beijing, Shanghai, and Guangzhou; international film producers in

Beijing; as well as local scholars and critics in Beijing.

2. Field Observation. Since piracy is closely related to crime organizations, one of the best ways to effectively yet safely collect information and arrive at meaningful and useful conclusions is through local contacts and field observation. I spent extensive time in parts of Hong Kong and China where most of the counterfeit products could be found.

3. Library and archival research. The qualitative interviews and observational research were supported by archival, legal, and statistical data and research.

List of Interviews

The following is a list of the interviewees and the location and time of the research fieldwork. Note that traditionally Chinese names begin with the surname. To differentiate those from the ones that follow a Western tradition of placing the given name before the surname, I capitalized the surnames.

1. Summer 1999: Field research, data collection, and in-depth interviews in Taiwan. In-depth interviews were conducted with:
   - Rudy Tseng, Vice President, Buena Vista Film Co. Ltd
   - Eric Shih, General Manager, Warner Bros.
   - Josephine Chen, Marketing Manager, Twentieth Century Fox Taiwan
   - Simon Huang, Marketing Manager-Taiwan, United Artists; Paramount; Universal; MGM
   - Frank Chen, Director, Government Information Office, Dept of Motion Picture Affairs, Taiwan
   - Wolf Chen, Vice President, Era Communications
   - WU Yii-feng, Director, Full Shot Communication Foundation
   - Wen-Chi Lin, Professor of Film Studies and Chair, English Dept., National Central University
   - Ru-Shou Chen, Assoc. Prof., Dept. of Motion Pictures, National Taiwan College of Arts
   - Neil Peng, Editor, *Entertainment Weekly*, *China Times*

2. Winter 1999: Field research in Hong Kong. Interviews:
   - Paul W. Hanneman, Senior Vice President, Twentieth Century Fox International
   - Sandra Low, Marketing Manager, Twentieth Century Fox Hong Kong
   - Joe Yan, Vice President, Buena Vista International
   - Sam Ho, Asst. Director, Asia/Pacific Anti-Piracy Operations, Motion Picture Association
   - Woody Tsung, Chief Executive, Motion Picture Industry Association

- Cecilia Yau, Director, Era Films (HK) Limited
- Ricky Fung, Chief Executive Officer, International Federation of the Phonographic Industry (IFPI)
- Patrick Chan, Senior Operations Manager, HK Film and Video Security Ltd. Affiliated with MPA
- Jimmy Choi, Director, Film and Video Dept., Hong Kong Arts Center

3. February/March 2000: American Film Market in Santa Monica, Calif. Interviews:

- Ann Hung, General Manager, China Star Entertainment Ltd.
- Samuel Ha, Sales Manager, Cineclick.com
- Thomas Chung, Group Managing Director, Media Asia Group
- Andrew Leung, Managing Director, Era Home Entertainment
- Boniface Chan, Managing Director, Era Productions (USA)
- Tina Shah, Global Film Distributors (for the Indian subcontinent)
- Winnie Tsang, Managing Director, Golden Scene
- Clarence Tang, Director, Golden Network Ltd.
- Jackie Kwak, Kangjegyu Film (Korea)

4. Summer 2000: Field Research in Hong Kong and China. Interviews:
Hong Kong

- John P. Alonte, Vice President, Warner Bros. International Theatrical Distribution
- Molly E. Kellogg, Vice President, Asia Anti-Piracy and New Market Development, Warner Home Video
- Michael J. Werner, Supervisor, China, Twentieth Century Fox International
- Tim Meade, Director, Sales and Marketing, China, Columbia Tri-Star Home Video
- Li Chow, General Manager, Edko Columbia Tri-Star Films
- Michael C. Ellis, Vice President and Director, Asia/Pacific Anti-Piracy Operations, Motion Picture Association International
- Louisa Chan, General Manager, UIP International
- William Kong, Executive Director, Edko Films Ltd.
- John Hsu, Director, Finance and Business Affairs, Intercontinental Group Holdings Ltd.
- Duncan E. E. Chang, President, Linfair Engineering and Trading Ltd.

Beijing, China
- HUANG Xiao Xin, Division Chief, The PRC Press and Publication Administration
- ZHANG Hui Guang, Vice Director, PRC National Anti-Piracy and Pornography Working Committee
- Peter Loehr, Managing Director/Producer, IMAR Film
- ZHANG Lihui, General Manager, Warner Home Video
- Randy Ma, China Representative, Motion Picture Association
- Yong Wang, China Legal Counsel, Motion Picture Association
- ZHANG Hui-jun, Professor and Vice President, Beijing Film Academy
- LA Peikang, President, China Film International
- HE Ping, Consultant, Columbia Pictures Film Production Asia
- JIANG Ning Yuan, Managing Director, United East Audio and Video
- SHEN Hao, Professor, Beijing Broadcast Institute

Shanghai, China
- Michael Ma, Manager, Public Relations, Shanghai Maya Online
- WANG Jianhua, Division Head, Government Press and Publication Office, Shanghai
- YU Guoguang, Division Head, Copyright Office, Shanghai
- XIE Baoxin, President and CEO, Shanghai Paradise Co. Ltd.
- WANG Hao, Professor, Shanghai Institute of Optics and Fine Mechanics

Tianjing, China
- LEE Jian Cheng, President, TianBao Optical Disc Production

Guangzhou, China
- J. Andrew Coombs, Executive Counsel, the Walt Disney Company
- ZHONG Xiong Bing, Director, Guangdong Freeland Movie and Video
- ZHAO Jun, Vice President, Guangdong Films
- Pioneer Chang, Director, Golden Image Video and Audio International
- WU Yi Hong, Chief, Guangdong Provincial Cultural Investigation

5. February/March 2001: American Film Market in Santa Monica, Calif. Interviews:

- Wolf Chen, President and CEO, Mata Entertainment, Taiwan
- Michael J. Werner, Co-Chairman, Fortissimo
6. November 2001: Beijing, China
  - HUANG Xiao Xin, Division Chief, The PRC Press and Publication Administration
7. April/May 2002: Taipei, Taiwan
  - Wen-Hsiang Lu, Deputy Director General, Intellectual Property Office, Ministry of Economic Affairs, Chinese Taipei
  - Jill Chu, Intellectual Property Office, Ministry of Economic Affairs, Chinese Taipei
  - Hank Kwuo, Executive Director, Foundation for the Protection of Film and Video Works, Affiliated with Motion Picture Association
  - Wolf Chen, President and ECO, Mata Entertainment, Taiwan
8. May 2002: Beijing, China
  - Randy Ma, Marketing Manager, Business Software Association, China
  - Jian-Hong Yu, Associate Professor and Assistant President, Beijing Film Academy
9. June 2002: Boston
  - Justin Lin, former Section Chief, Intellectual Property Office, Ministry of Economic Affairs, Chinese Taipei
10. July 2002: Beijing, China
  - Gongmin Jiang, Deputy Director General, Management Committee of Beijing Radio Film and TV Group

Appendix B

VCD/DVD Examination Check-Sheet

Hong Kong Film and Video Security Ltd.
Affiliated with Motion Picture Association

VCD/DVD Examination Check-Sheet

Title: _____   Purchase Date: _____
Location: _____

1.   *Packaging*
    1.1 Distributor Logo Yes/No   1.5   LBR No. _____
    1.2 Studio Logo   Yes/No   1.6   Mould Code No. _____
    1.3 Printing   Sharp/Poor 1.7   Others
    1.4 Hologram Label Yes/No   _____

2.   *Copyright Information*
    2.1 Copyright   2.3   US VCD
        Owner _____   Released Date _____
    2.2 Theatrical/Video   2.4   US Theatrical
        Distributor _____   Released Date _____

3.   *Content of VCD*
    3.1 Distribution   Yes   /   No
    3.2 Studio Logo   Yes   /   No
    3.3 Local Warning Edition Yes   /   No
    3.4 Starring   Yes   /   No

3.7 Subtitle	Chinese/English/Japanese/Others
3.8 Version	Chinese/English/Japanese/Others
3.9 Source	Promotional Tape/LD/Video Tape/Cinema/ Cable TV/TV/Hotel/In-flight Movie/Others
3.10 Data Input Date	_____
3.11 Others	_____

4.   Conclusion: *Counterfeit*   *Original*   *Infringing*

Examined By   _____   Place   _____
Date   _____   Time   _____

Source: MPA Hong Kong.

Appendix C

Hollywood Majors' Home Video Releases in China

The following are titles approved by the Ministry of Culture for release in Mainland China between 1 January 1996 and 23 June 2000.[1]

Warner Bros./SAST

Title	Copyright Holder	Local Distributor	Format
1. *Bodyguard, The*	Warner Bros.	Xianke	VCD, LD, DVD
2. *Fugitive, The*	Warner Bros.	Xianke	VCD, LD, DVD
3. *Rain Man*	Warner Bros.	Xianke	VCD, LD
4. *Little Princess, A*	Warner Bros.	Xianke	VCD, LD, DVD
5. *Love Affair*	Warner Bros.	Xianke	VCD, LD
6. *Pelican Brief, The*	Warner Bros.	Xianke	VCD, DVD
7. *White Sands*	Warner Bros.	Xianke	VCD, LD
8. *Police Academy 1–7*	Warner Bros.	Xianke	VCD, LD, DVD
9. *Under Siege 2*	Warner Bros.	Xianke	VCD, LD
10. *Somersby*	Warner Bros.	Xianke	VCD, LD
11. *Bridges of Madison County*	Warner Bros.	Xianke	VCD, DVD
12. *Batman and Robin*	Warner Bros.	Xianke	VCD, LD
13. *Client, The*	Warner Bros.	Xianke	VCD, LD

Continued on next page

Warner Bros./SAST—Continued

Title	Copyright Holder	Local Distributor	Format
14. *Fearless*	Warner Bros.	Xianke	VCD, LD
15. *Innerspace*	Warner Bros.	Xianke	VCD, LD
16. *J.F.K.*	Warner Bros.	Xianke	VCD, LD
17. *Outbreak*	Warner Bros.	Xianke	VCD, LD
18. *Final Analysis*	Warner Bros.	Xianke	VCD, LD
19. *All the President's Men*	Warner Bros.	Xianke	VCD, DVD
20. *American in Paris, An*	Warner Bros.	Xianke	VCD
21. *Robin Hood: Prince of Thieves*	Warner Bros.	Xianke	VCD
22. *Batman*	Warner Bros.	Xianke	VCD
23. *Time to Kill, A*	Warner Bros.	Xianke	VCD, DVD
24. *Batman Forever*	Warner Bros.	Xianke	VCD
25. *Tin Cup*	Warner Bros.	Xianke	VCD, DVD
26. *Ben Hur*	Warner Bros.	Xianke	VCD
27. *Tom and Jerry*	Warner Bros.	Xianke	VCD
28. *Black Beauty*	Warner Bros.	Xianke	VCD
29. *World of the Animals*	Warner Bros.	Xianke	VCD
30. *Doctor Hollywood*	Warner Bros.	Xianke	VCD
31. *Free Willy 1–2*	Warner Bros.	Xianke	VCD, DVD
32. *Gigi*	Warner Bros.	Xianke	VCD
33. *Forever Young*	Warner Bros.	Xianke	VCD
34. *Life of Emil Zola*	Warner Bros.	Xianke	VCD
35. *History of Rock 'N Roll*	Warner Bros.	Xianke	VCD
36. *Meeting Venus*	Warner Bros.	Xianke	VCD
37. *Memphis Belle*	Warner Bros.	Xianke	VCD, DVD
38. *Dave*	Warner Bros.	Xianke	VCD, LD
39. *Nico: Above the Law*	Warner Bros.	Xianke	VCD, LD, DVD
40. *Stolen Hearts*	Warner Bros.	Xianke	VCD, LD
41. *Sun Chaser*	Warner Bros.	Xianke	VCD, LD
42. *Dangerous Liaisons*	Warner Bros.	Xianke	VCD, LD, DVD
43. *Hard to Kill*	Warner Bros.	Xianke	VCD, LD, DVD

Continued on next page

Warner Bros./SAST—Continued

Title	Copyright Holder	Local Distributor	Format
44. *Mad Max: Road Warrior*	Warner Bros.	Xianke	VCD, LD, DVD
45. *Pale Rider*	Warner Bros.	Xianke	VCD, LD
46. *Dirty Harry*	Warner Bros.	Xianke	VCD, LD, DVD
47. *Eraser*	Warner Bros.	Xianke	VCD, LD
48. *Maverick*	Warner Bros.	Xianke	VCD, LD
49. *Vegas Vacation*	Warner Bros.	Xianke	VCD, LD, DVD
50. *Color Purple*	Warner Bros.	Xianke	VCD, LD, DVD
51. *Fair Game*	Warner Bros.	Xianke	VCD, LD
52. *Secret Garden, The*	Warner Bros.	Xianke	VCD, LD
53. *Dead Pool, The*	Warner Bros.	Xianke	VCD, LD
54. *Nuts*	Warner Bros.	Xianke	VCD, LD
55. *Richie Rich*	Warner Bros.	Xianke	VCD, LD
56. *Right Stuff, The*	Warner Bros.	Xianke	VCD, LD, DVD
57. *Battle of the Bulge*	Warner Bros.	Xianke	VCD, LD
58. *Yigeguafu He Sangeqiangsho**	Warner Bros.	Xianke	VCD, LD
59. *Roots 1–6*	Warner Bros.	Xianke	VCD, LD
60. *Lethal Weapon 1–3*	Warner Bros.	Xianke	VCD, LD, DVD
61. *Fu Cho Zhe**	Warner Bros.	Xianke	VCD, DVD

*Original titles in English not provided.

Warner/Thakral/Dongfang Film and Music

Title	Copyright Holder	Local Distributor	Format
1. *Fire Down Below*	Warner Bros.	Dongfang	VCD, DVD
2. *Demolition Man*	Warner Bros.	Dongfang	VCD
3. *My Fellow Americans*	Warner Bros.	Dongfang	VCD, DVD
4. *Conspiracy Theory*	Warner Bros.	Dongfang	VCD, DVD
5. *Passenger 57*	Warner Bros.	Dongfang	VCD, DVD
6. *Tango and Cash*	Warner Bros.	Dongfang	VCD, DVD
7. *The Goonies*	Warner Bros.	Dongfang	VCD
8. *Prince of the City*	Warner Bros.	Dongfang	VCD

Continued on next page

Warner/Thakral/Dongfang Film and Music—Continued

Title	Copyright Holder	Local Distributor	Format
9. *Something to Talk About*	Warner Bros.	Dongfang	VCD
10. *Lean on Me*	Warner Bros.	Dongfang	VCD
11. *New Jack City*	Warner Bros.	Dongfang	VCD, DVD
12. *Trial by Jury*	Warner Bros.	Dongfang	VCD
13. *Addicted to Love*	Warner Bros.	Dongfang	VCD, DVD
14. *Blade Runner*	Warner Bros.	Dongfang	VCD, DVD
15. *Curly Sue*	Warner Bros.	Dongfang	VCD
16. *Diabolique*	Warner Bros.	Dongfang	VCD
17. *The Glimmer Man*	Warner Bros.	Dongfang	VCD
18. *Free Jack*	Warner Bros.	Dongfang	VCD
19. *Space Jam*	Warner Bros.	Dongfang	VCD, DVD
20. *Private Benjamin*	Warner Bros.	Dongfang	VCD
21. *Arthur*	Warner Bros.	Dongfang	VCD
22. *Outland*	Warner Bros.	Dongfang	VCD
23. *Wizard of Oz*	Warner Bros.	Dongfang	VCD
24. *Action Jackson*	Warner Bros.	Dongfang	VCD, DVD
25. *Devil's Advocate*	Warner Bros.	Dongfang	VCD
26. *Accidental Tourist*	Warner Bros.	Dongfang	VCD
27. *Born to be Wild*	Warner Bros.	Dongfang	VCD
28. *Clara's Heart*	Warner Bros.	Dongfang	VCD
29. *Day for Night*	Warner Bros.	Dongfang	VCD
30. *Fandango*	Warner Bros.	Dongfang	VCD
31. *Five Days One Summer*	Warner Bros.	Dongfang	VCD
32. *Imaginary Crimes*	Warner Bros.	Dongfang	VCD
33. *Joe vs. the Volcano*	Warner Bros.	Dongfang	VCD
34. *Major League II*	Warner Bros.	Dongfang	VCD
35. *Major League III*	Warner Bros.	Dongfang	VCD
36. *Men Don't Leave*	Warner Bros.	Dongfang	VCD
37. *Quick Change*	Warner Bros.	Dongfang	VCD
38. *Rookie, The*	Warner Bros.	Dongfang	VCD
39. *Round Midnight*	Warner Bros.	Dongfang	VCD
40. *So Fine*	Warner Bros.	Dongfang	VCD
41. *Towering Inferno, The*	Warner Bros.	Dongfang	VCD
42. *World According to Garp*	Warner Bros.	Dongfang	VCD

Fox/CAV—Thakral/Dongfang Film and Music

Title	Copyright Holder	Local Distributor	Format
1. *The X Files—Movie*	Fox	Dongfang	VCD
2. *Dr. Dolittle*	Fox	Dongfang	VCD
3. *Hope Floats*	Fox	Dongfang	VCD
4. *A Life Less Ordinary*	Fox	Dongfang	VCD
5. *Romeo and Juliet*	Fox	Dongfang	VCD
6. *Brave Heart*	Fox	Dongfang	VCD
7. *Picture Perfect*	Fox	Dongfang	VCD
8. *Volcano*	Fox	Dongfang	VCD
9. *Great Expectations*	Fox	Dongfang	VCD
10. *Aliens*	Fox	Dongfang	VCD
11. *Kiss of Death*	Fox	Dongfang	VCD
12. *The Edge*	Fox	Dongfang	VCD
13. *Speed*	Fox	Dongfang	VCD
14. *Speed II*	Fox	Dongfang	VCD
15. *Abyss*	Fox	Dongfang	VCD
16. *Alien*	Fox	Dongfang	VCD
17. *Alien III*	Fox	Dongfang	VCD
18. *Wall Street*	Fox	Dongfang	VCD
19. *Bad Girls*	Fox	Dongfang	VCD
20. *Siege*	Fox	Dongfang	VCD
21. *Eddie*	Fox	Dongfang	VCD
22. *Home for Holidays*	Fox	Dongfang	VCD
23. *Bulworth*	Fox	Dongfang	VCD
24. *Toys*	Fox	Dongfang	VCD
25. *Prelude to a Kiss*	Fox	Dongfang	VCD
26. *One Fine Day*	Fox	Dongfang	VCD
27. *Firestorm*	Fox	Dongfang	VCD
28. *Imposters*	Fox	Dongfang	VCD
29. *Office Space*	Fox	Dongfang	VCD
30. *A Cool Dry Place*	Fox	Dongfang	VCD
31. *Commando*	Fox	Dongfang	VCD
32. *Big*	Fox	Dongfang	VCD
33. *Titanic*	Fox	Dongfang	VCD, DVD

Warner/UEAV/China Film AV

Title	Copyright Holder	Local Distributor	Format
1. *Boys on the Side*	Warner Bros.	China Film	VCD
2. *Contact*	Warner Bros.	China Film	VCD, DVD
3. *Executive Decision*	Warner Bros.	China Film	VCD, DVD
4. *Wyatt Earp*	Warner Bros.	China Film	VCD
5. *Perfect World*	Warner Bros.	China Film	VCD, DVD
6. *Presumed Innocent*	Warner Bros.	China Film	VCD, DVD
7. *Tequila Sunrise*	Warner Bros.	China Film	VCD, DVD
8. *Last Boy Scout, The*	Warner Bros.	China Film	VCD
9. *One Crazy Summer*	Warner Bros.	China Film	VCD
10. *Impulse*	Warner Bros.	China Film	VCD
11. *Dead Calm*	Warner Bros.	China Film	VCD, DVD
12. *Frantic*	Warner Bros.	China Film	VCD, DVD
13. *On Deadly Ground*	Warner Bros.	China Film	VCD, DVD
14. *Greystoke*	Warner Bros.	China Film	VCD
15. *City Heat*	Warner Bros.	China Film	VCD
16. *Cobra*	Warner Bros.	China Film	VCD, DVD
17. *Gauntlet*	Warner Bros.	China Film	VCD
18. *Murder at 1600*	Warner Bros.	China Film	VCD, DVD
19. *Stand and Deliver*	Warner Bros.	China Film	VCD
20. *Swing Shift*	Warner Bros.	China Film	VCD
21. *Wild America*	Warner Bros.	China Film	VCD
22. *Wildcats*	Warner Bros.	China Film	VCD
23. *Enter the Dragon*	Warner Bros.	China Film	VCD, DVD
24. *Giant*	Warner Bros.	China Film	VCD, DVD
25. *One Flew over the Cuckoo's Nest*	Warner Bros.	China Film	VCD, DVD
26. *Running on Empty*	Warner Bros.	China Film	VCD
27. *Star is Born, A*	Warner Bros.	China Film	VCD
28. *Victory*	Warner Bros.	China Film	VCD
29. *Client*	Warner Bros.	China Film	DVD
30. *Doc Hollywood*	Warner Bros.	China Film	DVD
31. *Eraser*	Warner Bros.	China Film	DVD
32. *Father's Day*	Warner Bros.	China Film	DVD
33. *Forever Young*	Warner Bros.	China Film	DVD
34. *JFK*	Warner Bros.	China Film	DVD
35. *Maverick*	Warner Bros.	China Film	DVD
36. *Pale Rider*	Warner Bros.	China Film	DVD

Continued on next page

Warner/UEAV/China Film AV—Continued

Title	Copyright Holder	Local Distributor	Format
37. *2010: The Year We Make Contact*	Warner Bros.	China Film	DVD
38. *A Perfect Murder*	Warner Bros.	China Film	VCD, DVD
39. *Under Siege*	Warner Bros.	China Film	VCD, DVD
40. *Point of No Return*	Warner Bros.	China Film	VCD, DVD
41. *City of Angel*	Warner Bros.	China Film	VCD, DVD
42. *Body Heat*	Warner Bros.	China Film	VCD, DVD
43. *Altered States*	Warner Bros.	China Film	VCD, DVD
44. *Mars Attacks*	Warner Bros.	China Film	DVD
45. *2001: Space Odyssey*	Warner Bros.	China Film	DVD

Buena Vista Home Entertainment/Thakral/CAV

Title	Copyright Holder	Local Distributor	Format
1. *Preacher's Wife*	BVHE	CAV	VCD
2. *Terminal Velocity*	BVHE	CAV	VCD, DVD
3. *Crimson Tide*	BVHE	CAV	VCD
4. *Metro*	BVHE	CAV	VCD
5. *The Rock*	BVHE	CAV	VCD
6. *Shine*	BVHE	CAV	VCD
7. *Ransom*	BVHE	CAV	VCD
8. *While You Were Sleeping*	BVHE	CAV	VCD, DVD
9. *Phenomenon*	BVHE	CAV	VCD, DVD
10. *Con Air*	BVHE	CAV	VCD
11. *Starship Troopers*	BVHE	CAV	VCD, DVD
12. *When a Man Loves a Woman*	BVHE	CAV	VCD
13. *Nothing to Lose*	BVHE	CAV	VCD
14. *Dick Tracy*	BVHE	CAV	VCD
15. *Jack*	BVHE	CAV	VCD
16. *Three Men and a Little Baby*	BVHE	CAV	VCD

Continued on next page

Buena Vista Home Entertainment/Thakral/CAV—Continued

Title	Copyright Holder	Local Distributor	Format
17. Spy Hard	BVHE	CAV	VCD, DVD
18. Sister Act	BVHE	CAV	VCD
19. Sister Act II	BVHE	CAV	VCD
20. Father of the Bride II	BVHE	CAV	VCD
21. A Simple Twist of Fate	BVHE	CAV	VCD
22. Joy Luck Club	BVHE	CAV	VCD
23. Mr. Wrong	BVHE	CAV	VCD
24. Bad Company	BVHE	CAV	VCD
25. Last Dance	BVHE	CAV	VCD
26. A Low Down Dirty Shame	BVHE	CAV	VCD
27. Before and After	BVHE	CAV	VCD
28. Father of the Bride II	BVHE	CAV	VCD, DVD
29. Dangerous Minds	BVHE	CAV	VCD, DVD
30. Arachnophobia	BVHE	CAV	VCD, DVD
31. Horse Whisperer	BVHE	CAV	VCD, DVD
32. Krippendorf's Tribe	BVHE	CAV	VCD
33. Nightmare before Christmas	Disney	CAV	VCD
34. Celebrate with Mickey	Disney	CAV	VCD
35. Toy Story	Disney	CAV	VCD
36. Aladdin	Disney	CAV	VCD
37. Lion King	Disney	CAV	VCD
38. Pocahontas	Disney	CAV	VCD
39. Beauty and the Beast	Disney	CAV	VCD, DVD
40. Quiz Show	Disney	CAV	VCD
41. Tall Tale	Disney	CAV	VCD
42. A Far Off Place	Disney	CAV	VCD
43. Santa Clause, The	Disney	CAV	VCD
44. Starring Donald	Disney	CAV	VCD
45. Rescue Ranger—Crimebuster	Disney	CAV	VCD
46. Olympic Goofy	Disney	CAV	VCD

Continued on next page

Buena Vista Home Entertainment/Thakral/CAV—Continued

Title	Copyright Holder	Local Distributor	Format
47. *Pluto's Greatest Hits*	Disney	CAV	VCD
48. *Fun with English*	Disney	CAV	VCD
49. *Deep Rising*	BVHE	CAV	VCD, DVD
50. *Winnie the Pooh and Christmas Too*	BVHE	CAV	VCD
51. *Mickey's Christmas Carol*	BVHE	CAV	VCD
52. *Bambi*	BVHE	CAV	VCD
53. *Face Off*	BVHE	CAV	VCD, DVD
54. *Doctor, The*	BVHE	CAV	VCD
55. *Our First Disney Video*	BVHE	CAV	VCD
56. *Guilty as Sin*	BVHE	CAV	VCD
57. *Billy Bathgate*	BVHE	CAV	VCD
58. *Paradise*	BVHE	CAV	VCD
59. *Feast of July*	BVHE	CAV	VCD
60. *Green Card*	BVHE	CAV	VCD
61. *One Good Cop*	BVHE	CAV	VCD
62. *Powder*	BVHE	CAV	VCD, DVD
63. *Innocent Man*	BVHE	CAV	VCD
64. *Consenting Adults*	BVHE	CAV	VCD
65. *Hand that Rocks the Cradle*	BVHE	CAV	VCD, DVD
66. *Miami Rhapsody*	BVHE	CAV	VCD
67. *Celtic Pride*	BVHE	CAV	VCD
68. *Flubber*	BVHE	CAV	VCD, DVD
69. *Jungle 2 Jungle*	BVHE	CAV	VCD, DVD
70. *Man of the House*	BVHE	CAV	VCD, DVD
71. *Tom and Huck*	BVHE	CAV	VCD
72. *That Darn Cat*	BVHE	CAV	VCD
73. *The Return of Jafar*	BVHE	CAV	VCD
74. *Romancing the Clone*	BVHE	CAV	VCD
75. *Greatest Treasure*	BVHE	CAV	VCD
76. *Winnie the Pooh— Making Friends*	BVHE	CAV	VCD

Continued on next page

Appendix C

Buena Vista Home Entertainment/Thakral/CAV—Continued

Title	Copyright Holder	Local Distributor	Format
77. *Winner Take Aladdin*	BVHE	CAV	VCD
78. *6 Days, 7 Nights*	BVHE	CAV	VCD, DVD
79. *Tron*	BVHE	CAV	VCD
80. *Donald and Company*	BVHE	CAV	VCD
81. *Donald's 60th Birthday Bash*	BVHE	CAV	VCD
82. *Dinning Out with Timon and Pumbaa*	BVHE	CAV	VCD
83. *Beauty and the Beast—The Enchanted Christmas*	BVHE	CAV	VCD, DVD
84. *Oh Holiday and Timon and Pumbaa*	BVHE	CAV	VCD
85. *Hercules*	BVHE	CAV	VCD
86. *Armageddon*	BVHE	CAV	VCD, DVD
87. *Dead Poet's Society*	BVHE	CAV	VCD, DVD
88. *Fun with English*	BVHE	CAV	VCD
89. *Splash*	BVHE	CAV	VCD, DVD
90. *Good Morning, Vietnam*	BVHE	CAV	VCD, DVD
91. *Mary Poppins*	BVHE	CAV	VCD, DVD
92. *Homeward Bound II: Lost in San Francisco*	BVHE	CAV	VCD
93. *Honey, I Shrunk the Kids*	BVHE	CAV	VCD
94. *Mighty Ducks*	BVHE	CAV	VCD
95. *D2—Mighty Ducks Are Back*	BVHE	CAV	VCD
96. *Benji the Hunted*	BVHE	CAV	VCD
97. *Heavy Weight*	BVHE	CAV	VCD
98. *Honey, I Blew Up the Kids*	BVHE	CAV	VCD

Continued on next page

Buena Vista Home Entertainment/Thakral/CAV—Continued

Title	Copyright Holder	Local Distributor	Format
99. *Straight Talk*	BVHE	CAV	VCD
100. *Mr. Margoo*	BVHE	CAV	VCD
101. *D3—Might Ducks*	BVHE	CAV	VCD
102. *Gordy*	BVHE	CAV	VCD
103. *Honey, I Shrunk Ourselves*	BVHE	CAV	VCD
104. *Snake Eyes*	BVHE	CAV	VCD, DVD
105. *101 Dalmatians Live*	BVHE	CAV	VCD, DVD
106. *Wish upon a Starfish*	BVHE	CAV	VCD
107. *Mickey's Summer Madness*	BVHE	CAV	VCD
108. *Homeward Bound Incred Journey*	BVHE	CAV	VCD
109. *George of Jungle*	BVHE	CAV	VCD
110. *Mulan*	BVHE	CAV	VCD
111. *The Richman's Wife*	BVHE	CAV	VCD
112. *White Fang*	BVHE	CAV	VCD
113. *The Many Adventures of Winnie the Pooh*	BVHE	CAV	VCD
114. *101 Dalmatians*	BVHE	CAV	VCD
115. *Pocahontas II— Journey to a New World*	BVHE	CAV	VCD
116. *Aladdin and the King of Thieves*	BVHE	CAV	VCD
117. *Mad Love*	BVHE	CAV	VCD
118. *My Father the Hero*	BVHE	CAV	VCD
119. *The Sixth*	BVHE	CAV	VCD
120. *Love DIY*	BVHE	CAV	VCD
121. *I'll Be Home for Christmas*	BVHE	CAV	VCD
122. *Enemy of the State*	BVHE	CAV	VCD
123. *First Kid*	BVHE	CAV	VCD
124. *Houseguest*	BVHE	CAV	VCD
125. *The Jerky Boys*	BVHE	CAV	VCD

Continued on next page

Buena Vista Home Entertainment/Thakral/CAV—Continued

Title	Copyright Holder	Local Distributor	Format
126. *My Favorite Martian*	BVHE	CAV	VCD
127. *Distinguished Gentlemen*	BVHE	CAV	VCD
128. *Money for Nothing*	BVHE	CAV	VCD
129. *Roommates*	BVHE	CAV	VCD
130. *Jungle Book: Mowgli's Story*	BVHE	CAV	VCD
131. *The Wonderful Icecream Suit*	BVHE	CAV	VCD
132. *A Pyromanian's Love Story*	BVHE	CAV	VCD
133. *Demon in the Bottle*	BVHE	CAV	VCD
134. *Max Q: Emergency Landing*	BVHE	CAV	VCD
135. *Winnie the Pooh— Learning, Sharing and Caring*	BVHE	CAV	VCD
136. *Around the World with Timon and Pumbaa*	BVHE	CAV	VCD
137. *101 Dalmatians I— Dalmatian Vacation*	BVHE	CAV	VCD
138. *Fox and Hound*	BVHE	CAV	VCD
139. *Ariel's Songs and Stories Heroes*	BVHE	CAV	VCD
140. *Winnie the Pooh Learning— Working Together*	BVHE	CAV	VCD
141. *The Rescuers*	BVHE	CAV	VCD
142. *Bonkers I—Going Bonkers*	BVHE	CAV	VCD
143. *Gargoyles—The Movie*	BVHE	CAV	VCD
144. *Winnie the Pooh Playtime— Cowboy Pooh*	BVHE	CAV	VCD

Continued on next page

Buena Vista Home Entertainment/Thakral/CAV—Continued

Title	Copyright Holder	Local Distributor	Format
145. *Goof Troop I—Trouble Afloat*	BVHE	CAV	VCD
146. *Inspector Gadget*	BVHE	CAV	DVD
147. *Romy and Michelle's High School Reunion*	BVHE	CAV	DVD
148. *The Rocketeer*	BVHE	CAV	DVD
149. *Instinct*	BVHE	CAV	VCD
150. *What's Love Got to Do with It*	BVHE	CAV	VCD
151. *I Love Trouble*	BVHE	CAV	VCD
152. *The Three Musketeers*	BVHE	CAV	VCD
153. *Son-In-Law*	BVHE	CAV	VCD
154. *The Sixth Sense*	BVHE	CAV	DVD
155. *The Aristocats*[2]	BVHE	CAV	VCD, DVD
156. *The Little Mermaid*	BVHE	CAV	DVD
157. *The Aristocats*	BVHE	CAV	DVD
158. *Ducktales I—Earth Quack*	BVHE	CAV	DVD
159. *Hideous Kinky*	BVHE	CAV	VCD
160. *Winnie the Pooh Playing—Detective Tigger*	BVHE	CAV	VCD
161. *Mighty Ducks the Movie*	BVHE	CAV	VCD
162. *Darkwing Duck I—Darkly Dawns Duck*	BVHE	CAV	VCD
163. *A Bug's Life*	BVHE	CAV	VCD
164. *The 13th Warrior*	BVHE	CAV	DVD
165. *Mumford*	BVHE	CAV	DVD
166. *Mystery, Alaska*	BVHE	CAV	DVD
167. *Encino Man*	BVHE	CAV	DVD
168. *Bringing Out the Dead*	BVHE	CAV	VCD, DVD
169. *Outrageous Fortune*	BVHE	CAV	VCD, DVD
170. *Tarzan*	BVHE	CAV	VCD, DVD

Continued on next page

Buena Vista Home Entertainment/Thakral/CAV—Continued

Title	Copyright Holder	Local Distributor	Format
171. *End of Days*	BVHE	CAV	VCD, DVD
172. *Pretty Woman*	BVHE	CAV	VCD, DVD
173. *Runaway Bride*	BVHE	CAV	VCD, DVD
174. *Aladdin III— Treasures of Doom*	BVHE	CAV	VCD
175. *Donald's Greatest Hits*	BVHE	CAV	VCD
176. *The Three Little Pigs*	BVHE	CAV	VCD
177. *The Insider*	BVHE	CAV	VCD, DVD
178. *The Hurricane*	BVHE	CAV	VCD, DVD

Columbia TriStar Home Entertainment/UEAV/CRC

Title	Copyright Holder	Local Distributor	Format
1. *City Hall*	Columbia	CRC	VCD
2. *Swan Princess*	Columbia	CRC	VCD
3. *Robocop 3*	Columbia	CRC	VCD
4. *Jumanji*	Columbia	CRC	VCD
5. *Alaska*	Columbia	CRC	VCD
6. *Absolute Power*	Columbia	CRC	VCD
7. *Bad Boy*	Columbia	CRC	VCD
8. *Extreme Measures*	Columbia	CRC	VCD
9. *The Fan*	Columbia	CRC	VCD
10. *Cliffhanger*	Columbia	CRC	VCD
11. *Dolores Claiborne*	Columbia	CRC	VCD
12. *Forget Paris*	Columbia	CRC	VCD
13. *Madame Butterfly*	Columbia	CRC	VCD
14. *No Way Back*	Columbia	CRC	VCD
15. *3 Ninjas High Noon at Mega Mountain*	Columbia	CRC	VCD
16. *The Dark Half*	Columbia	CRC	VCD
17. *The Big Hit*	Columbia	CRC	VCD

Continued on next page

Columbia TriStar Home Entertainment/UEAV/CRC—Continued

Title	Copyright Holder	Local Distributor	Format
18. *Murdered Innocence*	Columbia	CRC	VCD
19. *Donnie Brasco aka Lion's Den*	Columbia	CRC	VCD
20. *Shawshank Redemption, The*	Columbia	CRC	VCD
21. *Cats Don't Dance*	Columbia	CRC	VCD
22. *Fatal Combat*	Columbia	CRC	VCD
23. *Deadly Heroes*	Columbia	CRC	VCD
24. *Distant Justice*	Columbia	CRC	VCD
25. *As Good as It Gets*	Columbia	CRC	VCD
26. *It Could Happen to You*	Columbia	CRC	VCD
27. *Lone Star*	Columbia	CRC	VCD
28. *Desperate Measures*	Columbia	CRC	VCD
29. *New York Cop*	Columbia	CRC	VCD

Notes

1. MPA's Legal Counsel Wang Yong provided the list.

2. Note that *Aristocats* is listed twice here (155 and 157) with different translated Chinese titles: 155 is *Shen Mao Jio Shi Jie* and 157 is *Mao-r Li Xian Ji.*

Bibliography

Adler, Tim. 2002. "International Film." *Screen Finance*, 29 March.

Agence France Presse (AFP). 2002. "Taiwan Launches Anti-Piracy Crackdown on Computer Software." 1 May, at www.hindustantimes.com/neweconomy/internet010502b.shtml (accessed 11 June 2002).

Alleyne, Mark D. 1995. *International Power and International Communication*. New York: St. Martin's Press.

Amin, Ash, and Michael Dietrich. 1991. "From Hierarchy to 'Hierarchy': The Dynamics of Contemporary Corporate Restructuring in Europe." In *Towards a New Europe? Structural Change in the European Economy*, edited by Ash Amin and Michael Dietrich. Cheltenham, U.K.: Edward Elgar.

Ang, Swee Hoon. 2000. "The Influence of Physical, Beneficial and Image Properties on Responses to Parallel Imports." *International Marketing Review* 17(6): 509–524.

Appadurai, Arjun. 2000. "Grassroots Globalization and the Research Imagination." *Public Culture* 12(1):1–19.

Asia Pulse. 2001. "China's Demand for VCD Players to Hit 22.5 Million Sets in 2001." 7 February.

Asia Week. 2001. "Enterprise Cover Story: Hong Kong Cinema Grows Up." 10 July.

Askoy, Asu, and Kevin Robins. 1992. "Hollywood for the 21st Century: Global Competition for Critical Mass in Image Markets." *Cambridge Journal of Economics* 16:1–22.

Balio, Tino. 1996. "Adjusting to the New Global Economy: Hollywood in the 1990s." Pp. 23–38 in *Film Policy: International, National and Regional Perspectives*, edited by Albert Moran. London and New York: Routledge.

Barlow, John Perry. 2000. "Censorship 2000." *Nettime*, 12 July, at nettime-l@bbs.thing.net.

Beck, Ulrich, Anthony Giddens, and Scott Lash. 1994. *Reflexive Modernization: Politics, Tradition and Aesthetics in the Modern Social Order*. Stanford, Calif.: Stanford University Press.

Beck, Ulrich. 1994. "The Reinvention of Politics: Towards a Theory of Reflexive Modernization." Pp.1–55 in *Reflexive Modernization: Politics, Tradition and Aesthetics in the Modern Social Order*, edited by Ulrich Beck, Anthony Giddens, and Scott Lash. Stanford, Calif.: Stanford University Press.

217

————. 1994. "Self-Dissolution and Self-Endangerment of Industrial Society: What Does This Mean?" Pp. 174–183 in *Reflexive Modernization: Politics, Tradition and Aesthetics in the Modern Social Order*, edited by Ulrich Beck, Anthony Giddens, and Scott Lash. Stanford, Calif.: Stanford University Press.

Bello, Walden. 2001. "Introduction." Pp. xi–xviii in *The Future in the Balance: Essays on Globalization and Resistance*, edited by Walden Bello. Oakland, Calif.: Food First Books.

Benko, Robert P. 1987. *Protecting Intellectual Property Rights: Issues and Controversies*. Washington, D.C.: American Enterprise Institute for Public Policy Research.

Bettig, Ronald V. 1997. "The Enclosure of Cyberspace." *Critical Studies in Mass Communication* 14:138–157.

————. 1996. *Copyrighting Culture: The Political Economy of Intellectual Property*. Boulder, Colo.: Westview Press.

Blair, Helen, and Al Rainnie. 2000. "Flexible Films?" *Media, Culture & Society* 22:187–204.

Boyle, James. 1996. *Shamans, Software, and Spleens: Law and the Construction of the Information Society*. Cambridge, Mass.: Harvard University Press.

Brent, Willie. 2000. "Chinese Wary of WTO Entry." *Variety* 378, no.7 (3–9 April):76.

Bromley, Carl. 2000. "The House That Jack Built: How Valenti Brought Hollywood to the World. *The Nation*, 3 April.

Bromley, Simon. 1999. "The Space of Flows and Timeless Time: Manuel Castells's *The Information Age.*" *Radical Philosophy* 97: 6–17.

Brown, Steven D., and Rose Capdevila. 1999. "*Perpetuum Mobile*: Substance, Force and the Sociology of Translation." Pp. 26–50 in *Actor Network Theory and After*, edited by John Law and John Hassard. Oxford: Blackwell.

Burpee, Geoff. 1997. "Import Law Hits Stores in H.K.; Labels Laud Restrictions on Parallel Sales." *Billboard* 109, no. 32 (9 August): 34–5.

————. 1997. "Rights Confusion in Hong Kong: Parallel Imports Are the Central Issue." *Billboard* 109, no.16 (19 April):59–60.

Burpee, Geoff, and Steve McClure. 1996. "Parallel Import Fight Rages in Hong Kong." *Billboard* 108, no. 43 (26 October):1–2.

Business Software Alliance, et al. 1999. Joint Appeal to Members of the Legislative Council, HKSAR. Personal attendance of LegCo Session, January, 2000.

Calkins, Mary Lynne. 1999. "Censorship in Chinese Cinema." *Comm/Ent* 21, no. 2:239–328.

Callon, Michel. 1999. "Actor-Network Theory—The Market Test." Pp. 181–195 in *Actor Network Theory and After*, edited by John Law and John Hassard. Oxford: Blackwell.

————. 1980. "Struggles and Negotiations to Define What Is Problematic and What Is Not: The Socio-Logic of Translation." In *The Social Process of Scientific Investigation: Sociology of Sciences, Vol. IV*, edited by K. D. Knorr, R. Krohn and R. Whitley. Dordrecht: D. Reidel.

Callon, Michel, and Bruno Latour. 1981. "Unscrewing the Big Leviathan: How Actors Macro-Structure Reality and How Sociologists Help Them to Do So." In K. Knorr Cetina and A.V. Cicourel (eds.), *Advances in Social Theory and Methodology: Toward an Integration of Micro- and Macro-Sociologies*. Boston, London and Henley: Routledge and Kegan Paul.

Cassell, Philip, ed. 1993. *The Giddens Reader*. Stanford, Calif.: Stanford University Press.

Castells, Manuel. 1998. *End of Millennium*. Malden, Mass.: Blackwell.

————. 1997. *The Power of Identity*. Malden, Mass.: Blackwell.

————. *The Rise of the Network Society*. 1996. Malden, Mass.: Blackwell.

Chen, Kuan-Hsing. 1998. "Taiwanese New Cinema." Pp. 557–561 in *The Oxford Guide to Film Studies*, edited by John Hill and Pamela Church Gibson. New York: Oxford University Press.

Chen, Ru-Shou Robert. 1995. *Dian-Ying Di Guo: Lin Yi Zhong Zhu Shi (The Movie Empire: Another Gaze)*. Taipei: Wan Xiang.

China and Africa. 2002. "Imported Films: Disaster or Rebirth for the Chinese Film Industry?" www.chinafrica.com/200204/Forum-20024.htm (accessed 20 June 2002).

China Daily/Asia News Network. 2001. "China Merges TV, Radio and Film Firms into Media Group: Giant Company a Key Effort to Survive WTO Competition," December 9, at www.amic.org.sg/cmtv.html (accessed 23 June 2002).

China Online. 2002. "State Administration of Radio, Film & Television (SARFT)," China Online: The Information Network for China, at www.chinaonline.com/refer/ministry_profiles/c01050467.asp (accessed 24 June 2002).

————. 2000. "China's Real GDP Growth, 1979–1999," 7 January, at www.pnl.gov/china/stats.htm (accessed July 3, 2002).

China Times. 2002. "Bu Shuang Ran It Jia Tai Gao, Fan Fan Dao Ban Da Tran Jie" (Dissatisfied with the High Software Price, Anti-Anti-Piracy Unites). Taipei (7 May):9.

China Times.Com. 2002. "Zhong-Nauru Bang Yi Cheng Zhuei Yi" (ROC-Nauru Diplomatic Tie Only A Memory). July 23, at http://nettv.chinatimes.com/news/nauru/main.htm (accessed 31 July 2002).

CDR-Info. 2002. "Sony Drops Lawsuit; US Apex Agrees to pay DVD Royalties." 12 April, at www.cdrinfo.com/Sections/News/Details.asp? RelatedID=2222 (accessed 18 June 2002).

Christopherson, Susan. 1996. "Flexibility and Adaptation in Industrial Relations: The Exceptional Case of the U.S. Media Entertainment Industries." Pp.86–112 in *Under the Stars: Essays on Labor Relations in Arts and Entertainment*, edited by Lois S. Gray and Ronald L. Seeber. Ithaca, N.Y.: ILR Press.

Christopherson, Susan, and Michael Storper. 1986. "The City as Studio; The World as Back Lot: The Impact of Vertical Disintegration on the Location of the Motion Picture Industry." *Environment and Planning D: Society and Space*, 4: 305–320.

Chung, Winnie. 2002. "H. K. Exhibitor Lark Intl. Bows Distrib'n Unit." *The Hollywood Reporter*, 19 April.

Clark, Douglas. 2000. "IP Rights Protection Will Improve in China— Eventually." *China Business Review* 27, no. 3 (May/June):22–29.

Clifford, Mark L. 2002. "Facing Up to China," *Business Week Online*, at www.businessweek.com/2000/00_33/b3694009.htm (accessed 1 January 2002).

Cunningham, Stuart, and John Sinclair, eds. 2001. *Floating Lives: The Media and Asian Diaspora*. Lanham, Md.: Rowman & Littlefield.

Curtin, Michael. 2003. "The Future of Chinese Cinema: Some Lessons from Hong Kong and Taiwan." In *Chinese Media, Global Contexts*, edited by Chin-Chuan Lee. London: Routledge.

Dannen, Fredric, and Barry Long. 1997. *Hong Kong Babylon: An Insider's Guide to the Hollywood of the East*. New York: Hyperion and Miramax Books.

Davison. Mark J. 1997. "Parallel Importing of Copyright Material in a Digital Age: Why It Should Be Lawful and Why It May Never Be." *Federal Law Review* 25, no. 2:263–280.

Deleuze, Gilles. 1995. *Negotiations. 1972–1990*. New York: Columbia University Press.

Deleuze, Gilles and Félix Guattari. 1987. *A Thousand Plateaus: Capitalism and Schizophrenia.* Minneapolis: University of Minnesota Press.
———. 1977. *Anti-Oedipus: Capitalism and Schizophrenia.* New York: Viking Press.
Deutsche Bank. 2001. "A Business Guide to China & Hong Kong SAR." Deutsche Bank AG, Shanghai Branch.
DiOrio, Carl, and Don Groves. 2002. "Studios Water Overseas Markets: Warners Seeds China; UCI Grows Euro Garden." *Variety* (29 July–4 August 4):12 and 14.
Donahue, Suzanne Mary. 1987. *American Film Distribution: The Changing Marketplace.* Ann Arbor, Mich.: U.M.I. Research Press.
Dunkley, Cathy, and Dana Harris. 2001. "Foreign Sales Mavens See Their Empires Fade." *Variety,* 15–21 January:1, 103.
Dvorak, John C. 1999. "Piracy Panic." *Forbes,* 29 November:230.
The Economist. 2000. "Freedom of Speech." 5 August.
———. 1999. "Pirate's Paradise." 353, no. 8141(16 October):67.
———. 1999. "Chinese Cinema: VCDs Killed the Kungfu Star." 350, no. 8111 (20 March):67.
The Financial Times. 2000. "China—You Ought to Be in (Chinese) Pictures: Film Market to Open after WTO Entry." 10 October (Reprinted by *China Online*).
Fore, Steve. 1994. "Golden Harvest Films and the Hong Kong Movie Industry in the Realm of Globalization." *The Velvet Light Trap* 34:40–58.
Frantz, Robert. 2000. "Is the MPAA Serious?" *Byte.com,* 18 May.
Frow, John. 2000. "Public Domain and the New World Order in Knowledge." *Social Semiotics* 19, no. 2:173–185.
Fuller, Chris. 2000. "Copyright Violations." *Billboard* 112, no. 12 (18 March): 62.
Gershon, Richard A. 1997. *The Transnational Media Corporation: Global Messages and Free Market Competition.* Mahwah, N.J.: Lawrence Erlbaum Associates.
Gewertz, Ken. 2001. "Taiwan's Status Discussed: Foreign Minister Talks about Taiwan in the 'New Age.'" *Harvard Gazette,* 20 September, at www.news.harvard.edu/gazette/2001/09.20/15-taiwan.html (accessed 5 January 2002).
Giddens, Anthony. 1991. *Modernity and Self-Identity: Self and Society in the Late Modern Age.* Stanford, Calif.: Stanford University Press.
———. 1990. *The Consequences of Modernity.* Stanford, Calif.: Stanford University Press.
———. 1987. *The Nation-State and Violence.* Vol. 2 of *A Contemporary Critique of Historical Materialism.* Berkeley: University of California Press.
———. 1982. *Profiles and Critiques in Social Theory.* London: Macmillan.
———. 1977. *Studies in Social and Political Theory.* London: Hutchinson.
———. 1994. "Living in a Post-traditional Society." Pp. 56–109 in *Reflexive Modernization: Politics, Tradition and Aesthetics in the Modern Social Order,* edited by Ulrich Beck, Anthony Giddens, and Scott Lash. Stanford, Calif.: Stanford University Press.
Gomery, Douglas. 1998. "Hollywood as Industry." Pp. 245–254 in *The Oxford Guide to Film Studies,* edited by John Hill and Pamela Church Gibson. Oxford: Oxford University Press.
Graham, Stephen, and Simon Marvin. 1996. *Telecommunications and the City.* New York: Routledge.
Groves, Don. 2002a. "Confab Says DVD Pirates Tied to Drugs." *Variety* (19–25 August):22, 24.
———. 2002b. "Raid Snags Malaysian DVD Pirates." *Variety* (3–9 June):12.
———. 2002c. "Shanghai Breaks Through." *Variety* (18–24 March):13.
———. 2002d. "Distribs Unspool Split Screen." *Variety* (4–10 February):18.

———. 2001a. "Biz Blues May Run Deeper Than Per-plexing Answer." *Variety* (24–30 September):13.

———. 2001b. "H'wood Hopes for Huge Haul from Great Wall." *Variety* (18–24 June):7, 49.

———. 2000a. "Refocus Includes Exhibition Cutbacks." *Variety* 381, no. 3 (4 December):47.

———. 2000b. "Harvest Reaps China Deal." *Variety* 379, no. 12:41.

———. 2000c. "Village Roadshow Exits Hong Kong Exhib Biz." *Variety* 379, no. 11 (7 August):34.

———. 2000d. "Harvest Sows Asian Expansion." *Variety* 379, no. 2: 65.

Gu, Felicity Rose, and Zilai Tang. 2002. "Shanghai: Reconnecting to the Global Economy." Pp. 273–307 in *Global Networks Linked Cities*, edited by Saskia Sassen. New York: Routledge.

Guback, Thomas H. 1969. *The International Film Industry*. Bloomington, Ind.: Indiana University Press.

Hammond, Stefan. 2001. "Hollywood East." *Film Journal International* 104, no. 8 (August):145.

Hammond, Stefan, and Mike Wilkins. 1996. *Sex and Zen & a Bullet in the Head: The Essential Guide to Hong Kong's Mind-Bending Films*. New York: Fireside.

Hanson, Jeremy. 2000a. "Long-Distance Run." *Variety* 380, no. 10:28.

———. 2000b. "Hong Kong Claims Victory over Piracy." *Variety* 380, 8 (9 Oct.):14.

Haraway, Donna J. 1997. *Modest_Witness@Second_Millennium.FemaleMan©_Meets_ OncoMouse™: Feminism and Technoscience*. New York: Routledge.

Hardt, Michael, and Antonio Negri. 2000. *Empire*. Cambridge, Mass.: Harvard University Press.

Harvey, David. 2000. *Spaces of Hope*. Berkeley, Calif.: University of California Press.

———. 1990. *The Condition of Postmodernity*. Cambridge, Mass.: Blackwell.

Herman, Edward S., and Robert W. McChesney. 1997. *The Global Media: The New Missionaries of Corporate Capitalism*. London: Cassell.

Hillier, Jim. 1993. *The New Hollywood*. London: Studio Vista.

The Hollywood Reporter. 2002. "Fox Closes H.K. Office, Inks with Edko." 19 March.

Hoskins, Colin, Adam Finn, and Stuart McFayden. 2000. "Cultural Industries from an Economic/Business Research Perspective." *Canadian Journal of Communication* 25, no. 1:127–144.

Hoskins, Colin, Stuart McFadyen, and Adam Finn. 1997. *Global Television and Film: An Introduction to the Economics of the Business*. Oxford: Oxford University Press,

Hsing, You-tien. 1998. *Making Capitalism in China: The Taiwan Connection*. New York: Oxford University Press.

Huang, Wen-Zheng. 2002. "Guo Nei Ying Ren 19 Ri Jin Jian Zong Tong, Jian Ching Xian Zhi Xi Pian Kao Bei Shu" (Taiwan Filmmakers Will Meet with the President on 19 June, Requesting That the Limit on Print Copies Be Restored on Western Film Imports." *Yahoo News*, 15 June, at http://tw.news.yahoo.com/2002/06/15/entertain/ctnews/3302242.html (accessed 18 June 2002).

Hung, Alice. 2002. "Pop Stars Join Anti-Piracy Protest in Taiwan." *Reuters*, 4 April, at http://sg.entertainment.lycosasia.com/arts/seen/seenmu/6150.html (accessed 11 June 2002).

Intellectual Property Office, ROC Ministry of Economic Affairs. 2002. *International Cooperation*. 6 February, at www.moeaipo.gov.tw/cooperation/cooperation_c.asp (accessed 9 April 2002).

————, ed. 2000. *Profile of the Intellectual Property Office, MOEA.* Taipei: IPO, MOEA.

Intercontinental Group Holdings Limited. 2000. Company Brochure/Profile.

International Intellectual Property Alliance. 2003. "Copyright Industries Release Report on Piracy in 63 Countries." Press Release, 13 February, at www.iipa.com/pressreleases/2003_Feb13_SPEC301_PR.pdf (accessed 13 March 2003).

Irvine, Martin. 1998. "Global Cyberculture Reconsidered: Cyberspace, Identity, and the Global Informational City." www.georgetown.edu/irvinemj/articles/globalculture. htm (accessed July 2001).

Jameson, Fredric. 1998. "Notes on Globalization as a Philosophical Issue." Pp. 54–77 in *The Cultures of Globalization,* edited by Fredric Jameson and Masao Miyoshi. Durham: Duke University Press.

Jayakar, Krishna P. 1997. "The United States–China Copyright Dispute: A Two-Level Games Analysis." *Communication Law and Policy* 2, no. 1:527–561.

Jensen, Klaus Bruhn, and Nicholas W. Jankowski, eds. 1991. *A Handbook of Qualitative Methodologies for Mass Communication Research.* London: Routledge.

Jones, Arthur. 2002a. "Shanghai Fest Awaits Next News Bulletin." *Variety* (17–23 June):16.

————. 2002b. "Still No Decision on Royalties for DVD Makers." *Variety* (20–26 May):14.

————. 2002c. "Exhibs Dubious about New Regs." *Variety* (4–10 February):18.

Jones, Martin, and Deborah Dixon. 2001. "Capitalism for Itself: Organising and Instituting Circuits of Knowledge." Paper presented at the International Conference on Spacing and Timing, Palermo, Italy, 1–3 November.

Kahn, Joseph. 2001. "World Trade Organization Admits China, Amid Doubts." *NYTimes.com,* 11 November, at www.nytimes.com (accessed 23 June 2002).

Kan, Wendy. 2002. "Players." *Variety,* 29 April–5 May:A4.

King, R. Todd. 1999a. "The Video Compact Disc Market in China." At www.rtoddking.com/mit912_execsum.htm (accessed 29 December 2001).

————. 1999b. "The Film Industry in China." At www.rtoddking.com/mit228_introduction.htm (accessed 5 July 2002).

Ko, Ernie. 2001. "Discard the Myth about Diplomatic Relations," *The Taipei Times Online,* 4 July, at www.taipeitimes.com/news/2001/07/04/story/0000092689 (accessed 5 January 2002).

Landler, Mark. 2001. "Change Ahead as Taiwan Enters WTO," *NYTimes.Com.* www.nytimes.com/2001/11/10/business/worldbusiness/10TAIW.html?ex=10065780 45&ei=1&en=17314baee8b466a4 (accessed 10 November 2001).

Lash, Scott. 1994. "Reflexivity and Its Doubles: Structure, Aesthetics, Community." Pp. 110–173 in *Reflexive Modernization: Politics, Tradition and Aesthetics in the Modern Social Order,* edited by Ulrich Beck, Anthony Giddens, and Scott Lash. Stanford, Calif.: Stanford University Press.

————. 1994. "Expert-System or Situated Interpretation? Culture and Institutions in Disorganized Capitalism." Pp. 198–215 in *Reflexive Modernization: Politics, Tradition and Aesthetics in the Modern Social Order,* edited by Ulrich Beck, Anthony Giddens, and Scott Lash. Stanford, Calif.: Stanford University Press.

Lash, Scott, and John Urry. 1994. *Economies of Signs & Space.* London: Sage.

Latham, Robert. 2000. "Social Sovereignty." *Theory, Culture & Society* 17, no. 4:1–18.

Latour, Bruno. 1999. "On Recalling ANT." Pp. 15–25 in *Actor Network Theory and After,* edited by John Law and John Hassard. Oxford: Blackwell.

————. 1996. "On Actor-Network Theory: A Few Clarifications." *Soziale Welt* 47:369–381.

————.1993. *We Have Never Been Modern*. Cambridge, Mass.: Harvard University Press.

Law, John. 1999. "After ANT: Complexity, Naming and Topology." Pp. 1–14 in *Actor Network Theory and After*, edited by John Law and John Hassard. Oxford: Blackwell.

Law, John, and John Hassard, eds. 1999. *Actor Network Theory and After*. Oxford: Blackwell.

Lee, Chin-Chuan. 2003. "The Global and the National of the Chinese Media: Discourses, Market, Technology, and Ideology." In *Chinese Media, Global Contexts*, edited by Chin-Chuan Lee. London: Routledge.

Lee, Nick, and Paul Stenner. 1999. "Who Pays? Can We Pay Them Back?" Pp. 90–112 in *Actor Network Theory and After*, edited by John Law and John Hassard. Oxford: Blackwell.

Lee, Ya-Huei. 2000. "Mei Shang Ba Da Zai Taiwan Zhi Fa Zhan Yu Bian Zian Yan Jio, 1949–1999" (A Research on the Transition of Hollywood Majors in Taiwan, 1949–1999). Master's Thesis, National Chen-Chi University, Taipei, Taiwan.

Lent, John. 1990. *The Asian Film Industry*. Austin, Tex.: University of Texas Press.

Levitt, Theodore. 1983. "The Globalization of Markets." *Harvard Business Review* 61, no. 3:92–102.

Li, Cheuk-to. 1996. "Popular Cinema in Hong Kong." In *The Oxford History of World Cinema*, edited by Geoffrey Nowell-Smith. New York: Oxford University Press.

Lin, Wuu-Long, and Pansy Lin. 2001. "Emergence of the Greater China Circle Economies: Cooperation versus Competition." *Journal of Contemporary China* 10, no. 29:695–710.

Liu, Da-Nien, and Wen-Jung Lien. 1999. "The Trade Relationship between Taiwan and the U.S. since the Taiwan Relations Act." Paper presented at the International Conference on United States–Taiwan Relations: Twenty Years after the Taiwan Relations Act, Institute of European and American Studies, Academia Sinica, Taipei, Taiwan, 9–10 April.

Liu, Xiaomin, and Zhenlien Lee. 2000. *WTO Yu Zhong Guo Wen Hua* (*WTO and Chinese Culture*). Guangzhou, Guangdong, China: Guangdong Jin-Ji Chu Ban She.

Liu, Yu-Zhu, ed. 1999. *Wen Hua Shi Chang Shi Wu Quan Shu* (*Overview of Cultural Market Practice*). Beijing: Xinhwa.

Lo, Changfa. 1999. "Improving the Nature and Quality of Bilateral Trade Relations between Taiwan and the United States with the TRA." Paper presented at the International Conference on United States—Taiwan Relations: Twenty Years after the Taiwan Relations Act, Institute of European and American Studies Academia Sinica, Taipei, Taiwan, 8 April.

Logan, Bey. 1996. *Hong Kong Action Cinema*. Woodstock, N.Y.: Overlook Press.

Lu, Fei-i. 1998. *Taiwan Dian Ying: Zheng Zhi, Jin Ji, Mei Xuei 1949–1994* (*Taiwan Film: Politics, Economics, and Aesthetics, 1949–1994*). Taipei: Yuan Lio.

Lu, Guozhen. 2002. "Fan Fan Dao Ban Li Liang Da Wei Ran Qin Zuo Gong Yi Gai Shan Xing Xiang" (Effective Anti-Anti-Piracy Campaign, Microsoft Uses Charity to Improve Its Image). *Xin Xinwen* (*New Journalism*), 4 July, at http://tw.news.yahoo.com/2002/07/04/journal/3353730.html (accessed 6 July 2002).

Maltby, Richard. 1995. *Hollywood Cinema*. Oxford: Blackwell.

Martin, Michael F. 2000. "Whither Hong Kong?" *China Business Review* 27, no. 4 (July/August):16–20.

Maskus, Keith. 1999. "The National Bureau of Asian Research Regional Studies: IPR: 1999 Shanghai Conference." Paper prepared for the conference Intellectual Property Rights and Economic Development in Shanghai and the Lower Yangzi Region. Shanghai Academy of Social Sciences, 11–12 May.

Massey, Doreen. 1994. Space, Place, and Gender. Minneapolis: University of Minnesota Press.

Mastel, Greg. 2000. "U.S.–China Trade: Smooth Sailing or Choppy Waters?" At www. ustdrc.gov/research/China.pdf (accessed 12 January 2002).

Master, Greg. 2001. "China, Taiwan, and the World Trade Organization." *Washington Quarterly* 24, no. 3 (Summer):45–56.

May, Christopher. 1998. "Capital, Knowledge and Ownership: The 'Information Society' and Intellectual Property." *Information, Communication & Society* 1, no. 3:246–269.

Mazurkewich, Karen. 2000. "Hollywood Jumps In." *Far Eastern Economic Review*, 163, no.16:80–84.

Meyer, David R. 2002. "Hong Kong: Global Capital Exchange." Pp. 249–271 in *Global Networks Linked Cities*, edited by Saskia Sassen. New York: Routledge.

Miller, Toby. 1996. "The Crime of Monsieur Lang: GATT, the Screen, and the New International Division of Cultural Labour." Pp.72–84 in *Film Policy: International, National and Regional Perspectives*, edited by Albert Moran. London: Routledge.

Ministry of Economic Affairs, ROC. 1999. *Copyright Law of the Republic of China* (Amended and promulgated by the president on 21 January 1998). Taipei: IPO, MOEA.

Mok, Davena. 2000. "China Admits to Rampant Piracy." *Billboard* 112, no. 13 (25 March):54.

———. "Pirates Face Heavier Penalties in Hong Kong." *Billboard* 112, no. 4 (22 January 2000):12.

Mol, Annemarie, and John Law. 1994. "Regions, Networks and Fluids: Anaemia and Social Topology." *Social Studies of Science* 24: 641–671.

Morr, Alison. 1999. "Hong Kong's Copyright Ordinance: How the Ban on Parallel Imports Affects the U.S. Entertainment Industry and Hong Kong's Free Market." *Comm/Ent* 21, no. 2:393–432.

Morrison, Wayne M. 1996. "China–U.S.–Taiwan Economic Relations." *Congressional Research Service: Report for Congress, 96–534 E, 11 June*. At www.fas.org/man/crs/96-534e.htm (accessed 12 January 2002).

Movius, Lisa. 2002. "Imitation Nation: Is Piracy-Crazed China a Nightmare Vision of the Future, Or Just a Developing Country Going through Some Severe Growing Pains?" *Salon.Com*, 8 July, at www.salon.com/tech/feature/2002/07/08/imitation_nation/print.html (accessed 9 July 2002).

National Bureau of Standards. 2002. "IPR and Its Relevance to the Development of the Information Industry in Taiwan." 12 March, at http://stlc.iii.org.tw/earticles/NBS-R3.htm (accessed 16 April 2002).

National Research Council. 2000. *The Digital Dilemma: Intellectual Property in the Information Age*. Washington, D.C.: National Academy Press.

Nordstrom, Carolyn. 2000. "Shadows and Sovereigns." *Theory, Culture & Society* 17, no. 4:35–54.

The Office of National Anti-Piracy and Pornography Working Committee, PRC. 2000. *China Says "No" to Pornographic and Illegal Publications*. Beijing: China Publishing Journal.

Ong, Aihwa. 1997. "Chinese Modernities: Narratives of Nation and of Capitalism." Pp.171–202 in *Ungrounded Empires: The Cultural Politics of Modern Chinese Transnationalism,* edited by Aihwa Ong and Donald Nonini. New York: Routledge.

Ong, Aihwa, and Donald Nonini, eds. 1997. *Ungrounded Empires: The Cultural Politics of Modern Chinese Transnationalism.* New York: Routledge.

Palmer, Augusta. 2000. "BIZ: Taming the Dragon: Part II, Two Approaches to China's Film Market." *Indiewire,* 8 December, at www.indiewire.com/film/biz/biz_001208-ChinesePartII.html, accessed 28 December 2001.

Parker, Dana. 2000. "Copyrights vs. Free Speech: DeCSS Case May Be the First Test of the DMCA." *EMedia Professional* 13, no. 3:18.

Parkes, Christopher. 2000. "Hollywood Changes Tack and Gets in on the China Act: The Entertainment Industry Sees WTO Membership and Normalising of Trade Relations with the People's Republic as the Way to Get into the Last Great Untapped Market." *Financial Times* (28 March):4.

Patrizio, Andy. 2000. "DVD Player at Apex of Controversy." *Wired News,* 21 March, at www.wired.com/news/print/0,1294,35028,00.html (accessed 18 June 2002).

Patton, Paul. 2000. *Deleuze & the Political.* London: Routledge.

People's Daily Online (English). 2002. "IMAX Moves to Shanghai, Large Screen to Entertain Chinese." 28 June, at http://english.peopledaily.com.cn/20020628/eng20020628_98735.shtml (accessed 9 July 2002).

———. 2002. "Foreign Investors Rush to Chinese Silver Screen." 28 January, at http://english.peopledaily.com.cn/200201/28/print20020128_89491.html (accessed 20 June 2002).

———. 2002. "State Council Issues Regulation on Film Industry." 1 January, at http://english.peopledaily.com.cn/other/review.html (accessed 1 January 2002).

———. 2001. "State Radio, Film and Television Conglomerate Established." 6 December, at http://english.peopledaily.com.cn/200112/06/print20011206_86070.html (accessed 20 June 2002).

———. 2001. "Macedonia Set to Cut Ties with Taiwan." 1 June, at http://english.peopledaily.com.cn/200106/01/eng20010601_71571.html (accessed 1 January 2002).

Potter, Pitman B. 2001. "The Legal Implications of China's Accession to the WTO." *The China Quarterly* 167, no. 1:592–609.

The PRC Radio and Television Association, ed. 1996. *Zhong Guo Guang Buo Yin Shi Fa Guei Zheng Che Shi Yong Sho Ce (The PRC Radio, Film, and Television Regulations and Policies: A Practical Manual).* Beijing: The PRC Radio and TV publications.

Rawski, Thomas G. 2001. "China's GDP Statistics—A Case of Caveat Lector?" At www.pitt.edu/~tgrawski/papers2001/caveat.web.pdf (accessed July 3, 2002).

Republic of China Government Information Office. 2001. "Foreign Relations." October, at www.gio.gov.tw/Taiwan-website/5-gp/brief/foreign.htm (accessed 15 April 2002).

———. 2000. *Film Industry Report.* May, at www.gio.gov.tw/Taiwan-website/7-av/film_industry/mframes_eg.htm (accessed 6 January 2002).

———. 1999. *Dian Ying Pian Zhi Zuo Ye Chan Ye Bao Gao #8410 (Film Production Industry Report #8410).* Taipei: GIO.

———. 2001. *Motion Picture.* At www.gio.gov.tw/info/yb97/html/ch16_3.htm (accessed 9 December, 2001).

Republic of China Ministry of Economic Affairs, Intellectual Property Office. 2002. "International Cooperation." 6 February, at www.moeaipo.gov.tw/cooperation/cooperation_ c.asp (accessed 9 April 2002).

Richardson, Bonnie J. 1999. "Assessment of the Economic Effects on the United States of China's Accession to the WTO." ITC Investigation no.322–403, 23 February, at www.mpaa.org/legislation/press/99/99_2_23.htm (accessed 10 July, 2002).

Robertson, Tom, et al. 1999. An open letter to members of the legislative council regarding the order to amend the serious and organized crime ordinance. Personal attendance of LegCo session, January, 2000.

Ryan, Michael P. 1998. Knowledge Diplomacy: Global Competition and the Politics of Intellectual Property. Washington, D.C.: Brookings Institution Press.

Sassen, Saskia. 2002. "Locating Cities on Global Circuits." Pp.1–36 in *Global Networks Linked Cities*, edited by Saskia Sassen. New York: Routledge.

———. 2001. Lecture delivered at Cultures of Globalization, a Humanities Colloquium at Harvard University, 13 April.

———. 2000. Spatialities and Temporalities of the Global: Elements for a Theorization. *Public Culture* 12, no.1:215–232.

———.1998. *Globalization and Its Discontents: Essays on the New Mobility of People and Money*. New York: The New Press.

———. 1996. *Losing Control? Sovereignty in an Age of Globalization*. New York: Columbia University Press.

———. 1991. *The Global City: New York, London, Tokyo*. Princeton, N.J.: Princeton University Press.

Schwarzacher, Lukas. 2001. "Film Fest Shanghai'd by Politics." *Variety*, 18–24 June:7, 49.

Screen Digest. 2000. "Worldwide Video Software Markets Still a Solid Revenue Earner." (November):341.

———. 1998. "Worldwide Video Markets: Far East." November: 252. TableBase™, Copyright 2001, Accession# 1772028 (December 2001).

Sinclair, John, Elizabeth Jacka, and Stuart Cunningham, eds. 1996. *New Patterns in Global Television: Peripheral Vision*. Oxford: Oxford University Press.

Siwek, Stephen. 2002. "Copyright Industries In the U.S. Economy: The 2002 Report." The International Intellectual Property Alliance. At www.iipa.com/pdf/2002_SIWEK_FULL.pdf (accessed 11 June 2002).

Smith, Roger. 2001. "2000: Vid Biz Up, Dot-Com Down." *Variety*, 15–21 January:6.

———. 2001. "Pic Profits Defy All the Prophets." *Variety,* 1–7 January:1, 48.

Soja, Edward. 1996. *Thirdspace: Journeys to Los Angeles and Other Real-and-Imagined Places*. Cambridge, Mass.: Blackwell.

———.1989. Postmodern Geographies: The Reassertion of Space in Critical Social Theory. New York: Verso.

Stokes, Lisa Odham, and Michael Hoover. 1999. *City on Fire: Hong Kong Cinema*. London: Verso.

Strathern, Marilyn. 1996. "Cutting the Network." *Journal of the Royal Anthropological Institute* 2, no. 3:517–536.

Sun, Andy Y. 1998. "From Pirate King to Jungle King: Transformation of Taiwan's Intellectual Property Protection." Asia Pacific Legal Institute. At http://apli.org/apli.pub.htm (accessed 15 February 2002).

Sutter, Karen M. 2002. "WTO and the Taiwan Strait: New Considerations for Business." *China Business Review* 29, no.1 (January/February):28–33.

Tackaberry, Paul. 1997. "Intellectual-Property Laws in the Hong Kong S.A.R.: Localization and Internationalization." *McGill Law Journal* 42:580–602.

Tai, Andy. 2002. "MS Anti-Piracy Push Leads to Linux Adoption in Taiwan." 2 May, at www.kuro5hin.org/print/2002/5/2/22414/46236 (accessed 11 June 2002).

The Taipei Times Online. 2002. "Respect for IPR Key to New Economy." 7 May, at http://taipeitimes.com/news/2002/05/07/print/0000134982 (accessed 11 June 2002).

Taipei Times. 1999. "Taiwan's Film Industry Threatened by WTO Entry." *Taiwan Headlines,* November 23, at www.taiwanheadlines.gov.tw/19991124/19991124s2.html (accessed 9 December 2001).

The Taiwan Economic News. 2000. "Taiwan Tops 1999 U.S. Piracy List." 20 April, at www.taiwanheadlines.gov.tw/20000420/20000420b5.html (accessed 12 January 2002).

Tanzer, Andrew. 1998. "Tech-Savvy Pirates." *Forbes* 162, no. 5 (7 September): 162–165.

Tao, Zai-Pu. 2002. "Fan Dao Ban De Shen Ceng Jie Go" (The Deep Structure of the Anti-Piracy Campaign). *China Times,* May 7:15.

Television Digest. 1994. "Philips Switches CD-I Emphasis to Video CD." 34, no. 50 (12 December):12–13.

———.1993. "Latest Video CD Announcement Brings Even More Confusion." (Joint communiqué from Philips, Matsushita, Sony Corp., and JVC). *Television Digest* 33, no. 35 (30 August):13.

Teng, Sue-feng. 1996. "Small Is Big—The Battle over New Film Distribution Channels." *Sinorama,* March.

Thomas, Adam, and Stuart O'Brien. 2001. *Global Film: Exhibition & Distribution.* London: Informa Media Group.

Thompson, Kristin, and David Bordwell. 1994. *Film History: An Introduction.* New York: McGraw-Hill.

Tiefer, Charles. 2001. "Sino 301: How Congress Can Effectively Review Relations with China after WTO accession." *Cornell International Law Journal* 34, no. 1 (Winter):55.

Tien, Chia-chi. 2000. "Taiwan Hua Shang Fa Xing Ou Mei Wai Pian Zi Li Shi Fa Zhan Yan Jio" (A Historical Research on the Development of the Domestic Distributors of Imported Foreign Films). Master's Thesis, Yuan Zhi University, Taipei, Taiwan.

Teo, Stephen. 1997. *Hong Kong Cinema: The Extra Dimensions.* London: BFI.

To, Tony. 2000. "Thirty Years of Golden Harvest." *Variety* 379, no. 6: 42.

U.S. Census Bureau. 1999. *Statistical Abstract of the United States: 1999* (119th edition). Washington, D.C.

U.S. Department of State. 2002. "2001 Country Reports on Economic Policy and Trade Practices: Taiwan." Washington, D.C.: Bureau of Economic and Business Affairs, U.S. Department of State, February.

USTR Trade Summary. 2001. "Foreign Trade Barriers 410 Taiwan Trade Summary." At www.ustr.gov/html/2001_Taiwan.pdf, accessed 12 January 2002.

United States Trade Representative. 2000. "From the Cold War to the Wired World: The Clinton Administration Trade Record." At http://192.239.92.165/speech-test/barshefsky/factsheet.html (accessed June 2000).

Valenti, Jack. 2001. "Valenti Warns of Potentially Devastating Economic Impact of Copyright Theft." Jack Valenti Press Releases, 3 April, at www.mpaa.org/jack/2001/2001_04_03a.htm (accessed June 2001).

———. 2000. "Valenti Urged Congress to Support Copyright Protection in Internet Age." *Jack Valenti Press Release,* 15 June, at www.mpaa.org/jack/2000/00_06_15.htm (accessed June 2000).

————. 2000. "The New Digital Millennium." *The Business of Film*, February/March: 29.

Variety Deal Memo. 2000. "Intercontinental: Hong Kong Distrib Handles Disney Films, Lays Ground for China Push." 5 June:6–7.

Virilio, Paul. 1993. "The Third Interval: A Critical Transition." Pp. 3–12 in *Rethinking Technologies*, edited by Verena Andermatt Conley. Minneapolis: University of Minnesota Press.

Wang, Jing. 2001. "Guest Editor's Introduction." *positions* 9, no. 1:1–27.

Wang, Francis S. L. 1996. "Taming the Infringers: A Study of the Special 301 Process. Taiwan—A Case Example." At www.wangandwang.com/tameinfr.htm (accessed 14 January 2002).

Wasko, Janet. 1982. *Movies and Money: Financing the American Film Industry*. Norwood, N.J.: Ablex.

Wei, Yehua Dennis. 2002. "Multiscale and Multimechanisms of Regional Inequality in China: Implications for Regional Policy." *Journal of Contemporary China* 11, no. 30:109–124.

Weigand, R. E. 1991. "Parallel Import Channels—Options for Preserving Territorial Integrity." *Columbia Journal of World Business* 26, no. 1:53–60.

World Trade Organization. 2002. "Overview: The TRIPS Agreement." At www.wto.org/english/tratop_e/trips_e/intel2_e.htm (accessed 11 June 2002).

————. 2000. "Trading into the Future: The Introduction to the WTO. The Agreements. Intellectual Property: Protection and Enforcement." At www.wto.org/english/thewto_e/whatis_e/agrm6_e.htm (accessed June 2000).

Wu, Nelson H. 2002. "Multiplexes Eat Up B.O." *Variety*, 24–30 June.

Wu, Xianggui. 1992. "The Chinese Film Industry since 1977." Ph.D. Dissertation, University of Oregon.

Wyatt, Justin. 1998. "From Roadshowing to Saturation Release: Majors, Independents, and Marketing/Distribution Innovations." Pp. 64–86 in *The New American Cinema*, edited by Jon Lewis. Durham: Duke University Press.

Xinhua News Agency. 2001. "China Expands Radio, TV & Film Industries to Meet WTO Accession." 29 June.

————. 2000. "China Tops World in Production of VCD Players." 11 May.

Yeh, Hui-Lin. 2001. *Rushi Yu Zhishi Changquan Baohu* (*WTO and Intellectual Property Rights Protection*). Shanghai: Shi-Jie Tu-Shu.

Young, Laura W. 1996. "IP Protection in China and Taiwan: A Comparison." At www.wangandwang.com/nlj-comp.htm (accessed 14 January 2002).

Young, Laura W., and Francis S. L. Wang. 1996. "Taiwan's Efforts to Comply with TRIPs." At www.wangandwang.com/eaer-trp.htm (accessed 14 January 2002).

————. 1996. "Greater China Intellectual Property Protection: Taiwan's Efforts to Comply with TRIPS." At www.wangandwang.com/eaer-trp.htm (accessed 14 January 2002).

Yu, Gwo-chauo. 1993. "China, Hong Kong, and Taiwan: The Convergence and Interaction of Chinese Film." Unpublished Master's Thesis, University of North Texas.

Zelditch, M. 1970. "Some Methodological Problems of Field Studies." In *Qualitative Methodology: Firsthand Involvement with the Social World*, edited by W. F. Filstead. Chicago: Markham.

Zhao, Yuezhi, and Dan Schiller. 2001. "Dances with Wolves? China's Integration into Digital Capitalism." *Info* 3, no. 2:137–151.

Zhong Guo Shi Bao (China Times). 2002. "Da Lu Zhi DVD Bei Kong Qin Quan Ang He Jie" (Settlement Reached over the Mainland-Made DVD Player Infringement Law Suit). 8 May, p. 11.

Websites

Hong Kong Government Information Office
　www.info.gov.hk/
Hong Kong Trade Development Council
　www.tdctrade.com (updated 10 October 2001)
International Intellectual Property Alliance (IIPA)—www.iipa.com
　Copyright Industries in the U.S. Economy: Executive Summary
　　The 1999 Report
　　The 2000 Report
　　The 2001 Report
　　The 2002 Report
　2002 "Special 301" Recommendations
　　www.iipa.com/pdf/2002_Feb14_LOSSES.pdf (accessed 10 June 2002).
　USTR "Special 301" Decisions and IIPA Estimated Trade Losses Due to
　　Copyright Piracy and Estimated Levels of Copyright Piracy:
　　1996, 1997, 1998, 1999, 2000, 2001, 2002
　Country Reports:
　People's Republic of China 1996–2002
　　www.iipa.com/rbc/1996/rbc_china_301_96.html
　　www.iipa.com/rbc/1997/rbc_china_301_97.html
　　www.iipa.com/rbc/1998/rbc_china_301_98.html
　　www.iipa.com/rbc/1999/rbc_china_301_99.html
　　www.iipa.com/rbc/2000/2000SPEC301CHINA.pdf
　　www.iipa.com/rbc/2001/2001SPEC301CHINA.pdf
　　www.iipa.com/rbc/2002/2002SPEC301PRC.pdf
　Hong Kong 1996–1999
　　www.iipa.com/rbc/1996/rbc_hong_kong_301_96.html
　　www.iipa.com/rbc/1996/rbc_hong_kong_301_97.html
　　www.iipa.com/rbc/1996/rbc_hong_kong_301_98.html
　　www.iipa.com/rbc/1996/rbc_hong_kong_301_99.html
　Taiwan 1996–2002
　　www.iipa.com/rbc/1996/rbc_Taiwan_301_96.html
　　www.iipa.com/rbc/1997/rbc_Taiwan_301–97.html
　　www.iipa.com/rbc/1998/rbc_Taiwan_301_98.html
　　www.iipa.com/rbc/1999/rbc_Taiwan_301_99.html
　　www.iipa.com/rbc/2000/ Taiwan_2000.PDF
　　www.iipa.com/rbc/2001/ Taiwan_2001.PDF
　　www.iipa.com/rbc/2001/2001SPEC301TAIWAN.pdf
　　www.iipa.com/rbc/2002/2002SPEC301TAIWAN.pdf
The Internet Movie Database
　www.imdb.com/
JP Investment Clinic Web
　www.jpvest.com/23
Motion Picture Association of America

www.mpaa.org
Movie World Hong Kong
    www.movieworld.com.hk
Taipei Economic and Cultural Office in New York
    www.taipei.org/teco/cicc/currents/56/Selections/Html/?Selection4.m
Taiwan Democratic Progressive Party
    www.taiwandc.org/dpp/
Truemovie.com
    www.truemovie.com/records.htm
TVB
    www.tvb.com/tvbi/global/taiwan.htm
Twentieth Century Fox International, Asia/Pacific
    www.foxasia.com
World Intellectual Property Organization
    www.wipo.org/about-wipo/en/gib.htm
World Trade Organization
    www.wto.org 23CMC.htm
World Trade Organization/TRIPS
    www.wto.org/english/tratop_e/trips_e/intel2_e.htm

Index

actant. *See* actor
actor, in actor network theory, 15, 17–18
actor network theory. *See* ANT
Alonte, John, 125n7, 171, 185n10
Amélie, 129, 130, 138–39, 143, 144, 161
ANT (actor network theory), 17–18, 75,
  92, 189. *See also* Callon, Michel;
  Latour, Bruno
anti-anti-piracy alliance, 146, 149, 161–62
Appadurai, Arjun, 17, 36

Beck, Ulrich, 48
BSA, 149, 162
Business Software Alliance. *See* BSA

Callon, Michel, 15, 17, 164, 165n2, 165n4,
  191
Castells, Manuel, 1, 16, 17, 22–23, 30, 36,
  38n15, 39n29
Chen, Wolf, 115, 116, 117, 124, 126n11,
  126n12, 127–46. *See also* Era
  Communications; Mata Entertainment
China: economic growth, 44–47; film
  policy, 61–63; piracy in, 3, 8, 47, 65;
  VCD development in, 18, 50, 51–56,
  58n2, 84, 87; WTO accession of, 1, 4,
  31, 41, 42, 63, 64, 65–69, 77, 80, 82–
  83, 94
China Film Corporation: 61–63, 66, 68,
  139
Chiu, Fu-Sheng, 115, 127–28, 140
Chow, Li, 172

CMC Group, 116, 117, 126nn11–12, 129–
  31, 133–37, 145–46, 146n3
copyright: definition, 23–24; the protection
  of, 3, 13, 23, 28, 150, 188; regulation,
  3, 21–23, 30–36, 37n1, 77, 79, 80, 82,
  96n6, 96nn9–10, 105, 148, 150, 152,
  153–56, 162, 178, 180, 181–83, 185n13
copyright industries: in Hong Kong, 179;
  and piracy issues in China, 79, 95; in
  Taiwan, 47, 124, 148, 160;
  transnational, 18, 19n8, 77, 80, 147,
  191; U.S., 24–28, 37n7, 73, 95nn1–2,
  96nn3–5; in WTO/TRIPS negotiations,
  33
crisis industry, 100
Crouching Tiger Hidden Dragon, 70n11,
  91, 174–75

DeCSS, 21, 30, 37, 38n12
Deleuze, Gilles, 16, 74
Deltamac, 105, 116–17, 130, 131–33, 134,
  144
Democratic Progressive Party. *See* DPP
Digital Millennium Copyright Act
  (DMCA), 21, 24, 29, 37
disintermediation, 29
Disney/Buena Vista International (BVI),
  26–27, 70n3, 105, 108, 112, 115, 140,
  171–76
distribution: in China, 61–66, 68, 70,
  70n10; definition of, 1–2; in Greater
  China, 46, 189; in Hong Kong, 168–69,

231

About the Author

Shujen Wang teaches film and media studies in the Department of Visual and Media Arts at Emerson College. She is also a research associate at the Fairbank Center for East Asian Research at Harvard University. Her research interests include media globalization, piracy and international copyright governance, and issues surrounding space, power, and technology. Her works have appeared in such journals as *Theory, Culture & Society, Cinema Journal, Asian Cinema, Film Comment, Public Culture, Text, Journal of Communication Inquiry, Gazette, Visual Anthropology, Asian Journal of Communication,* and *Media Asia.* She is currently working on a book project examining copyright governance in the post-WTO Taiwan and China.